THE INHERITANCE

THE INHERITANCE

The Great Western Railway between the Wars

Tim Bryan

Ian Allan
PUBLISHING

For Jack and Katie

First published 2013

ISBN 978 0 7110 3682 6

Published by Ian Allan Publishing Ltd,
Riverdene Business Park, Hersham, Surrey KT12 4RG.

Printed in England

Visit the Ian Allan Publishing website at *www.ianallanpublishing.com*

Picture Credits
Individual picture sources are noted within the text. All uncredited pictures are from the collection of STEAM: Museum of the GWR. Further details of the collection are available at: *www.steampicturelibrary.com*

FRONT COVER The Terminus: Penzance Station Cornwall by Stanhope Alexander Forbes,1925. *Courtesy: Bridgeman Art Library/SSPL/ National Railway Museum*

BACK COVER A Great Western Railway publicity photograph used to promote the 'World's Fastest Train', the 'Cheltenham Flyer'.

HALF TITLE PAGE No 6000 *King George V* poses at the entrance to Middle Hill Tunnel, just west of Box Tunnel, shortly after the locomotive's completion in June1927.

TITLE SPREAD Platform 3 at Paddington on 21 August 1926, with the 'Torbay Limited' about to depart. Met Office reports noted that August was 'warm and mainly fine', something not reflected in the coats worn by passengers on the platform.

ABOVE Moving furniture by GWR at Maidenhead on 27 November 1935. *Philip Kelley collection*

LEFT A poster by Leonard Cusden advertising the 1928 edition of *Holiday Haunts*. Cusden went on to design many famous propaganda posters during World War 2. *Great Western Trust collection*

OVERLEAF Lines of coal wagons awaiting movement to Swansea Docks for export.

CONTENTS

FOREWORD

There have been many books written about the Great Western Railway, many of them covering the period between the two world wars. A good number have concentrated on the locomotives and rolling stock built by the company in the 1920s and 1930s, especially famous designs like the 'Castle' and 'King' express engines. Others have described the prestige express trains run by the GWR, such as the 'Bristolian' and the 'Cornish Riviera Limited'.

This is not however a book about locomotives or rolling stock; they are not ignored in the narrative, but they are considered instead as part of a bigger story, of how one of the most famous railway companies in the world fought its way through a tumultuous period of economic, social and political change. It tells how the GWR recovered from a world war, absorbed constituent

and subsidiary railways at the Grouping, and endured strikes, road competition and some of the toughest economic conditions ever seen in Britain. Despite all these difficulties the railway continued to innovate and lead, modernised its network and stations with the help of Government loans and, with clever publicity and marketing, remained a household name throughout.

As I worked on the book I soon became aware that it would need a much larger volume than this one to chronicle all the activities and developments in this fascinating period of railway history; I hope, however, that this account will give at least some impression of those difficult but exciting years for the GWR.

Tim Bryan
Swindon, March 2013

ACKNOWLEDGEMENTS

I am grateful to the staff of a number of libraries and archives for assistance provided during the research for this book, particularly those at the National Archives at Kew, the Somerset Heritage Centre at Taunton, Bristol Central Library, The Cardiff Story, Newport Reference Library and Swindon Central Library. I should like to thank in particular Elaine Arthurs, Collections Officer at STEAM, Museum of the GWR in Swindon, for putting up with my requests for information and help with the supply of images; thanks are due too to the volunteers at STEAM, past and present. Peter Rance, Tony Rivers, Laurence Waters and Paddy Baker, of the Great Western Trust at Didcot, were also extremely helpful in allowing me access to the collection there.

Phil Kelley generously allowed me access to his collection on GWR road vehicles, while Stephen Brindle of English Heritage was also helpful in locating information about the redevelopment of Paddington. I should also like to thank colleagues at the Heritage Motor Centre, Gaydon, particularly Lisa Stevens, Gillian Bardsley, Stephen Laing and Ralph Buckland.

The process of researching and writing is an antisocial activity, and I am grateful to my family for their forbearance during the completion of the book; I could not have done this without their support. Special thanks are due to my wife, Ann, for editing the manuscript and providing helpful comments about the style and content.

INTRODUCTION

Bookended by the horrors of the Great War and the looming shadow of the Second World War, the 1920s and 1930s are generally portrayed as a period of great uncertainty and turmoil, the effects of the Great Depression dominating the lives of many in Britain. The 21 years following the end of the Great War were an unsettling mix of triumph and tragedy for the Great Western Railway and its staff, and during this period the company made great efforts to restore itself to the pre-eminent position it had occupied in the years before 1914.

The two decades of railway and social history described in this book do not divide neatly into two parts; in the 1920s the GWR not only worked hard to recover from the trauma and heartache of the Great War but also coped with the upheaval resulting from the creation of the 'Big Four' companies in 1923, the Great Western being unique in that it was the only pre-Grouping company to retain its identity.

The creation of the 'Big Four' left the GWR with a rich inheritance in South Wales, as many of the railways absorbed owned substantial dock operations there. Much of the work done at Cardiff, Newport, Swansea and other docks centred on the export of coal mined in the Welsh valleys, and, initially at least, the coal trade proved a huge asset to the company. However, economic and political uncertainty in the 1920s led to industrial and social unrest. 'Not a minute on the day, not a penny off the pay' was the motto adopted by miners, and the General Strike of 1926 was the culmination of more than five years of industrial unrest both inside and outside the railway. As the coal industry struggled, production fell, and unemployment and poverty worsened. The effects of the strike and the long decline of the coal-mining industry were extremely serious for the GWR and would resonate within the company until nationalisation. Road competition also

LEFT A famous interwar photograph taken at Swindon locomotive shed and featuring a line-up of seven 'King' class locomotives. From left to right are Nos 6005 *King George II*, 6008 *King James II*, 6017 *King Edward IV*, 6020 *King Henry IV*, 6022 *King Edward III*, 6023 *King Edward II* and 6024 *King Edward I*.

RIGHT Sir Felix Pole, General Manager of the GWR from 1921 to 1929.

BELOW A Swindon Works print showing the company's floating crane moving a coal hoist from Cardiff to Barry in 1937.

TRANSFER OF NO. 12 HOIST (T/259) FROM CARDIFF TO BARRY
(APPROACHING THE JETTY AT BARRY).

NEG. D5·136

PHOTO'D 10. 9. 37.

For Drawing Office use only.........

grew steadily during the 1920s, and although the company made great efforts to provide both new and better bus services and also to modernise its goods operation through the use of motor vehicles, throughout the 1920s and 1930s the railway was fighting a losing battle with road hauliers, and car ownership rose steadily.

No portrait of the Great Western Railway between the wars would be complete without mention of the man who dominated the company during the 1920s — its General Manager, Felix Pole. Having guided the railway through some difficult years, Pole left the company in 1929 (unlike many managers, who died 'in harness') but left at a time when profits and standards of service were at their highest for many years.

Pole's successor, James Milne, presided over the railway during the darkest years of the Great Depression but was able to make use of Government loans being made available for railways to modernise themselves and in the process help to reduce the crippling unemployment that faced the country. The GWR plunged into an ambitious and far-reaching programme of modernisation, the like of which had not been seen since the years before the Great War, leading to the rebuilding of many of its major stations, notably Paddington, Bristol and Cardiff, as well as the widening and upgrading of many lines and a host of other

ABOVE The front cover of a GWR publication produced in 1936 to advertise the company's goods services for heavy and exceptional loads. *Great Western Trust collection*

BELOW Diesel railcar No 17, built to carry parcels, is passed by an express in Sonning Cutting in 1937.

improvements all over the network. The South Wales docks were also updated, in an attempt boost the coal trade.

A major development in the 1930s was the culmination of work begun by Felix Pole in the previous decade. GWR publicity and advertising had been gradually improving in quality, and by 1935 the company had begun to produce distinct and often stylish advertising material, including posters, books, leaflets and even jigsaw puzzles, celebrating and illustrating not only its services but also its locomotives and rolling stock — and, most importantly, the landscape and coastline of the areas it served in the West Country, the Midlands and Wales.

The 1920s and 1930s constituted a golden era for luxurious high-speed passenger trains on the GWR as the company battled to compete with the LNER and the LMS in particular. Until the advent of the streamlined services run by those companies' prestige expresses like the 'Cheltenham Flyer' and the 'Cornish Riviera Limited' represented the pinnacle of express travel. The GWR also pioneered the use of streamlined diesel railcars and in the 1930s operated its own air service.

As the only 'Big Four' railway company in a position to celebrate its centenary the Great Western might have been expected to make a fuss of its 100th anniversary in 1935. In the event the celebrations were rather low-key, although they heralded a short-lived upturn in fortunes, as revenues and traffic levels began to increase. However, the rising tension in Europe and deteriorating economic conditions were a prelude to the outbreak of World War 2, when the GWR would once again be called upon to play a vital role, as it had done two decades before.

TOP The three fishermen in the small boat seem more interested in the photographer than the Great Western ship the SS *St Helier* as it arrives at St Peter Port in Guernsey. *Great Western Trust Collection*

ABOVE The cover of the GWR publication *Speed to the West*, published in 1939.

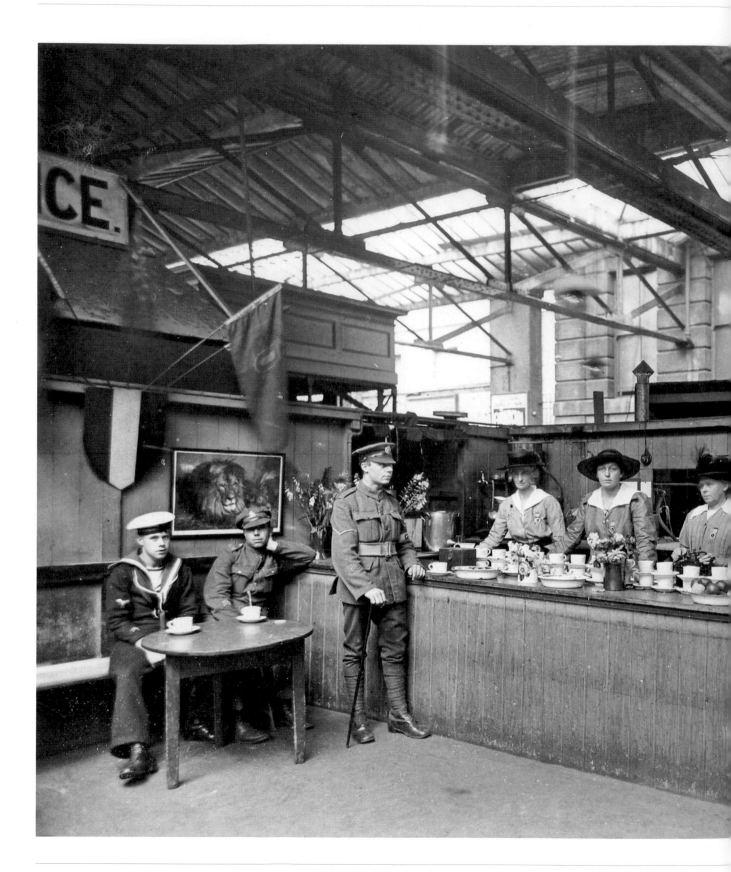

CHAPTER I

THE AFTERMATH

Great Western staff reporting for duty on the morning of 11 November 1918 did so in a state of anxious expectation. For almost a week it had appeared that Germany was on the point of surrendering, the final act in a long and bloody war which had taken its toll at home and abroad. Shortly before the official announcement of the peace Prime Minister David Lloyd George told the crowd outside 10 Downing Street that 'at eleven o'clock this morning, the war will be over. We have won a great victory and will be entitled to a bit of shouting.'[1] At the appointed hour the streets of the capital and other British cities, towns and villages were filled with revellers, happy to celebrate the end of the war.

In keeping with the widespread celebrations that broke out spontaneously in London, Brunel's great station at Paddington echoed to the sound of locomotive whistles adding to the cacophony of church bells, and bus and taxi horns. Although trains continued to run more or less on time, it is unlikely that there was much work done on the railway for the rest of the day or the following one as celebrations continued. At Swindon, Wolverhampton and a number of other locations men left work to join in with the celebrations. At a board meeting in December 1918 the General Manager told directors that other railway companies had experienced the same situation and 'the question of whether the workers should be paid for the time lost has been under discussion by the Railway Executive Committee'.[2]

A month later, when a good deal of the initial euphoria following the Armistice had subsided, the *Great Western Railway Magazine* summed up the prevailing mood by noting that while railway staff had rejoiced in the signing of the Armistice, they did not 'forget the enormous price in life and suffering, and sacrifice of all kinds which has had to be paid'.[3] The whole fabric of commercial life had, it warned, been 'torn asunder' by the war, and the whole process of demobilisation would require 'delicate handling if the shattered edifice of our industrial life is to be satisfactorily reconstructed'.[4] The sombre mood was heightened by no fewer than 12 pages of photographs showing GWR staff killed in the last months of the conflict as well as an account of the work done by a special fund set up by GWR clerical staff to provide assistance for 'comrades or relatives of comrades who have suffered in service of King and Country'. The fund committee had agreed to make a

The soldiers' and sailors' buffet at Paddington was open day and night from April 1915 until August 1919, with a staff of 80 ladies who catered for more than 80 million servicemen during the war.

'Yuletide' gift to widows or dependants of staff who had lost lives in the war, retaining over £2,600 for employees yet to return from military service.

With an end to hostilities the management of the company began to come to terms with the cost of the war, both in terms of infrastructure and rolling stock, and its staff. In the years leading up to the outbreak of the war in 1914, the GWR had transformed itself under the leadership of General Manager James Inglis and Locomotive Superintendent G. J. Churchward, boasting that it was the pre-eminent railway in Great Britain; the war had brought that transformation to a halt, with much still to be done, but in the aftermath of war any thought of new works was for the future.[5]

The GWR had effectively been nationalised for the duration of the war by the creation of the Railway Executive Committee (REC) under the terms of the 1871 Regulation of Forces Act, it being 'advantageous for them to do so for the welfare of the country in an emergency'.[6] The REC did not manage the day-to-day operations or financial arrangements of railways, as at the time it was thought inefficient and time-consuming. A circular issued to staff by General Manager Frank Potter on 5 August 1914[7] noted that the Government had, 'for the time being, taken over the control of the railway in connection with the mobilization of the troops'. The management of the railway and existing conditions of employment of staff would 'remain unaltered', he optimistically continued, implying the arrangement might be only temporary. By the end of the year, however, it was apparent that the war would not be over quickly, and the company was already facing significant difficulties, not only in operating its existing services but also in meeting the increased demands of the War Department.

By October 1914, more than 8,000 Great Western staff had already volunteered for the colours, the company optimistically promising that their jobs would be held open until their return from the war. Voluntary enlistment and, as the war progressed, conscription meant that the staff complement was severely depleted; the total number of men joining the forces throughout the course of hostilities was 25,479, 32.6% of the total prewar establishment.[8] The railway reacted by re-employing staff who had retired from the company and recruiting women to fill the places of men called up for military service. Although it tried to retain skilled staff, high casualty rates on the Western Front in March 1916 led to all unmarried men between the ages of 18 and 41 being liable for enlistment. Six months later the GWR was obliged to release all men under 26 except signalmen, shunters and other 'essential workers'. In 1918, a further 1,000 staff born in 1898 and 1899 were called up, leading to concerns that the railway was becoming dangerously understaffed.

The location for this photograph of an Allied tank is not recorded, but it is from an album recording the work of Swindon Works during the Great War.

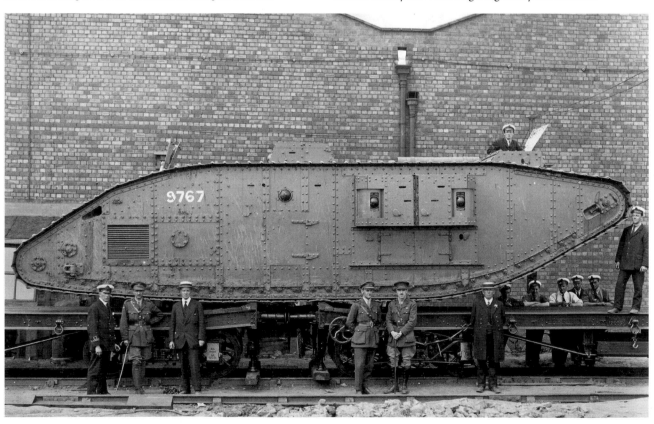

CONTINENTAL AMBULANCE TRAIN.
Built at G.W.R.Works. Swindon.1915.

TOP A view of an Ambulance Train built by the GWR in 1915 for Continental use. The image was published by the company as part of a set of postcards.

ABOVE Shells stand in stacks as they are loaded into the GWR gunpowder wagon at Swindon Works during World War 1. The wagons were lined with wood, while hinges and bolts were made of brass, to reduce the risk of sparks that might cause an explosion.

LEFT Frank Potter, GWR General Manager 1912–19. Potter joined the company as a goods clerk at Paddington in 1869.

As was the case with other railways and industrial concerns, many of the jobs left open for GWR staff were filled in their absence by women. When war broke out, the company had 1,371 women on its pay bill — 497 on railway work 'proper', as they called it (largely in clerical positions) and a further 874 in 'other capacities', including waitresses, hotel staff, charwomen and 'washerwomen'. By 1918, this figure had increased to 6,345, many employed not only in clerical posts but in operational roles such as porters, ticket collectors and carriage cleaners.[9]

Given the depredations of enlistment it is a testament to those staff that remained that the company did not suffer any major accident during the war and still managed to run an albeit reduced service to the public and large numbers of trains for the war effort. Although the London & South Western Railway, its network encompassing many more military bases and major embarkation ports, was most affected, the GWR still played a key part in the war effort. More than 63,000 special Government trains were run, including those carrying stores, supplies, ammunition and ordnance. This total also included the operation of 'Jellicoe Specials,' trains carrying coal for the Royal Navy. More than 80% of the steam coal required for the Admiralty originated in the Aberdare and Rhondda districts of South Wales, and by 1918 no fewer than 79 trains a week were being run between South Wales and Grangemouth in Scotland — a figure that increased as the end of the war drew nearer.

In addition to the many trains carrying troops and munitions to the Western Front, nearly 6,000 ambulance trains passed over the GWR system during the war; almost 3,000 of these called

at Great Western stations to discharge patients, Bristol Temple Meads being the busiest, handling 395 trains, largely due to its proximity to Avonmouth Docks, where many casualties from the Mediterranean and Far East were disembarked.

All this extra work had to be done in spite of severe coal shortages; as the war progressed, the demands of the War Office and Admiralty meant that the GWR along with other railways were forced to reduce services just to cope with war work. Despite the conflict, passengers still wanted to travel, but, to discourage them, fares were raised sharply, Sunday services reduced or withdrawn completely and excursions stopped for the duration. It was not surprising, therefore, that following the signing of the Armistice there was growing pressure to reinstate services to prewar levels as soon as possible.

Speaking at the first postwar Annual General Meeting of the GWR in February 1919, Company Chairman Viscount Churchill reported that, whilst the railway wanted to restore services, this could not 'be done to any material extent as matters stand at the present moment'.[10] Whilst shortages of staff still overseas was an issue, as was work still required to repair locomotives and rolling stock, the greatest concern was, he argued, a chronic shortage of coal. With only 2-3 weeks' stock instead of the normal 8-9 weeks' supply it was, he told shareholders, a source of 'constant anxiety' that the railway might not have enough coal to maintain even the current reduced level of services.

The victory of Lloyd George's coalition after the 'Khaki Election' of December 1918 ushered in a period of unrest and discontent in the first winter after the Armistice from which the Great Western was not immune. The demobilisation of troops was badly handled at first, and many of the three million men home from the war remained in camps, leading to mutinies and demonstrations that in many cases gained widespread public sympathy. Winston Churchill was forced to act and issue new orders, which meant that most men had returned to their families by the end of 1919. Nevertheless, the process was slow, and by July only 13,370 staff — just over half the GWR employees who had enlisted — had resumed employment with the company.[11] These returning staff had displaced 1,300 women and 940 temporary workers, although company records show that it was still necessary to retain the services of staff well past retirement age, the oldest being Mr T. Stephens, a 71-year-old foreman at Wolverhampton, whose services were to be retained until March 1920.

LEFT In 1919, the GWR bought a number of electric vehicles for delivering parcels and other goods. No E13 receives attention at Westbourne Park in 1920. *Philip Kelley collection*

BELOW LEFT Senior staff as portrayed In the *Great Western Railway Magazine* in 1919.

BELOW A fleet of GWR Commer lorries leaving the goods depot at Paddington, possibly during the rail strike of 1919. *Philip Kelley collection*

While the Government remained preoccupied with Peace Treaty negotiations in Paris, discussions and decisions about the future of Britain's railways after the war were postponed with a pledge from the Ministry of Transport that the 'period of control' would continue for another two years from Armistice Day, guaranteeing the GWR revenue based on its 1913 receipts. Despite giving the company some comfort in terms of time to rebuild, continued Government influence in the area of labour matters was to be of far-reaching importance. Although British workers had, in part, made the Allied victory in 1918 possible through their long hours of toil in munitions factories and other heavy industry, concessions gained during the war meant that in peacetime they felt more confident in flexing their collective muscle to gain further concessions from Government. The postwar industrial landscape had changed out of all recognition, and Great Western management now faced the prospect of negotiating with trade unions — something that would have been unthinkable a decade before.

Company correspondence was dominated by discussion of 'labour matters' in the aftermath of the war, and perhaps the most significant event early in 1919 was the Government's announcement of the adoption of the eight-hour day. This concession was a result of an undertaking given by Lord Ashfield, President of the Board of Trade, in August 1917 (following a threatened strike by footplate staff) that the matter would be considered at the end of the war. Within days of the Armistice being signed the Associated Society of Locomotive Engineers & Firemen (ASLEF) once again threatened strike action if the eight-hour day were not conceded, and on 1 February 1919 the principle was accepted by Government. In his memoirs Felix Pole, soon to be GWR General Manager, called the move an 'expensive concession', adding that the whole affair had been decided without any consultation with the railway companies or the Railway Executive Committee.[12] These politically expedient new arrangements markedly improved working conditions for staff but also left the Great Western with an estimated £1 million increase in its wage bill, as additional staff would now be required to maintain services.

Further negotiations and discussions took place as trade unions pressed home claims in an atmosphere of tension and discord. The alarm with which this was viewed by the company can be seen in an article in the March 1919 *GWR Magazine* wherein staff were warned that the workman was not 'a machine to be kept well-oiled with high wages and good housing' and that he might have 'an inflated idea of what company profits were'.[13] Unimpressed by this, the unions pressed numerous claims; in July 1919 directors were told that negotiations with the National Union of Railwaymen (NUR) and the Amalgamated Society of Railway Servants (ASRS) over wages and conditions of service had been agreed. They also heard of incidents occurring all over the system; carpenters and

The Armistice Day ceremony at Paddington on 11 November 1920.

cabinetmakers at Swindon refused to work under the piece-work system, and there were also disputes involving coal-weighers and signalmen at Swansea and dock porters at Plymouth.[14]

These more localised disputes were only a sideshow for larger negotiations occurring at a national level. The country had been hit by a wave of strikes, even police and prison officers in Liverpool and London withdrawing their labour, but in September 1919 the country was hit by a national rail strike. By the summer, discussions between Government and unions had dragged on for months. Progress had been made on staff terms and conditions, with various concessions over guaranteed days and weeks, overtime rates and paid holiday rates being decided. There was, unsurprisingly, less unanimity over wages. The wages of railwaymen had risen progressively during the conflict as a result of war bonuses, paid by Government as a result of the rapidly rising cost of living. In 1915, this had amounted to 3s a week extra for those earning less than 30s per week and 2s a week bonus for those on a higher wage. In 1917, the bonus was doubled; thus after the Armistice many railwaymen were earning considerably more than they had done before the war, and unsurprisingly, few were keen to lose these increases.

Unions had conceded in November 1918 that the level of what had become known as the 'war wage' should be based on the cost of living as published in the *Labour Gazette*. They also agreed that a sliding scale should be used, whereby wages were raised or lowered from time to time as the cost of living increased or decreased. This arrangement had of course appeared good while the cost of living was still increasing, but in March of 1919 it fell from 120% of prewar levels to 110%, which would have meant wages dropping on average 3s per week. This was not enforced by Government, as negotiations with unions were still continuing. Sir Auckland Geddes, President of the Board of Trade, was, however, keen on the 'standardisation' of wages, a term seen by most as a euphemism for 'reduction'; it was Geddes who eventually precipitated a strike when he issued unions with 'definitive' terms for settlement which for many would bring a reduction in wages, including a minimum wage of 40s instead of the current 51s.

What one historian has called Geddes' 'high-handed bearing'[15] was not well received by the National Union of Railwaymen (NUR), which rejected the proposals on 23 September, with a threat of strike action if new a offer was not received by noon on the 25th. A meeting that day between the NUR and the Prime Minister failed to produce an agreement, and at midnight the Great Western, along with almost every other railway in the country, was brought to a standstill. The nine-day railway strike that followed was every bit as bitter as the one that was to follow it in 1926, and while Government ministers painted the dispute as an anarchist conspiracy, it did not at that time develop into a larger General Strike. Accusations and counter-accusations were exchanged in the press (J. H. Thomas, Secretary of the NUR and a former GWR fireman, even appearing in a special film screened in cinemas across the country, arguing the railwaymen's case), and this, and other trade union support, meant that what Pole called a 'face-saving' agreement was not reached until 5 October, when its terms were revealed at a mass meeting held in the Albert Hall.

Existing pay levels were to be guaranteed until 30 September 1920, and no adult railwayman's wages would drop below 51s as long as the cost of living remained at or above 110% of prewar levels. Wages withheld from men while on strike would be paid on resumption of work, and it was also noted that 'men should work harmoniously with railway servants who have remained at, or returned to work, and Government and unions agree that no man shall be prejudiced in any way as a result of the strike'.[16] Feelings had certainly run high during the strike, the most serious incident, on 1 October, being an attempt to derail a passenger train between Hay Lane and Wootton Bassett, near Swindon; a heavily loaded Bristol–Paddington service hit a large pile of rail and timber taken from a ganger's hut but fortunately remained upright.

The unveiling of the GWR war memorial at Paddington in 1922. The bronze figure was by Charles Sargeant Jagger, the stonework by Thomas S. Tait. Inside the plinth was a sealed casket recording the names of the 2,524 GWR employees who were killed in the Great War.

The company magazine also reported attacks on volunteers working on the railway during the strike. At Paddington a porter assaulted a volunteer, receiving three weeks' hard labour for the attack, whilst at South Lambeth two other volunteers had acid thrown at them. A volunteer signalman working at Bradford in Somerset was knocked unconscious by a strike sympathiser who had told him 'it's the likes of you who are keeping us working men down,' reported *The Times*.[17] In a less serious incident at Swindon, strikers intending to tar the windows of a 'blackleg' managed to tar the wrong house. Upon discovering their mistake, noted the *GWR Magazine*, 'they cleaned off the tar as well as they could'.[18]

Great Western management had little influence on a strike they had not precipitated. Despite the use of volunteers they could run only a skeleton service and cope as best they could; this even included using volunteers to move 80 sheep, stranded by the dispute at Paddington goods depot, to a field at West Ealing. Besides income lost on passenger services its goods business suffered badly, and traffic was lost to road transport during the dispute — the beginning of a process that would profoundly change the business model and profitability of railways between the wars.

Pole wrote later that after the strike had been settled he had 'marvelled that conditions of service that were regarded as impossible before the war should have been granted in the most open-handed manner after the country had been impoverished by a war that had cost millions'.[19] What all this meant to Britain's railways, including the GWR, was that for the year 1920 operating expenses totalled £73,923,419 — a figure far in excess of the £23,260,765 spent in 1913, before takeover by Government.

For families of Great Western employees still grieving at the loss of loved ones killed or badly injured in the war there was more tragedy to cope with. Railway staff and their families were not immune from the effects of the great influenza epidemic that affected almost half the world's population, eventually killing many millions. In Britain the outbreak began in the early summer of 1918, peaking initially in November when in the worst week over 7,500 people died in London and other urban centres. After a brief respite there was a further outbreak early in 1919, increasing in intensity until March. London was particularly badly hit, a total of more than 15,000 deaths from influenza being recorded between 1918 and 1919. Seemingly fit and healthy men and women were struck down, often dying within days.[20] The March 1919 *GWR Magazine* told its readers that the influenza epidemic had 'taken full toll of victims from the Paddington Telegraph office staff,' reporting that three of its telephone operators had succumbed to the disease; one, Miss Elsie Lewis, had passed away on 4 February after an illness of only a few days.[21]

Some of the 230,000 British people who had died in the influenza pandemic had been weakened by war wounds or disease or illness brought on by the strain of the conflict at home or abroad. Although

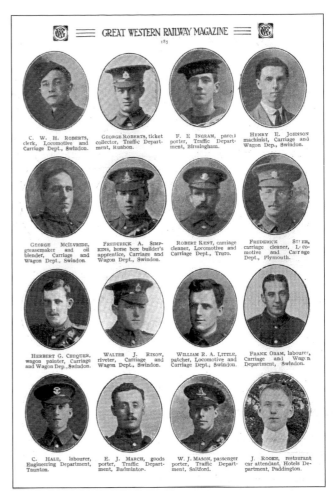

A page from the *Great Western Railway Magazine* in 1918, showing just 16 of the 2,524 GWR staff killed in action. This grim ritual was been repeated month after month from 1915 and continued even after the Armistice had been signed.

his eventual passing was not brought on by influenza, the death of the GWR's General Manager Frank Potter in 1919 was in no small part due to the stresses and strains of running the railway during the conflict. The first hint that the heavy pressure Potter had been under was affecting his health was given when it was announced in April 1919 that he had been advised to take a 'short rest' in Cornwall. Some clue as to why the job of General Manager was quite so taxing was then revealed in a leading article in the company magazine wherein it was noted that, unlike his counterpart on most other large railways, the General Manager of the GWR, 'in the conduct of the extremely onerous duties appertaining to his office, has not had an assistant or deputy'.[22] For some time past, the editor noted without irony, it had been apparent that the appointment of an Assistant General Manager was 'desirable'.

Never again would a General Manager be without an assistant, and the man chosen to step up to the new post was

A reminder of prewar glories. Churchward 'Saint' No 2933 *Bibury Court*, built at Swindon in 1911, stands at the end of Platform 1 at Paddington.

Charles Aldington, Superintendent of the Line. It seems likely that the GWR board did not expect Potter to return, for in the same article new incumbents of the Superintendent of the Line position and Principal Assistant to the General Manager were also announced. The new holder of the latter post was Felix Pole, the rising star of the company, whose 'knowledge of affairs and urbanity have given him an established reputation,' reported the *GWR Magazine*.

For those close to Frank Potter at Paddington his death in July 1919 was perhaps not entirely unexpected, the official announcement of his passing revealing that, despite previous reports that he had been advised to take a complete rest in February, he had not done so immediately, instead remaining in London to assist with staff negotiations and preparations for the GWR's Annual General Meeting. The 63-year-old, who had devoted his whole life to the railway and had risen up through the ranks, only reluctantly went to Cornwall to recuperate and died of heart failure at the company's Tregenna Castle Hotel on 23 July.

Charles Aldington, now elevated to the top job on the Great Western, was only six years younger than Potter and had begun his career on the railway at 14 as a junior clerk at Handsworth & Knowle station in 1876. Working his way up through the ranks (unlike many of his colleagues), he took the revolutionary step of leaving the company to join the Central London Railway in

1899, returning to Paddington three years later. Thanking well-wishers for their messages of support in the September 1919 *GWR Magazine*, Aldington told readers that he looked forward to the future with a belief that 'as during the war, Great Western men will prove themselves to be unsurpassed … in their loyalty of spirit and singleness of purpose for the country's welfare'.[23] Felix Pole described Aldington as a conscientious, hard-working and efficient railwayman but felt that, while he had always aspired to be General Manager, it soon became apparent that he found his new duties 'irksome'. Like all his predecessors he worked long hours, often in trying circumstances, and Pole reported that on one occasion he had grumpily told him: 'I was a fool to take this job'.[24]

Only months before Potter's death Aldington and Company Chairman Viscount Churchill had attended a memorial service at St Paul's Cathedral to honour the almost 19,000 railwaymen who had been killed in action, died of their wounds or who were missing in action. The ceremony, held on 14 May, included music played by an orchestra of 150 men and women drawn from various railways, including the Great Western, and similar services were held at Bristol, Cardiff and Birmingham to honour the contribution of railway staff to the war effort.

The overwhelming sense of grief and loss felt by families hit by the death of loved ones in the war was compounded by the fact that many had no grave to visit. The difficulties faced by the Imperial War Graves Commission in recovering and repatriating the bodies of those killed meant that cemeteries were built close to the battlefields. Unable to visit these, local communities and organisations and employees took the initiative in building their own war memorials closer to home. On the Great Western this process had begun in late 1915, when a 'Roll of Honour' was installed in a prominent position on Platform 1 at Paddington station. Designed by a member of staff, it consisted of a central panel which noted that the staff named on the Roll of Honour 'upheld the best traditions of their country, and their memory is revered alike by the Company and their comrades'.[25] The Roll was updated and revised from time to time until June 1922; framed examples were distributed to principal stations on the GWR system and, 90 years on, a number still survive.

Exactly a year after the guns fell silent for the last time, Great Western employees gathered at Paddington to mark the two-minute silence on the 11th hour of the 11th day of the 11th month. This first commemoration of the signing of the Armistice was a low-key affair, attended by around 200 staff and presided over by the stationmaster, Mr Weaver. A year later the GWR Magazine reported that more than a thousand members of the public, relatives and staff, including the Assistant General Manager Felix Pole, had gathered to place wreaths at the Roll of Honour and hear an address from the Reverend E. N. Sharpe from St James's Church in Paddington. The solemn gathering was repeated annually until 1934 but was not held that year, as Armistice Day fell on a Sunday and it proved difficult to find a choir for the ceremony. The new Vicar of St James's wrote to the company on his appointment in October 1935, asking if his services would be required on 11 November, but was told that it had been decided to discontinue the ceremony. GWR correspondence also reveals a regular request from the GWR Company Secretary to the Superintendent of the Line about the Armistice Day service, requesting that he 'kindly arrange, as before, as to the minimum movement in the station and the whistling and blowing off of steam during the service'.[26]

War memorials to fallen comrades were erected by staff at a number of other locations across the system, the highest number being within the company's railway works at Swindon. Many of the individual workshops had their own roll of honour or memorial, but one of the largest was the tablet recording the names of 217 staff from the 'A' Erecting Shop who had returned safely from the war, as well as the 18 men who had lost their lives. Company correspondence also reveals that the Great Western board of directors made a grant of £32 to clear an outstanding balance for the war memorial in the town, which had been erected by public subscription, and made a further grant from its Apprentice Fund to pay for a tablet listing the names of Swindon men who had lost their lives in the war to be made in the Carriage Works and installed at the Town Hall.

1   Hattersley, R.: *Borrowed Time — The Story of Britain between the Wars* (Abacus Books, 2007), p2

2   Great Western Railway: Minutes of Board Meeting held 6 December 1918

3   *Great Western Railway Magazine* December 1918, p171

4   *Ibid*, p171

5   For more detail see Bryan, T.: *The Golden Age of the Great Western Railway, 1892–1914* (PSL Books, 1991)

6   Gittins, S.: *The Great Western Railway in the First World War* (History Press, 2010)

7   GWR Circular, General Manager's Office, Paddington, 5 August 1914

8   Pratt, E. A.: *The War Record of the Great Western Railway* (Selwyn & Blount, 1922), p30

9   *Ibid*, p31

10   *Great Western Railway Magazine* March 1919, p35

11   Great Western Railway: Minutes of Board Meeting held 4 July 1919

12   Pole, F. J. C.: *His Book* (Town & Country Press), 1968, p104

13   *Great Western Railway Magazine* March 1919, p37

14   Great Western Railway: Minutes of Board Meeting held 4 July 1919

15   Mowat, C. L.: *Britain Between the Wars* 1918–1940(Methuen 1955), p39

16   *Great Western Railway Magazine* November 1919, p207

17   'Railway Volunteer assaulted', report in *The Times* 10 October 1919

18   *Great Western Railway Magazine* November 1919, p207

19   Pole, *ibid*, p109

20   Pugh, M.: *We Danced All Night — A Social History of Britain between the Wars* (Vintage Books, 2009), p6

21   *Great Western Railway Magazine* March 1919, p51

22   *Ibid* April 1919, p55

23   *Ibid* September 1919, p163

24   Pole, *ibid*, p38

25   Great Western Roll of Honour — STEAM collection

26   Letter dated 31 October 1927 — National Archives: RAIL253/256

CHAPTER 2

A NEW GREAT WESTERN

The two years following the settlement of the national railway strike in October 1919 were no less problematic and uncertain for the Great Western than the tumultuous period after the signing of the Armistice. Labour relations remained difficult, and the management of the railway wrestled with the enormous task of balancing a budget that had been strained even further by an increase in salary costs of over £1 million with the introduction of the eight-hour day.

There had been some tentative steps towards restoring at least some of the prewar services to which GWR passengers had been accustomed; a new summer timetable had been issued in May 1919 which included additional main-line, suburban and provincial trains. The timetable showed at least some accelerated services and the reintroduction of dining cars and slip coaches. The 10.15am Paddington–Penzance service reverted to a 10.30am start time, and although its revised schedule looked more like

the prewar 'Cornish Riviera Limited', the company did not for the moment feel confident enough to relaunch its pre-eminent express. The *Great Western Railway Magazine* also reported that a number of smaller stations like Dawlish Warren, closed for the duration of the war, had been reopened.[1] There could, however, be little real progress until Government made clear its intentions for railways at a national level. After four and a half years under Government control there seemed little likelihood that Britain's railways would revert to their prewar position whereby more than 100 independent companies competed in a wasteful and often uneconomic manner. A Parliamentary Select Committee had examined the problem in 1918, and its Chairman, Sir Eric Geddes, formerly Deputy General Manager of the North Eastern Railway and Minister of Munitions during the war, had the unenviable task of making recommendations for dealing with what became known as 'The Transport Problem'. Whilst no definite recommendation was suggested, a number of possible solutions were put forward, all involving some degree of amalgamation, and one even suggesting full nationalisation. These conclusions can hardly have been a surprise to the GWR board, and indeed an article in the company magazine noted that there had 'been a widespread feeling that reversion of prewar conditions, so far as railways were concerned, was hardly likely to take effect in its entirety'.[2] There was, however, some consternation when, in an election address in December 1918, Winston Churchill, then Secretary of State for War, suggested nationalisation as the best option. A critical article in *The Times* noted that while no one was 'prepared to return to the competition of private companies as it existed before the war' Churchill's 'startling' remarks did not help clarify a bigger issue that also involved canals, roads and the future use of the 'great fleet of motor lorries that will some day be released by the Armies'.[3]

There was no doubt some element of electioneering in Churchill's speech, and while his remarks were not subsequently publicly supported by the Prime Minister, the company nevertheless remained wary about the outlook; at its Annual General Meeting some months later the Chairman, Viscount Churchill, told shareholders that directors were ready and fully prepared to protect and safeguard their interests when any 'definite pronouncement' was made.

A further step towards the co-ordination of transport was taken in August 1919 with the passing of the Ways & Communications Act, which established a new Ministry of Transport, with Sir Eric Geddes as its first minister. With railways still remaining 'in the period of control' until September 1921, there was now time to produce definitive proposals for the future. Few were under any illusion that its task was easy; one of the civil servants involved in the process wrote a few years later that, from its inception, 'the new ministry certainly experienced its full share of criticism and publicity, no doubt due to the exceptional political and economic conditions of the time'.[4] For the Great Western — as with other large railways — the biggest challenge was how it would cope with the vastly increased costs

LEFT Churchward 'Star' No 4066 *Malvern Abbey* passes Twyford signalbox at the head of the down 'Cornish Riviera Limited' in 1925.

BELOW A train headed by 'Star' No 4019 *Knight Templar* includes a number of coaches still in wartime all-brown livery, as well as several Churchward 70ft 'Concertina' carriages.

ABOVE A cycle delivery tricycle, photographed at Ealing in January 1923. *Philip Kelley collection*

ABOVE RIGHT The bridge over the River Towy at Carmarthen, after rebuilding in 1925. The steelwork was by the Cleveland Bridge & Engineering Co of Darlington.

it now had to bear following the war, once Government control was removed. On top of the huge increases in staff wages, the costs of the materials essential to the business had rocketed. Coal, which had been 12s per ton in 1913, was now 36s a ton, and boiler plate just over 8s a ton before the war was now almost 30s a ton; even hay, required for Great Western shunting and delivery horses, had increased in price by £10 per ton.

Besides keeping a tight rein on expenditure, the only way the company would be able to survive was to generate additional income. Railways had been unable to raise their passenger fares or rates charged for the transport of goods, as these were controlled by the Ministry of Transport. By the beginning of 1920, however, it had become apparent to Government that, if drastic action were not taken, the taxpayer might well be subsidising railways at a level of around £50 million per year for the foreseeable future. This politically unpalatable problem was resolved by increasing rates for merchandise and mineral traffic from 15 January, in many cases doubling charges; passenger fares were similarly raised in August and September 1920.

Whilst this measure made some progress towards railways returning to balances somewhere nearer 1913 levels, it also, not surprisingly, raised the temperature of the national debate about the future of railways and of transport in general. Although some newspapers, like *The Times*, took a largely sanguine view regarding the inevitability of fare and rate rises, arguing that the railways were at 'breaking point' in terms of generating sufficient income to survive without Government assistance, they were also quick to criticise fare rises as 'holiday taxes'. Other papers took a more confrontational approach, running campaigns against 'iniquitous' railways like the GWR, which were accused of making a profit at the expense of travellers, with comments like 'the wasters don't care — they'll put up your fare'.[5]

Opponents were also quick to highlight the advantages of road transport and its competitiveness, in terms of both price and speed of delivery. *The Times* reported evidence given by the Transport Manager of Lipton's Tea at a Ministry of Transport committee in 1920; he told the committee that 'road transport today is beating the railways all the time' — a comment that could hardly be reassuring to the GWR management at Paddington.[6] There is little doubt that the company was stung by some of the more sensational criticism, even reprinting some of the wilder comments in the magazine; when the *Daily Mail* accused railways of profiteering, announcing that the increased cost of jam was down to higher transport costs, it felt compelled to respond with an article full of calculations showing that increased rates would amount to 1d per 6lb of jam.

The more serious matter of the future of British railways became clearer at the end of June 1920 with the publication of a Government White Paper. The idea of full nationalisation had been abandoned in favour of a proposal to reduce the 120 independent companies taken over by the Government in 1914 to seven new systems — Southern, Western, North Western,

Eastern, North Eastern, Scottish and London. Each of these broad groups would absorb the smaller and independent lines within its area, and while the aim was that this process should be voluntary, powers would be provided to force companies to amalgamate if necessary.

The White Paper also noted that the financial arrangements proposed would enable the new groups, combining all the revenue from absorbed companies, to earn the equivalent of their 1913 income; it also anticipated that, with careful management and economies of scale achieved through amalgamation, railways would eventually make surpluses, and it intended to share in these profits. There was, however, no mention of any guarantee, should substantial losses be made by the new railway groups — an omission that prompted *The Railway Gazette* to comment, 'If the State is to share profits, it must also share losses.'[7]

More contentious still were proposals regarding the management of the new systems; as well as the normal quota of shareholder directors, the Ministry of Transport suggested that the board should include staff members who were not nominated by the company but

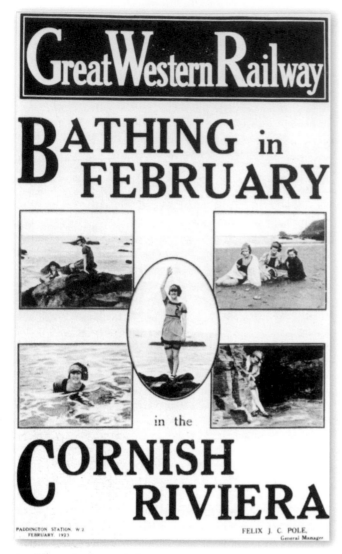

Great Western Railway

A well-known GWR poster which even today stretches the bounds of credibility but illustrates the company's ongoing promotion of Cornwall as a winter resort.

raised were communicated to staff in a long article in the *GWR Magazine* in early 1920; the RCA proposed an alternative scheme that included only five groups — North Western, North Eastern, Western, Southern and London. It also poured cold water on the laudable aim of Government to eliminate competition between the new groups, pointing out that 'any scheme of grouping, short of complete unification of the railway system as a whole, renders this impracticable'.[8]

It also came as no surprise that, despite dramatic changes in industrial relations following the war, railway companies were unwilling to accept the principle of 'workers elected by workers' being appointed to company boards, considering it 'unjustifiable' and 'from every point of view … objectionable'.[9] This issue, along with the proposal to establish national wage boards, highlighted the fundamental difficulty for Government, which, while wishing to return the railways to private ownership, still wanted to retain influence and control over them but (as the railways and other critics were quick to point out) did not want to provide them with any financial guarantees.

A further consideration in the months leading up to the introduction of the Railways Bill on 11 May 1921 was the amount of compensation due to railway companies for additional costs incurred as a result of the war. A committee set up by the Ministry of Transport and chaired by Lord Colwyn concluded that wear and tear on rolling stock, track, buildings and machinery had cost railways an estimated £150 million. Although Government had no legal obligation to pay, recognising the huge contribution made by railways like the GWR during the war (and following negotiations with the new groups), it agreed to pay a rather more modest £60 million, a figure formally noted in the 1921 Railways Bill.

The stress and strain of running the railway in such uncertain times gave the Great Western board yet another problem to contend with early in 1921. At the company's Annual General Meeting in February Viscount Churchill had reported that the General Manager was indisposed due to ill health; less than two years after taking over from Frank Potter, Charles Aldington suffered a stroke and, like his predecessor, was sent by the board to Cornwall to recuperate. In his absence, his assistant Felix Pole deputised, playing a key role in much of the discussion surrounding the detail of the amalgamation. When Aldington returned to London in May 1921, doctors advised against returning to work and insisted on his immediate retirement; reporting his resignation in the *GWR Magazine*, his successor, Pole, reminded staff that, for Aldington, life was so interwoven with the Great Western that 'it must have been a severe wrench for him to detach himself, especially on the threshold of such changes as the immediate future seems to hold'.[10]

Pole was to play an important role in shaping the detail of the Railways Bill when it was introduced into the House of Commons. The fierce criticism that followed the publication of the White Paper had resulted in the Act that reached the statute

elected by the workforce. In the matter of dealing with wages and working conditions, it was also proposed that national wage boards be set up, continuing the kind of system that had operated while railways remained under Government control.

Publication of the White Paper was followed by almost a year of debate, discussion and negotiation involving railways, trade unions, chambers of commerce and other industrial concerns. The railways, the future of which was so closely tied up with the proposals, had not been consulted in advance and, not surprisingly, had many objections to the original scheme. These objections were outlined in a formal letter to the minister from the Railway Companies Association (RCA), whose chairman was Viscount Churchill, also Chairman of the Great Western. The main issues book being a rather more circumspect affair; one contemporary writer noted that it represented a 'large measure of agreement between Government and the railways, the trading community and the trades unions',[11] but railway companies saw the end result as a real victory, maintaining the private ownership of the network. Given the huge financial difficulties facing the country after the Great War, the amalgamation scheme enacted in 1921 was probably the most expedient course of action, given that, as Adrian Vaughan has noted, the Government lacked the money to purchase the whole network, if it wanted to create a nationalised railway.[12]

Despite the publication of the draft Bill, there were still some twists and turns to be negotiated by the Great Western before the Act was formally passed in the summer of 1921 — and a good deal of work following that to integrate companies into the new Western group. There was, unsurprisingly, still considerable intrigue and much manoeuvring to be done even as the Bill was being discussed in Parliament. In the original Bill it had been proposed that the Western group should be made up of the Great Western and six other 'constituent' companies, namely the Barry, Cardiff, Rhymney and Taff Vale railways, the Cambrian Railways and the Alexandra Docks & Railway, along with a larger number of 'subsidiary' railways. This state of affairs did not sit well with Pole or the GWR directors, who were not happy to be bracketed

with these smaller companies, and following some lobbying the Great Western was elevated to a pre-eminent position as the only 'constituent' company in the group.

This was not the end of the story, however. Whilst a number of railways in South Wales were smaller operations than the GWR, the considerable income generated from coal and dock business made them powerful players, and there was some pressure to create a separate group for South Wales, while others were unhappy at losing their constituent status. While the committee stage of the bill was being discussed, Pole was contacted by A. S. Mills, the Great Western representative at the proceedings, who told him that the minister felt he should 'make some concession to Welsh sentiment' and that he had been asked if the company would relent to the point relating to the 'subsidiary' status of some Welsh railways.

In a shrewd move, Pole agreed, suggesting that the minister should be asked in return if the new group might be called the Great Western Railway, so that the old company need not be wound up. Thus it was that the 86-year-old GWR retained its identity, the

BELOW A photograph taken to record an experiment undertaken by the GWR in June 1922, when it used a Fordson tractor in place of a horse, hauling a normal horse lorry between Paddington and the docks. *Philip Kelley Collection*

OVERLEAF A lone shunting horse, the last to be used at Paddington, stands in the high-level goods yard in August 1925, while over the wall a number of fishermen wait in hope for a bite from the canal. *Philip Kelley Collection*

only railway in the grouping process to do so. Although the GWR and the other six constituent companies were listed in the Act as equals, in reality they were to be amalgamated with the Great Western, and the company was easily the 'predominant partner' in the whole arrangement.[13]

This arrangement also meant that, when it came to selection of directors of the newly constituted operation, the easiest course was the retention of existing GWR directors, who were joined by a further six — one being drawn from each of the other constituent companies.

The creation of the new Great Western Railway group, involving agreement of financial terms with the other six 'constituent' railways and the eventual absorption of the remaining 'subsidiary' lines, was a drawn-out affair, not being completed until the middle of 1923. The whole ('Grouping') process was overseen by an Amalgamation Tribunal, whose job it was to facilitate and ratify the amalgamation or absorption of 120 companies to form just four railways — the Great Western, the London, Midland & Scottish, the London & North Eastern, and the Southern. For the most part the GWR was able to agree terms with most of the railways it amalgamated with or absorbed, although some proved more difficult than others.

Whilst the combining of the six constituent companies (seven including the GWR) was on paper technically an amalgamation, it was in reality a takeover by the Great Western, and company correspondence leaves little doubt that GWR management at Paddington thought it so. Pole's memoirs note that, as it was the largest company, 'it was agreed that negotiations should be conducted by the GWR'.[14] No doubt among the directors of some companies, especially more profitable lines such as the Taff Vale Railway, this high-handed approach must have rankled, but they had little choice but to make the best of the arrangement and get the best deal they could.

Discussions centred on the agreement of terms for the exchange of stocks by the respective companies, as well as the level of compensation to be paid to directors of constituent companies displaced by the amalgamation. Whilst these high-level discussions were going on, at an operating level the Great Western had started the process of integration; at a meeting of Chief Officers in October 1921 it was announced that 'several constituent companies had been invited to co-operate with the Great Western Railway in securing additional traffic and effecting all possible working economies and improvements'.[15]

By March 1922, terms had been agreed with five of the six other constituent companies, the exception being the Barry Railway. An application was therefore submitted to the Amalgamation Tribunal for approval in March, although the General Manager was keen to proceed carefully, aware perhaps of the sensibilities of staff in companies about to be taken over; according to the minutes of a meeting held on 27 February 'it was not proposed to make any changes to the management of the constituent companies until after the amalgamation scheme had been approved by the Tribunal,

Churchward 4-6-0 No 2923 *Saint George* at Plymouth. The locomotive was built at Swindon in September 1907.

and that the departmental officers of the various undertakings would continue responsibilities until other arrangements [could be] made'.[16] The scheme submitted by the GWR was approved by the tribunal on 25 March 1922, a total of £54,500 being paid to directors who had lost their positions as a result of amalgamation. By holding out, the Barry Railway obtained improved terms for the holders of its stocks and shares, arguing that the company had had great potential, although contemporary commentators felt that in the end the terms finally offered were 'generous'.[17]

Once terms had been agreed with the Barry Railway the arrangements for its amalgamation into the GWR and a further scheme for the absorption of a number of smaller 'subsidiary' companies, including the Cleobury Mortimer & Ditton Priors Light Railway, the Princetown Railway, and the Port Talbot Docks & Railway, were also submitted to the tribunal. Over the succeeding months a number of other schemes followed in a similar vein, each culminating with agreement by the tribunal and a special meeting of the GWR shareholders and proprietors to ratify the financial arrangements. There was much to do for staff as each batch of companies was welcomed into the new operation, from dealing with staffing and timetabling to the most basic administrative tasks, such as the transfer and renaming of bank accounts.

THE GREAT WESTERN "Hooray! Never even blew me cap off!"

TOP Two Taff Vale Railway locomotives inherited by the GWR as part of the Grouping process; 'M' class 0-6-2 No 481 retains more of its TVR features than 'Westernised''U' class No 602.

ABOVE A much-reproduced cartoon, originally published in the *Western Mail*, illustrating the fact that the GWR was the only pre-Grouping company to retain its original name.

By June 1922, the General Manager was able to report to staff in the *GWR Magazine* that seven of the 'major' companies had been absorbed and that negotiations were almost complete on others. The lines still to be brought in were, he noted, 'relatively unimportant independent ones or lines already worked by the Company'.[18] Speaking at the Annual General Meeting some months earlier the Chairman, Viscount Churchill, expressed the hope that, by enabling the company to carry on its old name in the considerably extended area comprising the Western group, the 1921 Act had 'brought joy to the hearts of many who loved the Great Western'. He added, rather ruefully, that the terms agreed between the GWR and constituent and subsidiary railways had been arrived at 'after long and considerable negotiation'.[19]

In the case of some companies, negotiations were very long; under the terms of the Railways Act all arrangements for the amalgamation and absorption of railways into the four new railways should have been complete by 1 January 1923, but at the end of November 1922 the General Manager told his Chief Officers that terms had yet to be agreed with the Didcot, Newbury & Southampton Railway, the Exeter Railway, the Forest of Dean Central Railway, and the Midland & South Western Junction Railway (MSWJR).

By June 1923, the MSWJR was the only railway still to agree terms, and surviving correspondence shows that negotiations with the GWR were extremely protracted, the first meeting between officers of the two railways having been held as early as December 1921. At this initial meeting, Felix Pole had explained that the deal to be offered would be based on the income of the MSWJR in 1913. John Davies, the latter company's General Manager, argued that he should 'certainly expect that the GWR would go further than this' and that, in view of the geographical position of the MSWJR line for traffic purposes, 'the Great Western would deal with the matter in the most liberal way possible'.[20] In January 1924, the GWR

offered £25,542, a figure based on the 1913 net-revenue figure of £25,217 plus £325 interest. Although this figure appeared low, the financial position of the MSWJR was not good; it had borrowed heavily from the Midland Railway, and whilst, as the MSWJR argued, this meant that 'the railway was superior in condition to subsidiary lines generally' it also left the Great Western liable for a debt in excess of £200,000.

The offer was rejected by the MSWJR board in March 1922, but the smaller company's case was not strengthened when it became apparent that the London & South Western Railway, over which the MSWJR had running powers, intended to ask the GWR for money owed in respect of traffic receipts. A revised offer was made to the MSWJR board in April 1923 and put to a meeting of MSWJR shareholders in July. A newspaper report noted that the Chairman, Spencer J. Portal, in recommending the revised deal, 'painted a gloomy picture of the potential financial performance of the company in the future'. The terms were, he argued, the outcome of protracted negotiations and 'fair and reasonable'.[21] Not all shareholders agreed; Mr B. Read, representing the 3% debenture holders, told the meeting that of 500 stock holders 205 were ladies and 'to a great extent were not in a position to understand the meaning of all these schemes and papers and things that were sent to them'.[22]

The meeting voted against the proposal, but it was nevertheless sent for consideration to the Amalgamation Tribunal in September 1922, and this ruled in favour of the GWR. Davies reluctantly wrote to MSWJR shareholders on 4

ABOVE RIGHT A postcard view of a Midland & South Western Junction Railway porter.

BELOW A colour picture of a GWR carriage, reproduced in the *Great Western Railway Magazine*, published to celebrate the reintroduction of the prewar chocolate-and-cream livery.

October 1923 with details of division of shares, ending a saga which illustrated something of the complications involved in the amalgamation process — negotiations with fiercely independent railways with proud traditions and officers and shareholders who saw the absorption of their railway by a large and seemingly prosperous company like the Great Western as an opportunity to try and claw money back.

At a meeting held on 1 October 1923, the General Manager was able to report to staff that the scheme for absorption of the MSWJR had been approved by the tribunal, the minutes recording that 'the final amalgamation scheme having been passed ... the whole of the arrangements in regard to grouping under the Railways Act, 1921 so far as the Company were concerned had now been completed.'[23] Writing in the *GWR Magazine* in January 1924, Pole was able to note that as of that date the GWR was now 'one homogenous whole' and that it was a unified system with great potentialities and fine possibilities.'[24]

Pole had also on a number of occasions made reference to welcoming staff from amalgamated and absorbed companies into the GWR 'family', and on a practical level much work had been done in the early stages of the Grouping process. It could not have gone unnoticed, however, that in 1922 the Great Western announced that it was to resume the repainting of passenger stock in the old prewar chocolate-and-cream livery and would also use on both locomotives and carriages the traditional crest featuring the arms of the cities of London and Bristol, which did not reflect the heritage of any of the railways brought into the new Western group.

1   'Summer Train Services', *Great Western Railway Magazine* May 1919, p87

2   *Great Western Railway Magazine* February 1919, p17

3   'Trouble on the Railways', *The Times* 6 December 1918

4   Simnett, W. E.: 'Railway Amalgamation In Great Britain', *The Railway Gazette* 1923, p26

5   *Great Western Railway Magazine* August 1920, p200

6   *The Times* 22 July 1920, p13

7   'Second thoughts on the Government's railway proposals', *The Railway Gazette* 9 July 1920, p51

8   'The Future of Railways', *Great Western Railway Magazine* January 1920, p10

9   *Ibid* p10

10   'Resignation of Charles Aldington', *Great Western Railway Magazine* July 1921, p155

11   Simnett, *ibid*, p35

12   Vaughan, A.: *The Great Western at Work, 1921–1939* (PSL Books, 1993), p10

13   Railways Act 1921

14   Pole, F. J. C.: *His Book* (Town & Country Press, 1968), p54

15   Great Western Railway, Minutes of Chief Officers' Conference Meeting held 21 October 1921

16   Great Western Railway, Minutes of Chief Officers' Conference Meeting held 27 February 1922

17   Simnett, *ibid*, p53

18   *Great Western Railway Magazine* June 1922, p217

19   *Great Western Railway Magazine* March 1922, p90

20   Great Western Railway: Absorption of MSWJR (correspondence file) — National Archives: RAIL253/753

21   'MSWJR Company: The Amalgamation Scheme — Meetings of the Company', *Wilts & Gloucestershire Standard* 11 August 1923

22   *Ibid*

23   Great Western Railway: Minutes of Chief Officers' Conference Meeting held 1 October 1923

24   'The New Year — And Last', *Great Western Railway Magazine* January 1924, p1

CHAPTER 3

THE LEGACY

When Felix Pole took up his new position as General Manager in 1921 the two most important challenges facing him were (1) to stabilise the financial position of the Great Western as it moved into new trading conditions without the benefit of Government assistance as the period of control ended, and (2) to 'weld into one organisation'[1] the seven constituent and 26 subsidiary companies which as of 1 January 1923 were to constitute the enlarged GWR. Although the company had pulled off an astute and clever feat by manoeuvring itself into a position where it managed to both keep its original name and also the predominant position as the leader of the new Western grouping, the assorted group of railways it had inherited contained a wide range of operations from some of the most well-run and profitable lines in Britain to a number of small and financially vulnerable companies struggling just to stay in business.

Space does not permit a description of all the railways that formed this Great Western inheritance, but it is worth looking at some of the railways whose fortunes were now irrevocably linked to the GWR. The acquisition of these new lines added over 900 miles to the company's existing network, and no doubt management at Paddington involved in the process of amalgamation were quite familiar with the history and operation of many of the major lines that now formed part of the system. For rank-and-file staff, however, a good number of what the company had called 'foreign' lines were unfamiliar and geographically distant. More than a dozen of the most significant additions were profiled in a series of articles in the *Great Western Railway Magazine* in 1922 and 1923. A few years later, in 1926, Chief Goods Manager P. R. Gale produced a 142-page reference book, marked 'PRIVATE: FOR THE USE OF THE COMPANY'S OFFICIALS ONLY', which listed key dates, route mileages and other relevant information useful to stationmasters and goods and engineering staff; they were reminded that it was 'frequently necessary to ascertain the history of particular sections of the system, and this record is designed to meet this purpose'.[2]

The book also gave details of those lines that had been significant in the development of the Great Western Railway itself, and it is perhaps helpful to give the briefest description of its network as it stood just before the Railways Act was passed.

The Great Western gateway to the West Country: passengers await departure of their train from Platform 1 at Paddington. The station would be extended and improved during the interwar period, although proposals to completely rebuild the terminus in the 1920s were watered down after the General Strike.

In the case of a number of the other 'Big Four' companies the process included the amalgamation of a number of railways of a similar size, but the GWR was by far the largest of the Western-group 'constituent' companies named in the Act, with a route mileage of 2,784. By comparison, the two next-largest companies by mileage were the Cambrian and Taff Vale, with 280 and 124 miles respectively.[3]

In addition to Brunel's original route from Paddington to the West Country via Bristol the GWR had in the years before the Great War developed a route to Devon and Cornwall via Westbury, as well as another new route to Birmingham, completed in 1913; trains trundled through the Severn Tunnel to South Wales, serving its main towns of Cardiff, Newport and Swansea. Further west, the port of Fishguard, opened by the GWR in 1906, provided the company with access to Ireland via its steamer service. Great Western ships also served the Channel Islands from Weymouth.

The Great Western was a huge undertaking; before the Great War it had advertised itself as 'the line of a thousand stations', reflecting the fact that it owned not merely large and imposing facilities like those at Paddington, Bristol and Birmingham Snow Hill but also more humble stations on sleepy branch lines deep in the countryside. Many of the 92,000 staff on the pay bill in 1921 worked on these stations, in goods sheds and depots, signalboxes and offices, as well as in refreshment rooms or in one of the eight hotels owned by the company.

The vast majority of the railway's fleet of over 3,000 locomotives were built and maintained at its vast works at Swindon, where more than 12,000 people were employed; carriages, wagons and all

LEFT Penarth Docks, developed by the Taff Vale Railway in the 1860s and recorded by the GWR photographer in 1930.

BELOW Lunchtime in Rodbourne Road as just some of the staff from Swindon Works troop home in 1934. At the Grouping more than 12,000 of the town's men and women were employed by the Locomotive, Carriage & Wagon Department.

LEFT A view of a new general cargo berth opened at Cardiff Docks in the 1920s. From the ship moored alongside, timber pit props are being unloaded, by the crane nearest the camera, into the waiting wagons.

BELOW The *raison d'être* of the Barry Railway, the export of coal, is reflected in the depiction of a dockside coal tip as part of the company seal.

RIGHT A beautiful photograph of Rhymney Railway 'AP' class 0-6-2T No 36, built for the company by Hudswell Clarke in 1921. Subsequently rebuilt at Swindon, it would survive into BR ownership.

manner of other items for use on the railway were also constructed and maintained there. By 1922, the railway was also operating well over 100 motor vehicles, including buses and goods delivery vans, although horse power was still much in evidence on the network.

In 1921, the net income of the Great Western was over £6 million, a figure that dwarfed that for each of the other constituent railways; however, whilst the GWR paid a creditable 7¼ % dividend that year, the Barry Railway was able to offer its shareholders 10% in the same period, illustrating the fact that some constituents, although smaller, were nevertheless profitable businesses, largely because of their dock operations and links with the coal trade.

With the exception of the Cambrian Railways, five of the constituent companies that became part of the enlarged GWR had a history closely associated with the coal trade in South Wales. By far the largest of these in terms of annual income and staff was the Taff Vale Railway (TVR), whose original Act of Parliament was passed in 1836, only a year after the Great Western itself. In 1922, the company magazine called the Taff Vale 'one of the brightest gems in the sceptre wielded by the Great Western Railway'[4] and described in some detail the early history of a line that reflected to a large extent the development of the South Wales coalfield as a whole. The original route of the railway, from Cardiff to Merthyr, was opened in April 1841, but it grew steadily, absorbing smaller railways and most importantly extending its lines deep into the Rhondda and Aberdare valleys in order to transport the coal being extracted there to the coast.

At the time of the Grouping the Taff Vale system was recorded by the GWR as having a mileage of exactly 124 miles 42 chains, the handbook issued by the company noting the TVR main line 'proper' as consisting of the route from Cardiff to Merthyr (Plymouth Street station). Although coal trains had been unloaded at the docks in Cardiff, congestion and delays there prompted the TVR to develop docks at Penarth in the 1860s and lease the branch line linking it to the main network.

The Taff Vale also had more than 20 branch lines, many running along tributaries of the River Taff; among these were the Rhondda, Rhondda Fach, Clydach, Ynysbawl and Roath branches, as well as the Cardiff Bute West, Dock East and Dock West lines. Apart from a short section of route which ran through the more picturesque Vale of Glamorgan, the TVR ran largely through a densely populated industrial landscape, and the *Great Western Railway Magazine* noted with some irony that the railway 'could never claim attention as a line for the tourist or pleasure seeker'.[5] It could nevertheless claim with some justification that its passenger traffic was extremely heavy, colliers and their families making frequent use of trains to travel from the valleys to Cardiff for shopping, rugby and football matches and other events. In 1920, the railway carried over 10 million passengers, of whom more than a million used workmen's tickets.

The size and importance of the Taff Vale's coal business was without doubt the key to its financial success; it was paying a 5% dividend in the 1850s and a record 14.9% between 1880 and 1889 — the highest dividend paid by a British company over a sustained period. It was, however, unable to maintain these record figures, and labour difficulties and competition from other

railways such as the Barry affected its business; by 1913, mineral traffic transported annually by the railway amounted to almost 20 million tons, but this figure would shrink dramatically to just over 11 million tons by 1920, when the effects of a postwar slump in the coal trade really began to bite. Even so, in the years before amalgamation TVR shareholders were still receiving reasonable dividends in comparison with those issued by a number of other Welsh railways.

The congestion at Cardiff Docks that had led the Taff Vale to support developments at Penarth also led to pressure from a group of mine owners led by David Davies MP to build a new dock at Barry and railways to serve it. Not surprisingly, the newly promoted Barry Railway faced stiff opposition from both the Taff Vale and Rhymney railways, but in 1884 parliamentary approval was gained to build a 19-mile main line from Barry to Trehafod, north of Pontypridd, where a junction with the TVR gave access to the Rhondda. The Barry also had a number of short branches, including the mile-long line giving access to the Barry Island resort, a popular holiday destination in GWR days. The railway and docks opened in February 1889, and by 1892 the amount of coal traffic handled was already a third of Cardiff's. In the Great War the docks moved as much coal as Cardiff and Penarth combined, loading more than 6,000 Admiralty transport ships with coal.

With a total network of only just over 38 miles the Barry depended heavily on connections with other railways; in addition to links with the TVR it had connections with the Great Western at Bridgend, with the Brecon & Merthyr near Cardiff, and with the Rhymney and LNWR at Energlyn. The company's aggressive tactics in developing its services certainly led to commercial success, for between 1894 and 1920 it paid a dividend of between 9½ and 10%. Felix Pole wrote that the railway was 'notorious for its individualistic and somewhat piratical tendencies' and was 'antagonistic' to amalgamation;[6] however, despite its holding out for a better settlement in the Grouping negotiations, 'ultimately the Barry came into line'. The company was independent to the last, and at its last annual meeting in 1922 its Chairman, the Earl of Plymouth, told its shareholders that the company's progress had been 'one uninterrupted success from its commencement,' and that 'your Directors have every confidence that if it were possible for the Company to have remained as an independent undertaking, they might have anticipated a period of still greater prosperity'.[7]

Like the Barry, the Cardiff Railway was primarily a dock operation, the railway company coming into existence only in 1897, following the expansion of the Bute Docks in the 1880s and early 1890s. The docks had been growing for almost 60 years, but poor rail links had led to the development of rival ports at Barry and Penarth along with the railways that served them, drawing coal traffic away from Cardiff. The new Cardiff Railway had a main line of only around 12 miles, although the tangle of lines within the port itself amounted to 10 times this distance. One writer noted that, despite its name, 'the company controlled one of the great sea ports of the world, whereas the railway the company planned to feed it was insignificant in comparison, never achieved its aim, and was largely closed twenty years after its opening'.[8] Initially the railway ran north to connect with the Taff Vale and the Rhymney, and later it also had its own line to Treforest. Fierce competition with the TVR and the Rhymney was a major problem — so much so that it frustrated the aim of the Cardiff Railway (supported by Parliament) to bring much of the coal traffic to its docks. Despite the huge amounts of trade that passed through the docks, which handled not only coal but all manner of other cargoes, the railway company was not a profitable operation, paying a dividend of only 1% in 1921.

Apart from the GWR, the third independent company involved in the tightly packed jumble of railway lines around the port of Cardiff was the Rhymney. Unlike its rivals, however, the Rhymney Railway did not own or lease docks and spent most of its life fighting its corner against competitors, not only in the Cardiff area but also up in the 'hills' — the valleys where coal was mined. Describing the line for staff in 1922, the *Great Western Railway Magazine* remarked that 'the equipment of the line, particularly in regard to stations and other buildings has never been on a lavish scale, which is putting the position somewhat mildly'.[9]

The Rhymney Railway was nevertheless a relatively profitable operation, in 1920 carrying almost 4 million tons of coal over its 51 miles of main line; even the following year, by which time coal revenue had dropped significantly, it was still able to pay a 9% dividend. Its 123 locomotives were maintained at a modern works opened at Caerphilly in 1902, and the station there had been extended just prior to the Great War as a result of increasing passenger business. The line north from Rhymney to Nantybwch

ABOVE The crest of the Alexandra (Newport & South Wales) Docks & Railway. The company handled almost 6 million tons of coal at its docks in 1913.

BELOW The massive sea lock at Newport Docks, opened in 1914, was, when built, the largest in the world, at 1,000ft long and 110ft wide, and was capable of handling the largest cargo boats. The pumps required to raise the water level in the lock could move 5 million gallons of water per hour.

ABOVE RIGHT GWR 2-4-0 No 810 at Oswestry, formerly the headquarters of the Cambrian Railways. The locomotive had been built in 1873 and would be withdrawn in 1926. An example of Armstrong's final design of 2-4-0, it was one of four based at Wolverhampton shed and was thus not too far from home when photographed.

connected with the London & North Western, giving the Rhymney access to collieries and ironworks at the north end of the valleys, and the LNWR direct access to Cardiff via RR lines. It therefore came as no surprise that, when the 1921 Railways Act was under discussion, the LNWR tried to move the Rhymney into the LMS group. The General Manager of the Rhymney, E. A. Prosser, told Felix Pole that the LNWR had offered him double the 'personal terms' he would get from the GWR.[10]

The last of the constituent railways situated in South Wales — and the smallest — was the Alexandra (Newport & South Wales) Docks & Railway. Like the Barry Railway this was predominantly a dock company but had its own line that enabled coal from the western section of the South Wales coalfield to be transported to Newport for shipping. In 1922, the track mileage operated by the company amounted to barely 19 miles, well over half of this total comprising running powers over the Brecon & Merthyr and Rhymney lines between Newport and Pontypridd. Despite having so little track of its own, the Alexandra company still managed to negotiate, for its permanent staff, reciprocal 'privilege ticket' arrangements with all the other companies, which, as one GWR docks official later argued, 'no doubt saw the humorous side'.[11]

The Alexandra company opened its first dock in 1875, and upon its completion the local business community was keen to link it with the rapidly growing coal industry, especially in

the Rhondda Valley. This was achieved by the construction of the Pontypridd, Caerphilly & Newport Railway to Pontypridd, opened in 1884 and bought by the Alexandra (Newport & South Wales) Docks & Railway three years later. Passenger trains were run by the company between Newport and Pontypridd, but these were taken over by the GWR in 1899, leaving the Alexandra to run between Pontypridd and Caerphilly only. Alexandra Docks lines also connected directly with the Great Western in Newport at Alexandra Dock and Maesglas junctions; there was also a connection with the Brecon & Merthyr at Bassaleg. Some measure of its modest size as a railway operation can be gained from the fact that it owned only 38 locomotives, four carriages and 642 freight wagons, while many of its 1,830 staff worked not on the railway itself but within the bustling confines of the docks at Newport. Nevertheless, the volume of traffic traversing the system was impressive; in 1913, some 5,910,898 tons of coal was delivered to the port for export — the largest quantity it had ever handled in the prewar era.[12]

The final constituent was the Cambrian Railways, which, like the newly enlarged GWR, noted a writer in the *Great Western Railway Magazine* in 1922, was an amalgamation of a number of formerly independent lines. Over the course of more than half a century it had grown into a large concern, incorporating railways from both sides of the English/Welsh border. Thus (ironically, in

view of its name) a considerable proportion of its lines ran through English counties, and indeed its administrative headquarters and workshops were situated in the town of Oswestry, in Shropshire. The Cambrian Railways Act of 1865 had brought together a number of railways, including the Oswestry & Newtown, the Newtown & Machynlleth, the Llanidloes & Newtown and the Ellesmere, Oswestry & Whitchurch; the following year another act brought the Aberystwyth & Welsh Coast Railway into the Cambrian fold, giving the company a network of nearly 170 miles.

Although the Cambrian became a relatively large concern, as many of its lines traversed sparsely populated parts of Mid-Wales, its financial position was never that strong. This situation was not assisted by the acquisition of a number of other small and sometimes ramshackle lines, such as the Van Railway, the Tanat Valley Light Railway and the Mawddwy Railway. The Van Railway, noted the GWR Goods Manager in his 1926 survey, was a 6¾-mile line opened in 1871 to serve lead mines near Llanidloes that had been reopened and worked by the Cambrian from 1 August 1896, having been entirely closed in 1892; 'It is not now operated for passenger traffic,' he concluded.[13] The Cambrian had also acquired two narrow-gauge railways that are now well known as heritage lines — the Vale of Rheidol and the Welshpool & Llanfair — and these too became part of the GWR operation after the Grouping. Matters did improve for the Cambrian in the years before the Great War, its historian noting that 'a concern, which was born under, and for many years continued to struggle for its very existence with, the most embarrassing financial conditions … gradually acquired a more robust economic constitution'.[14]

'There are many physical difficulties to contend with on the Cambrian line from which many other companies are immune,' argued the GWR in 1922.[15] These difficulties included 288 miles of single track, which required 70 stations where trains could cross, and railways built across beautiful but challenging landscapes. Although there were only six tunnels on the whole railway, there were instead some fearsome gradients to contend with, including 4½ miles at 1 in 52 encountered by trains at Talerddig. The railway was certainly not engineered to the high standards expected by the Great Western, and in July 1922, the Chief Engineer reported that a 'large amount of maintenance work would be necessary in the course of the next few years in the renewal of bridges on the Cambrian section, there being upwards of 600 timber structures on that section'.[16]

In public, at least, Great Western management was keen to stress the 'development possibilities' of the Cambrian Railways network, especially in the expansion of train services to serve the Cambrian Coast resorts of Aberystwyth, Barmouth, Harlech and Pwllheli. In private, however, it cannot have been impressed by the company accounts and traffic statistics; in 1913, the Cambrian had carried 3 million passengers and 1 million tons of goods — figures that deteriorated in the years before the Grouping. Indeed there was some dismay at Paddington that the Cambrian had been even considered as a 'constituent' company at all, but political expediency by a Government anxious to avoid any difficulties from Welsh Nationalist politicians may well have played some part in the decision, especially considering the situation in Ireland at the time. At any rate, Cambrian shareholders were no doubt delighted that they would gain from the Grouping, receiving a guaranteed dividend for the first time.

As the various absorption schemes were approved by the Amalgamation Tribunal smaller companies joined the enlarged Great Western. The Brecon & Merthyr Tydfil Junction Railway, authorised in 1859, was one of the more complicated railways absorbed at the Grouping. Although the line was originally intended to link the two towns named in the railway's title, the final route was rather more complicated. In the north a 26-mile main line ran from Brecon to join the Rhymney at Deri Junction, from where the railway had running powers over just over two miles of line as far as Bargoed South, from where it ran a further 15 miles to Bassaleg on its own metals. From Bassaleg the B&M had running powers over a further two miles of Great Western Railway route giving access to High Street station at Newport. In 1861, the Brecon & Merthyr also acquired the old Rumney Railway, which gave it access to coal traffic and a route via the Barry Railway to its docks. The railway competed with — and also had connections with — almost all the other railways in South Wales, including the Alexandra, Barry, Cambrian, LNWR, Neath & Brecon, Rhymney and Taff Vale, and the line's complex nature and severe gradients made it difficult for the company to be profitable.

Although relatively short, with a 40-mile route network, the Neath & Brecon Railway, one of those that had connections with the Brecon & Merthyr in the mountains of South Wales, was well run and in 1921 still able to pay shareholders a 4% dividend. Dating back to 1864, when it began life as the Dulais Valley Mineral Railway, a 10-mile line north of Neath, it became the Neath & Brecon three years later when it acquired powers to extend the line to Brecon and built a number of small branches linking collieries on the route. The N&B had connections with the Cambrian Railways at Three Cocks Junction, where it also linked with the LNWR, which had running powers over the Neath & Brecon, giving it access to Swansea. This arrangement was to continue after the Grouping, although the LMS would discontinue its passenger services in 1930.

The profitability of the Neath & Brecon depended heavily on coal mined in 15 collieries close to the line; most of the coal extracted in the area, at locations such as Ystradgynlais, was anthracite, and by 1920 more than 25% of the 4½ million tons of this fuel produced was being carried on the railway.[17] Most of the coal transported was sent to Swansea, Port Talbot or Barry docks for export, and this remained a vital part of traffic until the late 1930s, when foreign competition caused many pits to close. The

mountains of Breconshire also provided a further Welsh staple for transport. Many of the thousands of sheep reared locally were transported by rail, and in 1921, the Neath & Brecon transported more than 17,000 to market. Although the N&B was still paying a dividend to its shareholders, the acquisition of this small company was hardly likely to make any significant impact on the finances of the new Great Western; despite carrying more than 720,000 passengers and over 600,000 tons of coal in 1921, its annual profit was just £43,159!

The majority of the railways absorbed by the GWR at the Grouping were based in Wales. There were, however, a number of important English companies that were brought under GWR control in 1923, as well as other, less important lines. Described by one writer as 'an unavoidable nuisance'[18] to the Great Western, the Didcot, Newbury & Southampton Railway was something of an anomaly, as, although it was an independent company, its 44-mile route had been worked from its inception by the GWR. This arrangement was not without its problems, and one DNS shareholder in 1890 made reference to the hostile and disparaging attitude of 'openly contemptuous' GWR staff, describing a journey on the line as a 'trip across the wilderness'.[19] Running from Didcot through thinly populated rural Berkshire to Newbury and then on to Winchester, where it connected with the London & South Western, the railway had originally been promoted as a cross-country line, the north–south route of which would enable Welsh coal to be transported to Southampton. However, it never generated the levels of traffic necessary to justify the high cost of construction, and the cost of maintaining the route, which included many cuttings, embankments and bridges, was prohibitive.

The Cleobury Mortimer & Ditton Priors Light Railway could not have been more of a contrast; built under a Light Railway Order in 1901 that 'turned what had seemed an unlikely dream into a feasible proposition',[20] it opened in 1908, promoters promising the possibility of 200,000 tons freight annually. The

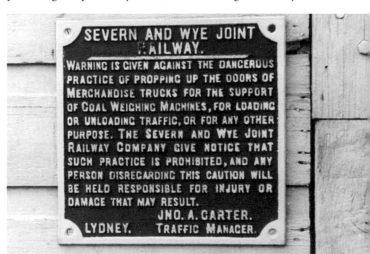

This cast-iron notice produced by the Severn & Wye Railway was still in evidence at Speech House Road station in 1960. The Severn & Wye was incorporated in 1894 as a joint venture by the GWR and the Midland Railway and continued as a joint company after grouping. *Author's collection*

line followed a 12-mile route from Cleobury Mortimer, west of Kidderminster, to Ditton Priors, where it served local basalt quarries. Over its short length the railway featured 13 level crossings and many gradients, although there were no signals, as the 'one engine in steam' system was used. Although the stone traffic was initially healthy, business fell off as tarred roads became more commonplace after the Great War. Company receipts in 1913 were only £3,069, meaning no dividend for shareholders; by 1919, income had risen to £10,632, enabling the company to pay shareholders a very modest dividend of 1½%.

The difficult financial situation faced by the Midland & South Western Junction Railway (MSWJR) has been described in the previous chapter, as have its efforts to squeeze more money out of the Great Western in the Grouping process. The protracted negotiations meant that the company was the last to be absorbed into the GWR, retaining an extra nine months of independence but in the process greatly irritating staff at Paddington and Swindon. The company had been the result of the combination of two companies – the Swindon, Marlborough & Andover Railway and the Swindon & Cheltenham Extension Railway, – and its route ran from Andoversford, on the GWR Banbury–Cheltenham line, to Red Post Junction, on the LSWR Waterloo–Exeter main line.

Open throughout in 1883, the MSWJR experienced financial difficulties almost from the outset, passing into receivership in 1892 and remaining thus until 1897. The company's General Manager, Sam Fay, seconded from the LSWR, did much to turn around its fortunes, although its finances could never be described as solid, especially when they depended largely on a large loan from the Midland Railway. When first the line was promoted the GWR had done everything it could to block the scheme, and, to add insult to injury, when constructed, the railway ran through the heart of the GWR at Swindon, its line crossing over the main London–Bristol route just west of the great railway works — something that must have rankled with Great Western management.

The full list of the 26 'subsidiary' railways finally absorbed by the GWR between 1 January 1922 and 1 July 1923 is given in Appendix I; in the months leading up to the Grouping, and in the years following, Great Western staff and management faced the difficult task of melding all these companies with such different histories, finances and staff into a 'Greater' Great Western.

ABOVE RIGHT Few passengers are in evidence in this photograph taken in May 1935 of Winchester (Chesil), on the old Didcot, Newbury & Southampton Railway. *STEAM / H. C. Casserley collection*

RIGHT A Midland & South Western Junction Railway 4-4-0 built by the North British Locomotive Co carries its new GWR number (1122) but is otherwise still in original condition as it departs Swindon Town station shortly after the Grouping.

1   Pole, F. J. C.: *His Book* (Town & Country Press), 1968, p63

2   Gale, P. R.: *The Great Western Railway* (Chief Goods Manager's Office, Paddington, 1926)

3   MacDermot, E. T.: *History of the Great Western Railway* Volume II (Great Western Railway, 1927), p243

4   *Great Western Railway Magazine* June 1922, p333

5   *Ibid*, p340

6   Pole, *ibid*, p54

7   Rimell, R. J.: *The History of the Barry Railway Company, 1884–1921* (Western Mail, 1923), p103

8   Mountford, E. R.: *The Cardiff Railway* (Oakwood Press, 1987), p5

9   *Great Western Railway Magazine* June 1922, p448

10   Pole, *ibid*, p51

11   Brown, F., speaking at 'The Docks of the Great Western Railway' — Meeting No 156 of the Great Western Railway (London) Lecture & Debating Society, held 18 January 1923

12   Alexandra (Newport & South Wales) Docks Statistics — Newport Reference Library collection

13   Gale, *ibid*, p92

14   Gasquoine, C. P.: *The Story of the Cambrian* (Woodhall, Mishall, Thomas & Co, 1922), p136

15   *Great Western Railway Magazine* June 1922, p177

16   Great Western Railway: Minutes of Chief Officers' Conference Meeting held 21 July 1922

17   For further information on the history of anthracite mining in South Wales see www.welshcoalmines.co.uk/index.html

18   Body, G., quoted in *Encyclopaedia of the Great Western Railway*, edited by Will Adams (PSL Books, 1993)

19   Sands, T. B.: *The Didcot, Newbury & Southampton Railway* (Oakwood Press, 1971), p23

20   Price, M. R. C.: *The Cleobury Mortimer & Ditton Priors Light Railway* (Oakwood Press, 1995)

CHAPTER 4

THE MARITIME INHERITANCE

The fortunes of the Great Western Railway had been linked to marine developments from almost the earliest years of the company's existence. Brunel's original line from London to the West had been promoted in part to advance the fortunes of the port city of Bristol, and even before his railway was complete Brunel was designing the *Great Western*, a steamship to take some of the railway's passengers across the Atlantic to the United States. In the course of the following 80 years the railway 'took energetic action'[1] to develop its marine business, constructing docks and harbours at locations such as Milford Haven, Neyland and Weymouth, and in the years before the Great War it spent considerable sums of money establishing a brand-new harbour for Irish traffic at Fishguard, in West Wales.

With the passing of the Railways Act 1921 the relatively modest Great Western Docks Department grew dramatically within the space of a year; the acquisition of South Wales companies like the Alexandra (Newport & South Wales) Docks Railway and the Barry and Cardiff railways, along with a number of smaller concerns, meant that the GWR had at a stroke become

RIGHT A striking aerial view of Cardiff Docks, showing the pier-head building. Built in 1897 as the headquarters of the Cardiff Railway, this building became the offices for the GWR Docks Department after the Grouping. It is now an exhibition centre for the Welsh Assembly.

BELOW A busy scene at Weymouth harbour in the 1920s. The Great Western began operating steamer services from the port to the Channel Islands in July 1889.

one of the world's largest dock-owning companies. Speaking at a lecture at Paddington in January 1923, Mr F. Brown, Commercial Assistant to the new Docks Manager, noted that, in the previous year, the Great Western had become 'deeply absorbed' in docks. This phrase, he joked, was carefully calculated to satisfy two schools of thought — those who regarded the company as acquiring South Wales dock undertakings and those who, 'with that diffidence and modesty which characterise all with South Wales associations, incline to the view that South Wales acquired the Great Western company'.[2]

Although South Wales ports were capable of handling cargoes of all types, inward- or outward-bound, the fortunes of those brought into the Great Western empire at the Grouping were to a great extent tied to the growth and prosperity of the South Wales coalfield. In 1913, the year before the outbreak of the Great War, more than 56 million tons of coal was mined in South Wales, of which 41 million tons was then exported through ports on the Bristol Channel coast. Some idea of the scale of the operation can be seen in the statistics for each port.[3]

ABOVE A '56xx' 0-6-2 tank engine on a freight. This class was used extensively on South Wales coal trains.

TOP RIGHT The different sizes and grades of coal can be clearly seen in this photograph of loaded coal wagons at Swansea. The sheer number of wagons to be seen illustrates just how important the coal trade was to the company between the wars.

ABOVE RIGHT A photograph of a coaling appliance at Cardiff Docks, taken in May 1926. The cabin for the 'hoist man' can be seen high on the side of the coal tip.

Coal Exported from South Wales Docks 1913	
Port	Million tons
Barry	11
Cardiff	10½
Newport	6
Swansea	4½
Penarth	4½
Port Talbot	2¼
others	2¼

Just how important financially this new marine inheritance was to the GWR can be judged by the fact that its dock properties represented £15 million of capital, or 10% of the whole operation. Of £60 million tons of freight carried on the railway, 48 million tons passed through its docks, equating to 4 out of every 5 tons of goods moved. As a result, by the time agreements had been reached with most of the South Wales 'constituent' companies early in 1922, the company was already putting in place new arrangements to run the enlarged Docks Department. Felix Pole reported to the Chief Officers in February that he intended to 'appoint a new dock manager to take charge of the whole of the South Wales Docks and be responsible for the traffic working and financial results'.[4]

Various sub-committees dealing with issues linked to the Grouping, such as Traffic Matters and Finance, were established, and it was noted that Mr Vickery of the Alexandra Docks Co was to be consulted when dealing with questions relating to South Wales docks. It was no surprise then, that at a board meeting a month later, on 7 April, Pole reported that a recommendation was to be made to appoint a Chief Docks Manager (Mr Vickery) and

a Docks Assistant to the Chief Engineer (Mr Waddell)[5] and that reorganisation should take place as soon as possible, followed by the retirement of the general managers of the Barry, Cardiff, Rhymney and Taff Vale companies.

John Herbert Vickery was an experienced railwayman who had begun his career on the London & South Western as a goods clerk; he had come to Newport in 1913, managing the docks and railway through the difficult war years.[6] The new GWR Docks Department was set up in the pier-head building at Bute Docks in Cardiff, and while the Docks Manager was responsible for much of what went on in the South Wales ports, his work also required the support of the Chief Engineer at Paddington and the Chief Mechanical Engineer at Swindon.

Although coal had been mined in the mountains and valleys of South Wales for centuries it was not until the coming of railways that the industry began to grow rapidly and the potential for export was finally realised. As late as 1782 a customs officer at Cardiff said: 'We shall have no coals exported from this port, nor ever shall, as it would be too expensive to bring it down from the internal part of the country.'[7] Within a century, dock and railway companies had evolved a system for bringing coal from the valleys, and before recounting the history and facilities at some of the larger docks it would be helpful to describe in more general terms the way in which the coal business was organised.

The coal that was so hard won by miners was loaded at the collieries and brought by train down the valleys; before being moved into the docks, wagons were normally delivered to one of the many yards provided for the reception of full and empty wagons belonging to collieries or other private owners. In 1923, it was estimated that there were around 500 miles of sidings — sufficient to accommodate a staggering 30,000 to 40,000 coal wagons. These sidings were located as close as possible to the docks and were used both to sort wagons ready for loading and also to stable them temporarily — a process that was sometimes unavoidable; due to bad weather, ships for which coal was destined often did not arrive on time, while on other occasions coaling berths at the docks were already occupied, and vessels had to wait their turn to be loaded. There were also periods when export markets were slow, and coal was dispatched to ports by colliery companies before it had actually been sold.

One of the reasons that it was necessary to sort loaded wagons was that coal sent for export came in many different varieties, including Large, Nuts, Grain, Peas, Beans, Small and Duff, and trains often arrived at docks 'in the manner they have been passed out from the colliery, various sorts of coal very frequently all higgledy-piggledy and these needed to be sorted on arrival'.[8] In the case of around 30% of the loads, the various types of coal were mixed as they were loaded onto ships — a process that was both time-consuming and complicated.

With a few exceptions the equipment and methods used to load coal at the docks like Barry, Cardiff and Newport were broadly similar. In 1929, the GWR was able to boast that its coal-shipping appliances in South Wales 'number nearly 200 and include coal hoists, coaling cranes and belt conveyors. All are "quite modern" and include the highest and most efficient hoists in the country.'[9]

Once sorted in the reception sidings, coal wagons were moved by dock locomotives to railway lines leading to coal-loading hoists. These sidings were usually built on an incline which allowed wagons to descend by gravity to a weighbridge close to the ship's side. The wagon and its contents were weighed, and the weight was recorded on a 'tipping note' before a chain was attached to the wagon by the quaintly named 'jigger-man'. Operating a hydraulic capstan, he pulled the loaded truck off the weighing machinery and onto the cradle of the coal hoist at the level of the quay. The use of capstans to move wagons around was very dangerous, and as a result, the GWR Docks Department Rule Book prohibited staff from stepping over chains or ropes attached to wagons without permission, noting that 'proper care must be exercised in getting between trucks for the purpose of coupling and uncoupling them, and shunting poles or sticks MUST be used when practicable. In no circumstances should anyone be allowed to pass between the buffers of trucks.'[10]

Another dock worker, known as the 'cradle man', now secured the wagon with a chain and signalled to the 'hoist man' or 'top man' that all was ready. Seated in a small cabin high on the side of the hoist, the latter operated hydraulic equipment that slowly raised the cradle carrying the wagon to the required height. Riding with the coal wagon, the cradle man then knocked out a pin, allowing the wagon door to open. The cradle was then raised, allowing the coal to tumble out with a roar and a cloud of dust, down a chute and into the hold of the ship. Even before this operation was finished the empty wagon was being lowered, not to quay level but to an empty high-level siding, from there running by gravity across a viaduct to another weighbridge, where it was weighed again and the weight added to the tipping sheet. Meanwhile the cradle was lowered back to ground level to start the process once more, and the empty wagon taken back to the reception sidings to be returned to the colliery. In the ship's hold a further band of 'coal trimmers' worked in what must have been awful conditions; it was their job to shift coal away from the hatch where it had been loaded into the ship so that it could be safely stowed for the voyage.

By the 1920s, this whole process had become very efficient, and up to 60 wagons of coal could be weighed, hoisted, tipped, re-weighed and passed back to empty sidings in an hour.[11] In some ports a number of hoists were movable, so that two or more could be operated at the same time on one vessel, although dock staff were divided as to whether movable hoists were a commercial proposition, as loading into different hatches wasted time because the loading and the trimming of coal did not proceed uniformly. In a bid to win and retain as much business as possible, dock management did all they could to maintain rapid loading times, and throughout the 1920s the *Great Western Railway Magazine*

printed examples of 'good work' done at ports, including a record shipment of over 14,000 tons of coal loaded in a single day at Port Talbot on 7 May 1923.[12]

A large number of the hoists were capable of lifting and tipping to a height of 70-76ft above the water, enabling them to be used to load coal into the bunker hatches of the liners and freighters using docks to replenish their own supplies. Although most Welsh steam coal was relatively hard, the GWR introduced 'anti-breakage' technology to try to reduce damage to coal being dropped into the holds of ships. At Cardiff it utilised Lewis-Hunter coaling equipment, which was different from the conventional coal hoist; loaded wagons were tilted at ground level and the contents tipped into a large box, this box being then swung into hold by the crane, opened and the coal unloaded, the idea being to avoid breakage by having two short drops instead of one larger one. Problems with the speed of loading and the reliability of the equipment meant that the cranes had 'few friends among their old acquaintances', F. Brown told staff in 1923.[13]

Although Cardiff had been chosen as the location of the new GWR Docks Department Headquarters, by 1923 it was argued that it no longer 'held first place for coal shipping' and that, 'in the last few years before the war, Barry held the honours'.[14] The dock complex at Cardiff was, however, substantial — and fitting for the

LEFT There is much detail in this view of the rather unloved Lewis-Hunter coal cranes at Cardiff. In the middle distance coal is being tipped into the box that was then loaded into the hold of the ship; in the foreground a boy leans on his bicycle behind the wagon weighbridge.

BELOW In addition to ancillary vessels such as dredgers and tug boats, the Great Western employed a number of divers to check and maintain lock gates and other equipment. The team seen at work here was based at Barry.

BOTTOM All the South Wales docks were ports of call for passenger vessels. Here the United States Lines' *George Washington* is seen calling at Cardiff's Queen Alexandra Dock on 29 July 1928. The vessel was the largest to have visited the South Wales docks at this time.

Welsh capital. Together Bute East and Bute West docks covered an area of over 60 acres in total and had been in operation for more than 60 years. The Roath and Queen Alexandra docks dated back to 1887 and 1907 respectively, the latter, at 52 acres, being the largest in the complex. And although Cardiff exported millions of tons of coal, it also dealt with all manner of general cargoes, including foodstuffs such as barley, grain, flour and frozen and chilled meat; a huge flour mill owned by Spillers was served by a floating suction plant capable of unloading grain at a rate of 120 tons per hour, either into a warehouse or direct into railway wagons. A large cold store, occupying some 30,000sq ft, was also provided for perishable products such as fruit and vegetables, and, in common with other South Wales ports, Cardiff had numerous warehouses for storage.

After the lifting in 1928 of an embargo that had been imposed following outbreaks of foot-and-mouth disease in Europe and in North and South America, the Bute Docks at Cardiff were licensed for the importation of cattle, receiving large consignments from Ireland, Canada and South Africa.[15] The facilities provided also contained lairage, abattoirs and an auction ring, as well as rail loading platforms.

The docks at Penarth, close to Cardiff, were of a more modest size but still capable of exporting more than 4 million tons of coal annually in the early 1920s. The operation had been acquired by the Taff Vale Railway on a 999-year lease in 1863. The dock covered an area of around 25 acres and utilised the same coal-

tipping equipment as neighbouring docks; the GWR boasted that the four movable coal hoists at Penarth constituted one of the finest dispatch berths in the country.

At Newport, docks were built on land between the Usk and Ebbw rivers, the first being opened as early as 1842; by the beginning of the 20th century substantial investment by the Alexandra (Newport & South Wales) Docks & Railway Co had provided the town with a large, modern and very efficient port. The largest dock, the Alexandra South, opened in 1882, was later extended so that by 1922 it was 4,000ft long and 1,000ft wide. The West Quay was equipped with coal hoists, and behind them ran the tangle of rail lines needed to supply them; in 1923, the docks exported 6,769,493 tons of coal — a high-point that would never be exceeded. On the other side of the dock the East Quay had berths for general cargoes, with warehousing behind.

All along the South Wales coast (or close to it) were a large number of iron and steel works and other manufacturing companies generating considerable trade in general cargo, particularly raw materials. Over 1,500,000 tons of ore was imported at South Wales ports in a single year, and the total import of steel bars and export of manufactured iron and steel, galvanised sheets, tinplate and other products amounted to nearly 2 million tons per year. Newport was the main port for supplying the Ebbw Vale steelworks with iron ore, and in 1923 it imported 349,770 tons of ore, along with 286,618 tons of 'semi-manufactured' iron and steel.[16] It also handled bauxite from North Africa, for use by the British Aluminium Co.

While Cardiff, Newport and Swansea were best known for the export of coal and the handling of general cargoes, steamer lines also used them as ports of call for services to the Mediterranean, India, the Far East, Africa, Australia, New Zealand, Canada and the USA. In the case of Newport, details of sailings read like a world atlas. In 1927, monthly sailings left the docks for destinations such as Bombay (courtesy of the Brocklebank Line), Kobe in Japan (Alfred Holt Line) and Cape Town (Clan Line and Ellerman Lines). Rio de Janeiro could be reached using a three-weekly service operated by the Royal Mail Steam Packet Co, and it was noted that there were 'irregular' sailings to Constantinople and the 'Patagonian ports'.

One of the proudest boasts of Newport dock staff was that they could accommodate the largest cargo ships in the world. A fortnight before the outbreak of war in 1914, the Alexandra company had completed the construction of what was promoted as the largest sea lock in the world, measuring 1,000ft long and 110ft wide. Pumping massive amounts of water in and out of the locks required powerful equipment, and at Newport the steam-powered turbo pumps used could shift up to 5 million gallons of water an hour if required. The

Dockside cranes unload meat at Cardiff Docks, where it would be loaded into GWR wagons for distribution elsewhere.

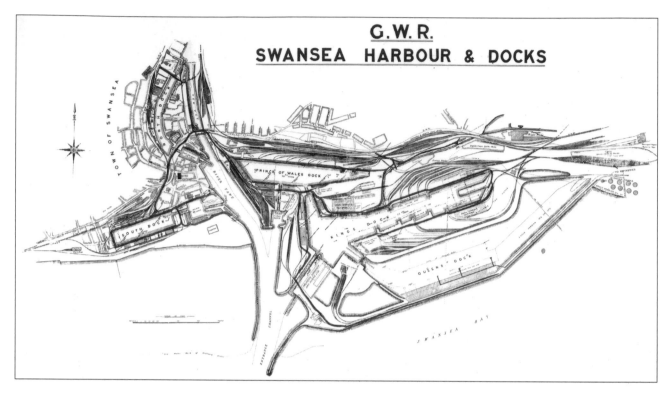

ABOVE A company plan of Swansea Docks. By 1929, the extensive port facilities included 835,137sq ft of warehouse space.

BELOW All South Wales ports had timber as a staple import — in particular for pit props, used extensively in the coal mines in the valleys. This massive stack of props was pictured at Swansea.

ABOVE FAR RIGHT Loading motor cars bound for Ireland at Fishguard Harbour in May 1937.

equipment at Newport and other South Wales docks, along with other items such as cranes, capstans, generating equipment and lock gates, were maintained by dock engineering workers and 'outstation' staff from Swindon Works.

Writing not long after nationalisation of the railways in 1948, O. S. Nock observed that 'while it is generally acknowledged that railway engineers are jacks of all trades one would not ordinarily include the dredging of channels for ocean-going ships even among their manifold activities'.[17] In fact the GWR employed a number of dredging vessels in most of its South Wales ports to keep locks, channels and docks clear of mud and silt. In Newport it faced an additional problem, as the River Ebbw, which flowed seaward from a heavily worked mining valley, carried significant amounts of fine coal in suspension. Past the entrance to the docks it flowed into the Bristol Channel, and coal and suspended matter were deposited on a mud bank close to its confluence with the River Usk. Just how polluted the river had become is illustrated by the fact that coal was reclaimed during the dredging process and reused elsewhere.

Barry Docks could claim the record for the largest total shipment of coal among all the dock systems absorbed by the Great Western, 11 million tons having been shifted in 1913. This compared with 10½ million at Cardiff and 6 million at Newport in the same year. The Barry Docks undertaking had been authorised in 1884, and the first docks were opened in 1889, a further dock being completed in 1898. By 1922, the 'wet' docks occupied an area of more than 114 acres; GWR publicity

emphasised the fact that the port's principal business was 'the shipment of coal', and there were 41 fixed and movable coal hoists distributed between the two docks.

General cargoes were also handled at Barry, although the majority of this kind of business was dealt with down the coast at Cardiff. Nevertheless, the dock was equipped with 47 hydraulic cranes and a 'spacious' transit shed, 'admirably designed' for the storage of imported grain and other general merchandise.[18] Barry Docks also had three graving docks (two of which were owned by private firms, the other being the property of the railway), which were used to inspect and repair ships using the port — something repeated elsewhere in the South Wales docks.

The docks at Port Talbot, authorised as late as 1894, were well situated to serve an important part of the South Wales coalfield; more than 2½ million tons of coal was exported per year, and although the coal hoists were similar to those used at other ports, Port Talbot also employed a system whereby loaded wagons tipped coal onto conveyor belts which then transported coal to chutes and onto ships. This equipment was speedy, but its effectiveness was reduced by delays in trimming coal in the ships.

Port Talbot's docks also served the Iron and steel industry, including the blast furnaces of Guest Keen and Baldwins, as well as the copper-smelting works of the Rio Tinto Company which developed in the area. The profitability of the port was, however, limited by the dimensions of the lock entrance, which was neither long enough nor deep enough to admit larger vessels.

The most westerly of the docks that eventually became part of the GWR were at Swansea, although these were not included in the original Grouping process. Separate negotiations were held with the harbour trustees, and in 1923, the General Manager was able to announce that Royal Assent had been given to the Act vesting the undertaking of the Swansea Harbour Trust to the GWR and the absorption of the docks operated as of 1 July that year. In 1913, coal exports had amounted to 4½ million tons, Swansea dealing with much of the output of the West Glamorgan coalfield, which, in addition to Welsh steam coal, included large deposits of anthracite — a fuel that in the 1920s was in great demand.

Swansea was often described as the 'metallurgical centre of the world' and the home of the copper-smelting and tinplate trade; in the period between the two world wars almost three-quarters of the tinplate made in Great Britain was produced in works within a dozen miles of the Swansea docks, and half a million tons of tinplate and galvanised sheet were exported from the port each year. As well as these well-established industries, Swansea was at the centre of the new trade in oil and motor spirit. The Anglo-Persian Oil Co invested heavily in the business, and traffic in crude and refined oil and motor spirit in and out of Swansea Docks amounted to well over 2 million tons per annum; by 1929, GWR publicity was promoting Swansea as the 'greatest oil port in the kingdom'.[19] Oil was discharged from tankers at the Queen's Dock into storage tanks and then pumped to refineries at Llandarcy, about 4 miles away.

ABOVE Passengers disembark from the GWR tender *Sir Francis Drake* and make for their train to Paddington in April 1924, while their luggage remains piled on the deck of the boat.

RIGHT Advertisement for GWR dock facilities, 1935. *Author's collection*

In the process of amalgamation the Great Western had also acquired other South Wales docks at Briton Ferry, Llanelly and Burry Port, where considerable quantities of coal were loaded into smaller vessels for coastwise rather than export traffic. The Docks Department also managed smaller ports away from the South Wales area, including Brentford, Bridgwater, Fowey, Lydney and Newquay. In addition it had acquired the tiny dock at Aberdovey, which had originally been owned by the Cambrian Railways; its harbour was tidal, with a deepwater wharf and three jetties, and dealt with the import of cement, artificial manures, and timbers, and the export of slate.[20]

Of the marine facilities that had formed part of the GWR's Marine Department before the war and the Grouping, Fishguard Harbour fared least well, the outbreak of hostilities having curtailed the development of the port as a deepwater facility. The

South Wales ports provided coal for ships of all sizes as they journeyed around the world. The GWR photographer recorded the arrival of the whaling ship *Antarctic* as it called at Cardiff before setting off for the South Atlantic in 1929.

cattle pens and only an occasional crane at work, which 'could with ease handle ten times its present volume of traffic'.[21]

The loss of Ocean Mail traffic at Fishguard was balanced by an increase in business at Plymouth, where eastbound ocean liners called on their way up the English Channel to Southampton. By the Grouping there was 75 acres of dock, with 20,000ft of quay; GWR tender boats ran back and forth across Plymouth Sound, ferrying passengers, mail and luggage to waiting trains, and the introduction of conveyors to move luggage from the boats to the carriages of Ocean Mail specials made the company's operation at Plymouth both efficient and popular.

The final port run by the railway between the wars was Weymouth, which remained the GWR's terminal for all Channel Islands traffic, both passenger and goods; during the interwar period it was rebuilt by the company with the assistance of the local council and, despite its somewhat difficult and cumbersome layout, continued to be busy all year round.

After 1923, the GWR's management believed that one provision of the new Railways Act was that docks should be self-supporting or that reasonable efforts should made in that direction. While the inheritance of such a vast docks empire clearly had many advantages, few in the company believed that the success of the docks operation could be sustained without further investment; in the years following the Grouping the GWR would spend considerable sums of money in maintaining its new assets against a backdrop of worsening economic conditions and a decline in the coal trade, ensuring that by 1939 the docks were in a 'much higher state of efficiency than before' and 'capable of dealing with a greatly increased volume of trade'.[22]

difficult political situation in Ireland in the years after the Great War also had a severe effect on cross-channel traffic, although just as serious was the emergence of Southampton as the main port for transatlantic liner traffic rather than Liverpool, as it had been before 1914. This move meant that there was little hope of Fishguard attracting any Ocean Mail or passenger business; Irish boat-train traffic did eventually improve, but throughout the inter war period the port remained a reminder of 'what might have been'. Visiting Fishguard, O. S. Nock painted a striking picture of a harbour station with long, empty platforms, silent

1   Nock, O. S.: *The Great Western Railway — An Appreciation* (Heffer, 1951), p80

2   Brown, F., speaking at 'The Docks of the Great Western Railway' — Meeting No 156 of the Great Western Railway (London) Lecture & Debating Society, held 18 January 1923

3   Appleby, H. N.: *Great Western Ports* (Great Western Railway, 1929)

4   Great Western Railway: Minutes of Chief Officers' Conference Meeting held 27 February 1922

5   Great Western Railway: Minutes of Chief Officers' Conference Meeting held 27 March 1922

6   Hutton, J.: *The Newport Docks & Railway Company* (Silver Link Publishing, 1996), p121

7   Brown, *ibid*

8   *Ibid*

9   Appleby, *ibid*, p115

10 Great Western Railway: *Rules and Regulations for Observance by Employees: Docks Department* (GWR, Paddington, 1937), p40

11 Chapman, W. G.: *'Twixt Rail & Sea: A Great Western Railway Book of Docks, Seaports and Shipping* (Great Western Railway, 1927), p49

12 *Great Western Railway Magazine* June 1923, p271

13 Brown, *ibid*

14 *Ibid*

15 Lee, B.: *Cardiff's Vanished Docklands* (Sutton Publishing, 2006), p24

16 Alexandra (Newport & South Wales) Docks statistics, 1921–1927, Newport Reference Library collection

17 Nock, *ibid*, p82

18 'Lines Absorbed by the GWR, No 3: The Barry Railway', *Great Western Railway Magazine* March 1922, p283

19 Appleby, *ibid*, p27

20 Great Western Railway: *Docks of the GWR* (GWR Docks & Marine Department, 1925), p29

21 Nock, *ibid*, p181

22 Appleby, *ibid*, p8

CHAPTER 5

GREAT WESTERN PROGRESS

Having negotiated the perils of the immediate postwar period and the upheaval following the introduction of the Railways Act 1921, Great Western management and staff began to look forward. Whilst no one was under any illusions about the task facing them, there was a good deal of optimism, promoted in no small part by the new General Manager, Felix Pole.

Pole was born in the Wiltshire village of Little Bedwyn in 1877, the son of the local schoolmaster; he joined the Great Western at the age of 14, starting his career as a telegraph clerk at Swindon Junction station. Within two years he was able to gain promotion and moved to Paddington, where he worked in the offices of both the Electrical Superintendent and the Chief Engineer before a further promotion in 1903 to the General Manager's Office. Here his skills as a communicator soon became apparent; he took on the editorship of the staff journal, the *Great Western Railway Magazine*, transforming it into a readable and informative publication and increasing its circulation from 2,000 to 25,000 copies per month within a few years. Although he did not have any formal technical or engineering training or qualifications, his 'energy and industry were limitless,' according to one admirer in 1921; his 'practical mind, sound judgment, quick grasp, remarkable memory … and, above all, a complete mastery of every subject he handled' marked him out as someone destined to climb to the highest rung of the Great Western ladder.[1]

In 1912, Pole was promoted to become Head of the Staff & Labour Department in the General Manager's Office, dealing with some difficult employment issues. Within a year he was Chief Clerk to the General Manager, a post he retained during the challenging years of the Great War, his poor eyesight making him unfit for military service. After the death of Frank Potter in 1919,

Pole was able to cement his reputation as an able and well-liked administrator as assistant to Charles Aldington. The latter's ill-health meant that Pole had to deputise for the General Manager at a critical time for the company, so that, when Aldington's retirement was announced, few in the railway world were surprised at Pole's appointment to the top job. The editor of the *Great Western Railway Magazine* summed up the general mood when he noted: 'The expected has happened. A hundred amongst us had long since prophesised the event'.[2]

The top job paid a top wage; Pole received £6,000 per annum,[3] but over the next eight years he would earn every penny. He made no secret of his admiration for one of his predecessors, James Inglis, whom he described as the 'finest General Manager the Company had ever had',[4] having seen at first hand the progress

FAR LEFT Between the two world wars the GWR provided assistance with staff housing, especially in the London area, where accommodation was expensive. It experimented by setting up a housing company in 1922 to advance loans directly to staff and subsequently made loans, at low interest rates, to co-operative schemes managed by employees to build houses. This image shows one of the houses in the Acton village.

LEFT Sir Felix Pole. Having managed the GWR through some of the most difficult and turbulent years in its history, he left it in a relatively strong position, despite the effects of the General Strike.

ABOVE Normally this picture of George Jackson Churchward is cropped to show only head and shoulders, but this original photograph reveals the wood block floor of one of the workshops at Swindon, where it was taken, and the simple office chair upon which he is sitting.

ABOVE The official portrait of No 4073 *Caerphilly Castle*, recorded in photographic grey following completion in 1923.

RIGHT The cover of *Caerphilly Castle* by W. G. Chapman. The book was published in 1924 and was reprinted three times that year after the first edition sold out rapidly.

made in the years before the Great War when, with Inglis at the helm, the GWR had transformed itself into a modern railway. Pole was keen to continue the modernisation of the railway but was also mindful that, in order to do this, he would have to make changes to the company's management structure. The new General Manager was aware that there were many matters over which he was either not consulted or about which he was informed only after they had been submitted to the board of directors. This was because the Chief Mechanical Engineer, Chief Civil Engineer, Secretary, Solicitor and Chief Accountant enjoyed direct access to independent committees of directors, allowing them to discuss and agree large programmes of expenditure or matters of principle without any recourse to the General Manager.

Pole was determined to assert his authority as what he called the 'principal executive officer' and, with the blessing of the Chairman, Viscount Churchill, set about creating a more modern staff structure. He began by reviving the Chief Officers' Conference, a management group of the most senior officers on the railway, originally set up in 1913 by Frank Potter, to co-ordinate and control spending across the whole organisation. As Adrian Vaughan noted, under this system 'each Chief would be told what he could spend — and what money he had to save'.[5]

Not surprisingly, this move did not sit well with some, in particular the Chief Mechanical Engineer, George Jackson Churchward, who saw his job as the most important on the railway. Controlling not only the huge works at Swindon but also locomotive sheds and depots, as well as management of the locomotive fleet and footplate and shed staff, Churchward was

indeed a powerful figure, and one not used to being told what to do. Described by Pole as 'a man of dominating personality', he had before the war been the leader of a 'little band of malcontent chief officers'[6] that had done their best to prevent expenditure by Inglis by building up large hidden departmental reserves which could have been used to pay a higher dividend or pay for further improvements to the railway. Already uncomfortable with the new power trade unions were wielding in the postwar world, and faced with a General Manager who was clearly not willing to compromise, he now decided that it was time to go, stepping down from his post on 31 December 1921, three months before he had been due to retire.

The creation of an enlarged Great Western provided a good opportunity to review the organisation of the company; its structure had developed piecemeal over the years and consisted of a number of departments, including Traffic, Goods, Civil Engineer, Signal & Telegraph, Locomotive and various others. Each department was self-contained, with a divisional structure under the central administration covering distinct geographical areas of the railway. Pole believed that this structure was over-centralised and not suitable for a modern railway; there was little co-ordination between departments, and not all the divisional areas actually coincided. Realising that in such a conservative organisation as the GWR change would be difficult, he began gradually, inviting chief officers and their wives to a weekend conference held in September 1921 at the Fishguard Bay Hotel, where much work was done 'in congenial conditions'.

New arrangements were discussed at a GWR board meeting in January 1922, when it was confirmed that areas supervised by the divisional managers of the Traffic, Goods, Locomotive and Engineering departments should be co-ordinated but only 'as and when opportunity offered'. If this development seems equivocal, the matter of 'the co-ordination of train and engine working' between the Locomotive and Traffic departments discussed between the Superintendent of the Line and the Chief Mechanical Engineer was even more ambiguous. C. B. Collett, Churchward's replacement as Chief Mechanical Engineer, fought a rearguard action to prevent the Superintendent of the Line's department from gaining control of the day-to-day running of locomotives and their rostering; the board minutes note only 'increased co-operation', reflecting that the pre-eminence of the Locomotive Department was maintained.[7]

Further changes were implemented on 16 May 1922, when the formation of the Cardiff Valleys and Central Wales divisions was announced following approval earlier in the month by the board. The former combined all of the old Cardiff and Rhymney lines, along with sections of the Barry, Taff Vale and Alexandra Docks lines, obtaining 'maximum advantage from the unification of the railway system'.[8] The new Central Wales Division encompassed all of the lines formerly operated by the Cambrian Railways and was intended to be the blueprint for the way in which Pole hoped the whole railway would eventually be reorganised, but the deeply entrenched conservative attitudes of many GWR staff meant that more than 15 years would elapse before his idea of truly independent and autonomous divisions became a reality.

The General Manager made no secret of his frustration at some of the conservative management at work on the railway, especially amongst some of the railways absorbed at the Grouping, noting that 'live men are not very conspicuous amongst them'. He also observed rather wistfully that 'it must not be supposed that officers of lines which had been keen rivals at once settled down to brotherly co-operation'.[9] Pole was keen, however, to promote what he called the '*esprit de corps*' of the new railway, and it was no doubt at his suggestion that the July 1922 issue of the company magazine included a letter from the stationmaster at Caerphilly, who argued that the success of the newly expanded GWR was 'of great concern to the men now, and they would jealously guard the traditions of the Great Western by yielding faithful and efficient service'.[10]

It seems that staff from some constituent railways were concerned with matters rather less serious than the well-being of the new GWR. In December 1922, the Chief Officers' Conference heard that complaints had been received from members of supervisory staff formerly employed by the Barry, Taff Vale and Rhymney railways, who had asked for the renewal of Second Class passes issued to them, 'on the grounds of discomfort occasioned by them having to travel in Third Class trains used by colliers and other workmen'.[11] Management took pity and allowed staff to travel in Second Class carriages where these were available, but the matter was typical of the many minor issues that needed resolution in the course of harmonising staff terms and conditions as well as ensuring that the larger railway business prospered.

It has been argued that the relative strength of most of the railways absorbed by the Great Western enabled it to be the first of the new 'Big Four' companies to move forward, and the most positive indication thus far came with the introduction of the new summer timetable in 1923. This was the result of a good deal of work at Paddington to review and remodel train services, with the aim not only of reintroducing some prewar trains but also of improving express and cross-country services and revising local and branch services. The 250-page timetable included more than 30 additional non-stop expresses, including the 11.10am from

Paddington to the Cornish Riviera, which made its first stop at Exeter, and two further new trains, both departing Paddington at 10.20 — one running non-stop as far as Birmingham and thence to the Cambrian Coast, the other an express running non-stop to Birkenhead. There were also new trains to South Wales and additional services to both Builth and Llandrindod Wells — a response to what the company called the 'national movement for British spas'. Branch-line and local services were also revised, extra trains being run using steam railmotors, while the new timetable further gave details of additional boat trains to and from Weymouth to coincide with a new daytime service to the Channel Islands.

The Great Western made efforts to compete with its rival the LNER in July 1923 when it accelerated the 2.30pm Cheltenham–Paddington service, a run that became known unofficially as the 'Cheltenham Flyer'. The train stopped at Gloucester and Stroud *en route* and called at Swindon at 3.40pm, departing at 3.45pm. It was timed to arrive at Paddington at 5pm, having covered the 77½ miles in 75 minutes at an average speed of 62mph. The company could claim the fastest start-to-stop run in Britain, although in truth, on an easily graded route and with powerful Churchward and Collett locomotives hauling a relatively modest train, the task facing crews was not a difficult one. This publicity exercise set the stage for more records to be broken in the 1930s, when competition with the LMS and LNER was keener.

In September 1923, there was further good news when the Irish Mail service via Fishguard and Rosslare was reintroduced. The political situation in Ireland had severely affected the Great Western's train and steamer services since the Easter Rising of 1916, and the company was not immune from the consequences of what had become an increasingly brutal battle between the British Government and Irish republicans.[12] This was vividly illustrated in July 1920, when the Great Western board heard that, in line with Irish railway workers' refusal to deal with military traffic, a number of GWR staff at Rosslare had refused to unload a consignment of barbed wire from a Fishguard steamer and

had been suspended; the wire had remained on the vessel, and other Rosslare porters had been suspended for refusing to handle barbed wire on subsequent trips.[13] The signing of a peace treaty in December 1922 and the establishment of the Irish Free State was described the following April in the *Great Western Railway Magazine* as an 'event without precedent in the history of British railways', for it meant that Fishguard–Rosslare services had new customs regulations to contend with, the Free State being now a 'foreign country'. Given the bloody fighting that had characterised the previous six years in Ireland, it was clearly no coincidence that the new trains run in September included through carriages from Aldershot — a large military barracks and headquarters of the British Army. A few months later, however, the company was able to report that quantities of cargo and livestock shipped from Ireland had been 'exceptionally good'.

If the improvements in train services on the Great Western were not enough, the company boosted its position still further in 1923 with the introduction of the 'Castle' class locomotive, designed by the new Chief Mechanical Engineer, C. B. Collett. This was not, however, the first major new design to have been built at Swindon following the war, this honour falling to Churchward's new '47xx' 2-8-0, introduced in 1919. There was much debate over the appointment of Collett, who had been Churchward's second-in-command and had already worked for the company for nearly 30 years; some at Swindon believed that William Stanier, only a year younger but a more gifted locomotive engineer, should have been given the top job, but the conservative nature of the company and its well-established promotion hierarchy prevailed.

ABOVE RIGHT The broad-gauge replica *North Star*, pictured in May 1925. The replica included some original parts retrieved from the works and from members of the public. One of the buffers had been used as a stool in a house near Bath, and one of the nameplates was returned to the factory by a local doctor, who had used it as a decoration for a fire screen.

BELOW A beautiful Collett-era corridor carriage, No 7624, built in 1924.

What cannot be disputed is that the 'Castle' class and the publicity surrounding its introduction captured the imagination of both the public and the press. For many the 'Castle' was the most graceful express locomotive produced by the company, and no doubt this was due in part to the fact that it was based on Churchward's 'Star' class, also regarded as a high-point in Great Western locomotive design.

Much debate has centred on Collett's perceived lack of expertise in locomotive design, but in the early 1920s at least, he did not need to innovate; it was sufficient merely to co-ordinate and continue the standardised locomotive policy introduced by his predecessor before the Great War. Precluded from building a significantly larger locomotive, a consequence of weight restrictions imposed by the Civil Engineer, Collett instead asked his design team to come up with a new locomotive that took the 'Star' as its foundation; the chassis was almost identical save that it was a foot longer, allowing the locomotive to be fitted with a larger side-window cab, to give the crew protection sorely lacking on the 'Stars'. A new boiler, based broadly on Churchward designs, was utilised, steam being fed through external (rather than internal) pipes to outside cylinders that were an inch bigger than those on the 'Stars'. Provision of these larger cylinders brought an increase

in tractive effort to 31,625lb at 85% boiler pressure (compared with the 27,800lb of the 'Stars'), making the new locomotive the most powerful express passenger design in the British Isles.

The first 'Castle', No 4073 *Caerphilly Castle*, made its debut in August 1923, its copper-capped chimney, brass safety-valve cover and beading around the cab and wheel splashers, along with 'artistic lined-out panels and boiler bands', rendering it a 'veritable blending of grace, dignity and power'.[14] Felix Pole and the GWR's publicity staff were quick to capitalise, making much of the boast that it was the 'most powerful locomotive in the world'; within months of its completion, the second 'Railway Book for Boys of All Ages' was published, entitled *Caerphilly Castle*. But the book was not just about No 4073; it also included chapters on how steam locomotives worked, Swindon Works and a lot more besides. The title, explained author W. G. Chapman, was 'selected for the reason that the super-locomotive so named, and recently produced at the GWR Company's works at Swindon, constitutes the last word in railway locomotive construction'.

The first batch of 'Castles' eventually numbered 10 locomotives, all named after famous castles located within GWR territory. Fittingly the last of these was No 4082 *Windsor Castle*, a locomotive that would feature on Royal trains for many

The front cover of a leaflet issued by the GWR. It noted: 'There is, of course, no reason and little if any economy in passengers' loading themselves with eatables and drinkables for consumption on the train,' as GWR restaurant cars offered 'refreshments nicely served at quite moderate charges'.
Great Western Trust Collection

years to come. In May 1924, *Caerphilly Castle* was displayed on the Great Western stand at the British Empire Exhibition at Wembley; the exhibition was intended to show the variety of industry across the Empire and Dominions and remained open for six months. The GWR stand was situated within the Palace of Engineering, *Caerphilly Castle* being positioned in close proximity to the LNER Pacific *Flying Scotsman*; there was also a working signalbox manned by GWR signal staff, along with various models of the docks recently acquired by the company. Importantly, there was also a kiosk distributing GWR publicity material and selling two new products — the book on *Caerphilly Castle* and the first jigsaw puzzle to be produced by the company, which also featured the locomotive. It was estimated that more than 750,000 people visited the footplate of No 4073 while it was on display, and, when the exhibition was repeated the following year, still more were able to view sister locomotive No 4079 *Pendennis Castle*, which appeared as part of a rather more ambitious display staged to mark the centenary of the Stockton & Darlington Railway; this also featured a 20-ton coal wagon and the replica broad-gauge locomotive *North Star*, which had been specially built at Swindon for the main Stockton & Darlington Centenary celebrations, held at Shildon in July 1925.

It is estimated that, in 1924 and 1925, in excess of 20 million people visited the Empire Exhibition, and the Great Western did good business by running more than 800 excursion trains carrying almost 400,000 passengers.[15] A shortage of hotel rooms in the capital in June 1924 prompted the company to offer special eight- and 15-day season tickets, allowing passengers to travel to the exhibition from more distant locations.[16] In the same month the *Great Western Railway Magazine* reported that, in connection with a 'Rodeo' competition being held at the exhibition, a special train had been run from Bristol, conveying 233 horses and 34 'cowboys' along with two further vans of luggage; a separate train was required to transport 160 steers, which presumably were also part of the show.

Whilst the exhibition was clearly an attraction, passenger business elsewhere on the Great Western continued to improve. The publication of the new timetable in 1924 revealed further changes and the introduction of what the company called 'standardised' departure time — a tradition that was to continue well into the modern era. Passengers would in future be able to rely on the fact that, from Paddington, all services to the West of England would depart at 30 minutes past the hour, trains to Birmingham and the North leaving at 10 minutes past the hour, to Bristol at 15 minutes past, to the West Midlands at 45 minutes past and to South Wales at 55 minutes past. By keeping West of England departures on the half hour the company avoided having to alter the 'Cornish Riviera Limited', the traditional 10.30am departure time of which had been heavily publicised for some years.

The Great Western carried out its own extensive trials with the 'Castle' class, and the results were extremely encouraging; Felix Pole had already been keen to extract maximum publicity from the boast that the 'Castles' were the most powerful locomotives in Britain, especially in comparison to the LNER's Gresley 'A1' Pacifics. In April 1925, the rivalry between the two companies was further increased by a series of locomotive exchanges in which *Pendennis Castle* was run on the East Coast main line between King's Cross and Doncaster and LNER 'A1s' were tried on the Paddington–Plymouth section of the 'Cornish Riviera Limited'. Whilst it is generally acknowledged that the LNER locomotives were not at their best, be it in terms of performance or coal consumption, the GWR engines recorded superlative performances, and *Pendennis Castle* proved easily capable of hauling a heavy 16-coach train up the gradients out of King's Cross — something that is said to have surprised even LNER staff.

A few months later No 4082 *Windsor Castle* found itself even further north, participating in the Stockton & Darlington centenary cavalcade, along with a number of other GWR locomotives, including the *North Star* replica. It has been suggested that LNER fitters may have carried out some undercover espionage work on

the 'Castle' while it was there, taking vital measurements which eventually led to Gresley's making improvements to the valve gear on his locomotives that would ultimately see them and their streamlined successors eclipse GWR designs in the 1930s.[17]

The high-profile developments in the Locomotive Department were supported by further investment elsewhere in the company; there was considerable ground to be made up, not only to return the railway to prewar standards but also to complete a number of projects that had been delayed by the conflict. A report produced by the Company Secretary as early as 1920, outlining potential new works in South Wales, also contained a long list of proposed schemes elsewhere on the system, including quadrupling of the line between Didcot and Wootton Bassett, provision of a new parcels depot at Paddington, doubling of the Cornish main line and the Falmouth branch, construction of new stations at Bristol and Newton Abbot and replacement of a number of locomotive sheds, including Aberystwyth and Stourbridge.

The report also identified as a major priority the construction of a rail bridge over the River Severn; the war had shown that the existing 'long under-seas' tunnel was a real bottleneck in the company's attempts to increase traffic to and from South Wales. The gradients in the tunnel limited the length of trains that could be safely worked to a maximum of 60 wagons with two locomotives and two brake vans. The density of traffic passing through the 4½-mile tunnel had increased appreciably, from 49 trains a day in 1913 to 65 a day in 1919, and, because trains

Prior to the Grouping, Aberystwyth station had struggled to cope with the holiday traffic arriving at the resort, and its modernisation was a high priority for the GWR. This postcard view shows the new buildings completed in 1924. *Author's collection*

had to be banked, ventilation in the tunnel was 'unsatisfactory'.[18] The solution was a bridge crossing the Severn (not far from the site of the current road bridges), providing a link between the existing South Wales main line near Portskewett and, on the English side, a new main line to Bristol. The greatest difficulty was, of course, the cost; even an outline cost of such a project was over £5 million, and the Great Western did not have such capital. With the advent of the Railways Act 1921 and the proposed absorption of South Wales companies by the GWR, the bridge scheme and a list of other suggested schemes in South Wales were, not surprisingly, re-evaluated in the light of the acquisition of railways and docks in the area.

In 1923, the Severn Bridge scheme was not even mentioned in a programme of works authorised by the board, that involved expenditure of £10 million; among contracts placed were those for the rebuilding of the goods depot at Bristol, the reconstruction of Newton Abbot station, the provision of a new locomotive shed at Stourbridge and improvements to the ex-Cambrian stations at Aberystwyth, Barmouth and Oswestry. Well over £427,000 was also to be spent on a number of smaller schemes, and there was to be considerable additional investment in South Wales. Wrote Felix Pole in 1924: 'When the Company assumed complete control of the Docks in South Wales, no time was lost in overhauling and supplementing the mechanical appliances and facilities for handling the immense amount of traffic to be dealt with.'[19] This resulted in an expenditure of almost £2 million, which included considerable sums on new sidings for coal traffic at Barry, Cardiff, Newport and Swansea, as well as a good deal of work in Cardiff to improve the layout and to provide a new hydraulic power plant.

The company also invested heavily in a lengthy campaign to persuade colliery owners in South Wales to adopt the use of larger modern 20-ton coal wagons. For many years coal had been shifted from pit to port in elderly 10- or 12-ton wooden-bodied wagons, and it was estimated that there were more than 100,000 privately owned wagons of this type in use in the early 1920s. In 1922, the matter was discussed by GWR management, and it was agreed that the General Manager and Chief Docks Manager should take soundings from colliery firms and submit a joint report outlining the steps needed to promote the use of high-capacity wagons. In September the following year Pole wrote to South Wales coal owners and received positive responses from more than 30 firms seeking further information. The General Manager had pointed out that the cost of building two 10-ton wagons was approximately 50% higher than that of building one 20-ton wagon. Other

A GWR 'Saint' 4-6-0 emerging from the west portal of the Severn Tunnel. A report published by the GWR in 1920 suggested a number of options to alleviate congestion in the tunnel, among them electrification (to speed up the trains) and the construction of a second bore close to the original. Both ideas were dismissed on cost grounds.

advantages, he argued, were that pressure on siding space would be reduced, as would the cost of repairs. However, as Pole reflected some years later, 'Human nature being what it is … it was useless to expect any change unless some inducement was offered,' so, as a further incentive, the GWR offered traders a rebate of 5% of the cost of moving coal on the network if 20-ton wagons were used.[20]

The scheme did not, of course, rely solely on the design and introduction of new wagons; considerable planning and investment were required in order to modify infrastructure at both the collieries and the railway-owned docks. GWR directors authorised the expenditure of 'practically two millions of new money to provide for necessary new and powerful coal hoists and reconstruction of existing appliances and alterations to lines feeding them,' noted a Great Western publication on its docks in the 1920s.[21] Pole was keen to press ahead with the introduction of the wagons and duly set up a committee to oversee the work. At a meeting in November 1923, referring to the minutes of an earlier meeting at Cardiff wherein it was recorded that the conversion of coal-tipping equipment might take up to seven years, he told managers: 'Any such period of time will certainly not be accepted by the board. We should aim to do the work in one year.'[22] Coal-tipping appliances at Barry, Cardiff, Newport, Penarth, Port Talbot and Swansea were identified, and the work was undertaken straightaway, whilst further capital was spent on the construction of new tipping equipment.

Pole duly got his way, and the first wagons were in use within the year. In March 1924, it was reported that initial contracts had been arranged with three firms — the Gloucester

ABOVE Although this photograph was produced to illustrate coal breakage in different types of wagon, it provides a graphic contrast between the new 20-ton wagons and the older wooden variety.

BELOW A '28xx' 2-8-0 at the head of a lengthy train of new 20-ton coal wagons. *Author's collection*

Wagon Co, the Birmingham Carriage & Wagon Co and the Bute Works Supply Co — for the supply of 250 wagons each, at a price of £280 per wagon.[23] By August the first trainload of these wagons had been delivered to a colliery at Maesteg, and it was reported that 'working arrangements and tipping facilities' had proved 'satisfactory', despite some initial teething problems, when the first proper train was run from the pit to Port Talbot Docks, on 27 August.

By 1925, new equipment was in use at Barry, Cardiff, Newport and Swansea, and the adoption of 20-ton wagons was well under way. In April 1927, the coal-tipping appliances were reported as being in a 'high state of efficiency', but colliery owners were reluctant to invest heavily in the new rolling stock, especially in the years after the General Strike. In February 1928, the *Great Western Railway Magazine* included an article on the successful introduction of high-capacity coal wagons on German railways. However, it noted: 'A very heavy expense has been incurred in equipping the South Wales docks with specially designed hoists for 20-ton wagons, and the poor response of traders in making use of the larger carrying unit is extremely disappointing.'[24]

ABOVE A 1935 advertisement for 20-ton coal wagons built by Metro-Cammell.

RIGHT While undoubtedly atmospheric, the cover of this 1920s leaflet promoting the Cornish Riviera lacks the style and verve of later publicity material. *Great Western Trust collection*

1 'The New General Manager — Mr Felix J. C. Pole', *Great Western Railway Magazine* July 1921, p156

2 *Ibid*

3 Channon, Geoffrey: 'Felix J. C. Pole' entry in the *Oxford Dictionary of National Biography* (Oxford University Press, 2004)

4 Pole, F. J. C.: *His Book* (Town & Country Press, 1968), p39

5 Vaughan, A.: *The Great Western at Work, 1921–1939* (PSL Books, 1993), p13

6 Pole, *ibid*, p41

7 Great Western Railway: Minutes of Board Meeting held 6 January 1922

8 *Great Western Railway Magazine* October 1924, p367

9 Pole, *ibid*, p63

10 *Great Western Railway Magazine* July 1922, p267

11 Great Western Railway: Minutes of Chief Officers' Conference Meeting held 15 December 1922

12 Hattersley, R.: *Borrowed Time — The Story of Britain between the Wars* (Abacus Books, 2007), pp35-62

13 Great Western Railway: Minutes of Board Meeting held 9 July 1920

14 Chapman, W. G.: *Caerphilly Castle* (GWR, Paddington, 1924), p40

15 Great Western Railway: *British Empire Exhibition Wembley — Souvenir of the Great Western Railway*. (GWR, Paddington, 1924 and 1925)

16 *Great Western Railway Magazine* June 1924, p279

17 Semmens, P.: *History of the Great Western Railway, 1. Consolidation 1923–1929* (Allen & Unwin, 1985), p64

18 *Memorandum on New Works in South Wales* (GWR Secretary's special report, March 1920) — National Archives: RAIL267/323

19 Great Western Railway: *British Empire Exhibition Wembley — Souvenir of the Great Western Railway* (GWR, Paddington, 1925), p40

20 Pole, *ibid*, pp72-73

21 Great Western Railway: *Docks of the GWR* (GWR Docks & Marine Department, **n.d** p30

22 Great Western Railway: Minutes of meeting held at Paddington 2 November 1923

23 Great Western Railway: Minutes of Chief Officers' Conference Meeting held 17 March 1924

24 *Great Western Railway Magazine* February 1928, p55

CHAPTER 6

THE GENERAL STRIKE

When Viscount Churchill stood up to address shareholders at the GWR's Annual General Meeting in February 1924 he did so with considerable optimism and pride regarding the position of the railway. He was able to report that it had carried over 12 million more passengers and over 7 million tons more freight than in the previous year, a result which reflected both the positive effects of the Grouping and a reduction in rates and charges, introduced in April 1923, which had brought goods rates down from 112% to 75% of prewar levels and passenger fares down from 75% to 50% above those of 1914. This move, aimed at stimulating business, had increased traffic but had not, Churchill noted, completely covered the losses caused by the reduction in rates.

It was nevertheless a good result, and, with a profit of over £8 million (and by dipping into reserves to the tune of £150,000), the company paid its shareholders an 8% dividend — the same figure as in the previous year. The Chairman was also able to announce that Felix Pole had received a knighthood for his services to the railway and the very positive position in which it now found itself owed much to his efforts. Quite apart from his enthusiasm for publicising the GWR and its services, Pole had proved adept at managing and modernising the railway; one key figure noted in the Annual Report was that costs were down by almost £500,000, despite the fact that the railway had expanded following the Grouping. Minutes of the Chief Officers' Conference are full of references to cost reductions; as early as 1921 staff were instructed that, if traffic did not increase sufficiently, 'receipts may be protected by drastically reducing expenditure'.[1] Pole also used his monthly 'From the General Manager' article in the company magazine to remind staff about the need for economy. A folder titled 'Economy & Co-operation — A Few Words to Great Western Employees' was issued to all staff; it highlighted the cost of some of the basic items used on the railway, including lamps, brooms and shunters' poles, and included a reminder that 'there are a thousand and one ways in which economies can be effected'.[2] The folder also vividly illustrated the huge costs of keeping the GWR in business,

One of the best-known bridges in the South Wales coalfield was the Crumlin Viaduct, constructed for the Taff Vale extension of the Newport, Abergavenny & Hereford Railway. Miners' cottages in smoky Ebbw Vale are visible in the background.

reminding staff that, on average, the railway used 3½ tons of coal and 1½ gallons of petrol per minute of every day.

Pole's leaflet also tellingly noted that 'Railway revenue follows the trade of the country: when trade is bad, railway revenue falls'. The encouraging results reported at the AGM were not to last, and by the summer revenues had begun to drop alarmingly. In a gloomy article in the company magazine in June, Pole noted that the excellent prospects anticipated earlier in the year had evaporated, this being due in no small part to strikes on and off the railway. A two-week dispute involving enginemen had dealt a 'heavy blow' to the railway industry, he argued, as had a national dock strike which had brought the South Wales docks to a standstill and prevented Ocean Mail traffic from being unloaded at Plymouth.[3] This and other disputes in the South Wales docks had clearly taken their toll on the Chief Docks Manager, J. H. Vickery, whose retirement was announced in April, his departure the result of the 'strain he has felt in consequence of the arduous duties and anxieties of the last few years, especially with the amalgamation of the docks and recurrent labour troubles'. In June 1924, an unofficial strike by staff in London caused a 'considerable stoppage,'[4] and Pole was moved to ask whether labour disputes were going to 'wreck the railway industry'.

By the end of 1924, freight traffic was well down, the most worrying factor being a dramatic decrease in coal traffic. The decline in coal exports reflected difficulties facing the British economy in the years after the Great War; despite a resurgence, the underlying outlook for the 'old' industries of coal, iron and steel, shipbuilding and textiles that had underpinned British exports for years was not good. Competition from abroad had grown, and in a world where oil was increasingly used for power, there was less demand for coal.

Another blow to the coal trade came with the resumption of exports from the Ruhr. Countries that had previously drawn large supplies from South Wales instead began taking cheaper German coal; exports of Welsh coal to mainland Europe were badly hit, France and Italy each reducing their imports by over 1 million tons in 1924 alone. When shareholders met in February 1925, the Chairman painted a far gloomier picture than he had a year previously; revenues were down, and although merchandise traffic was up, coal business was down by over £4 million. Whilst describing a 'very unsatisfactory result'[5] he was able to announce that shareholders would still be receiving a 7½% dividend, maintained by £850,000 of company reserves — a sign that the management of the GWR thought that the difficult economic conditions were only temporary and that better times lay ahead. This optimism soon evaporated, however, and in May the General Manager told senior staff that directors were 'seriously

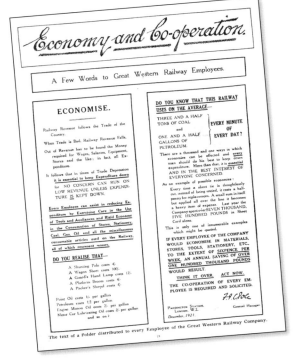

ABOVE The cover of a leaflet issued to all staff in 1926, as reproduced in the *Great Western Railway Magazine*.

LEFT The calm before the storm: a handbill advertising excursions to the capital from stations in the Bristol area in January 1926. *Author's collection*

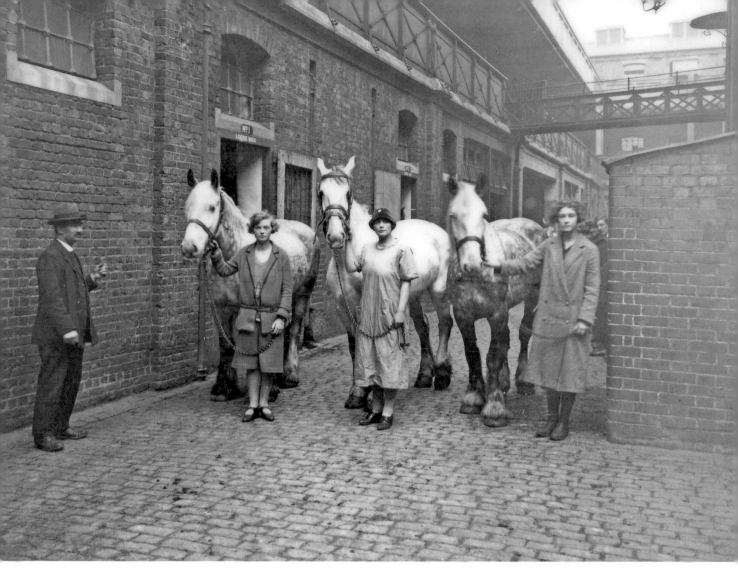

With no staff to feed and water them, GWR horses stabled at Paddington were cared for by volunteers in the General Strike.

concerned about the unsatisfactory financial results' and that they would 'undoubtedly have to face further adverse criticism when figures are submitted to the next board meeting'.[6] A plan to reduce expenditure by £1 million was tabled, including cuts to all departments of the railway.

Given that wages had in 1924 accounted for 71.53% of the company's expenditure, a reduction in staff was also inevitable. Meeting with unions, the company presented three options — redundancies, an 'all round' percentage reduction in salaries and wages, or the suspension of the guaranteed week. Staff representatives were unwilling to agree to either a pay cut or the end of the guaranteed week, and it seemed that discussions might end in industrial action. There did, however, appear to be some understanding of the difficult position the GWR was in, and, reluctantly, the unions agreed that redundancies were the only option. Further negotiation led to an agreement that casual and temporary staff would be discharged initially. When it was no longer possible to meet targets by dismissing these staff, employees with the shortest period of service were to be made redundant. The notice of dismissal also contained a clause that the company

would reinstate staff to existing posts, or posts of approximately equivalent nature, when 'circumstances improved'.

While the GWR was negotiating its way through the difficulties of reducing its workforce, more serious labour troubles were developing nationally. The problems in the coal industry had been exacerbated by Winston Churchill's decision to return Britain to the Gold Standard in April; while making the pound stronger this also made exports more expensive, and the slump in the coal trade became a crisis. In an effort to improve profits, colliery owners gave notice that a wages agreement negotiated when business was good would now be terminated at the end of July 1925. The proposed settlement involved a pay cut for miners and an end to the seven-hour day — a concession won as recently as 1919.

The miners were in no mood to compromise, having suffered badly since the war, and rejected the deal. When employers claimed losses were running at more than £1 million a month and that the settlement would make British coal more competitive in

GREAT WESTERN RAILWAY.

WE WANT ALL WAGONS
WATCH WASTE.

1. Watch every wagon.

2. Keep wagons moving.

3. If you cannot keep wagons moving, tell someone who can.

4. Deal as promptly with empty as with loaded wagons.

5. Avoid delay to wagons at Stations, Yards, Sidings and Works

6. See no delay occurs in advising arrival of wagons and confirming advices. This may be done verbally, by messenger or telephone, or by telegraph or post.

7. Increase average wagon load.

8. Increase average miles travelled daily.

9. Improve distribution by furnishing accurate wagon reports.

10. Co-operate unselfishly in carrying out instructions.

11. Call immediate attention to delay to wagons in the possession of other Departments.

12. Impress Traders with importance of releasing wagons on arrival, as this co-operation is for mutual benefit.

13. Ask Traders to give 24 hours' notice of empty wagons required.

FELIX J. C. POLE,
General Manager.

GREAT WESTERN RAILWAY.

NOTICE TO THE STAFF.

The National Union of Railwaymen have intimated that railwaymen have been asked to strike without notice to-morrow night. Each Great Western man has to decide his course of action, but I appeal to all of you to hesitate before you break your contracts of service with the old Company, before you inflict grave injury upon the Railway Industry, and before you arouse ill feeling in the Railway service which will take years to remove.

Railway Companies and Railwaymen have demonstrated that they can settle their disputes by direct negotiations. The Mining Industry should be advised to do the same.

Remember that your means of living and your personal interests are involved, and that Great Western men are trusted to be loyal to their conditions of service in the same manner as they expect the Company to carry out their obligations and agreements.

FELIX J. C. POLE,
General Manager.

PADDINGTON STATION,
May 2nd. 1926.

7765-5-26.

---

the world market, union leaders argued that coal owners' profits between 1921 and 1925 had been £58.4 million.[7] The involvement of the Trades Union Congress led to threats of an embargo on the movement of coal by transport workers. Prime Minister Stanley Baldwin, having said that there would be no further subsidy for the mining industry following discussions with both sides, capitulated on 31 July, announcing that there would be an investigation into the mining industry and that financial assistance would be given until the spring, by which time the inquiry would be completed.

The result of 'Red Friday', as the press dubbed it, was to postpone what many saw as an inevitable clash between miners and owners. In September a Royal Commission chaired by former Home Secretary Herbert Samuel was set up to investigate the coal industry. The inquiry took place in an atmosphere of increasing hysteria and tension, newspapers and politicians warning that a general strike might trigger a communist revolution. In January 1926, Pole wrote of a 'cloud' hanging over the coal industry, expressing his hope that the work of the Commission would 'disperse that cloud' through a 'display of mutual common sense and a supreme co-operative effort for peace'.[8] Speaking later the same month, he argued: 'The man who says that we are bound to have a strike this year is doing an incalculable amount of mischief, not only on this country but throughout the world.'[9]

In *Peeps at Great Railways*, published in 1926, Gordon Home wrote that, as the GWR main line ran along the southern edge of the South Wales mining district, the results of the 'underground labours' of the miners could be seen only in the 'long trains of trucks loaded with the hard steam coal which brings great wealth into England if not to the miner, who lives in the ugliest villages among the mountains under which he digs'. Before long, he hoped, 'something will be done to make this statement out of date'.[10]

While miners and their families struggled to survive on low wages, life for the wealthy continued much as normal; the company magazine reported in February 1926 that extra trains had been necessary to convey students back to public schools after the holidays, while undergraduate traffic to Oxford had entailed 'many extra carriages', and additional staff had been sent to deal with college baggage.[11]

Railway unions made no secret of their support for the miners, and, as the clocked ticked down towards the publication of the Royal Commission report, feelings ran high, resulting in a number of small disputes affecting the GWR. A strike at various stations in Dorset prompted the General Manager to issue a circular which reprinted letters from local traders complaining that because of labour problems they were considering the use of road transport in the future. One wrote that 'difficulties recently experienced at your station do not encourage us to send more goods by rail than we can avoid'. Pole was not pleased, warning staff: 'You have been quarrelling with your bread and butter. Resolve not to do it again.'

The ever-optimistic Viscount Churchill had concluded his speech to shareholders in 1926 by expressing his hope that the outlook had 'distinctly improved', but in reality matters were about

FAR LEFT Company records of the 1920s are full of references to shortages of GWR wagon stock. Matters were bad enough for the General Manager to issue this handbill to staff, in an attempt to ease the situation.

LEFT The letter issued to GWR staff by the General Manager on the eve of the General Strike, urging them to remain at work.

BELOW Volunteers and soldiers, their rifles, uniforms and helmets piled up on the platforms, wait to unload the goods from wagons shunted into the station at Paddington. The recently arrived train includes a rather motley selection of older clerestory carriages.

to get significantly worse. On 6 March, the Samuel Commission published its conclusions, recommending a reorganisation of the coal industry but also arguing that a pay cut for miners was unavoidable. For the Miners' Federation, whose slogan had been 'Not a penny off the pay, not a minute on the day', this was unacceptable. With only weeks of subsidy left for the coal industry (which had cost the Government £23 million rather than the £11 million originally thought), mine owners announced the rates they would be paying miners from 1 May 1926. These amounted to savage cuts in pay; for men working underground it meant a reduction of 2s 6d per day.[12] For men on a 'pitiably low' wage it was a cut too far. On 30 April, those who refused terms were locked out, and the coalfield ground to a halt. Unlike in 1921, when they had been deserted by union colleagues, the miners were supported by the TUC, and, despite last-minute negotiations with the Government, on 1 May 1926 it finally authorised a general strike.

The strike was to start at midnight on 3/4 May. At Paddington Sir Felix Pole and his staff had already made contingency plans, although the General Manager treated 'the forthcoming struggle' as one in which the principles of chess might be applied, aiming to keep one step ahead of his opponents. Not all unions gave formal notice of strike action, although C. T. Cramp of the NUR did write to Pole on 1 May, telling him that his union, 'in common

with others affiliated to the Trades Union Congress', had agreed to 'give its support to the miners during the present lock-out'.[13] As he wrote later in his memoirs, Pole believed that GWR men should not be allowed to strike without a 'word of advice', and so on Sunday 2 May he asked Nicholls, Superintendent of the Line, to telegraph a notice to be posted at stations and depots, urging them to 'hesitate before you break your contracts of service with the Old Company' and reminding them that their 'means of living and personal interests' were involved.[14]

As midnight passed it seemed that few heeded Pole's call; at Paddington the crew of the 11pm Southall goods arrived with their train and then took the locomotive back to the shed. Within five minutes the huge goods depot was silent. The general feeling amongst staff appeared to be that 'the working man ought to show its gigantic combined power for once; not to punish, or destroy, but just as a warning that there were certain things it would not tolerate'.[15] Some, particularly signalmen, did not leave their posts immediately at midnight but instead completed their shifts before joining the strike.

When Pole arrived at Paddington on the morning of Tuesday 4 May the station was 'dead', with practically all men on strike. The solidarity of the strike surprised even the TUC, the 2½ million workers on strike nationally leaving millions more struggling to work without public transport, resulting in chaos on the roads. Hundreds flocked to enlist as volunteers at Paddington; by 7pm there were more than the company could cope with, and so a halt was called to recruitment for the day. The volunteers were a real mixture — elderly retired GWR staff, university students and even

BELOW A passenger shakes the hand of one of the crew as he passes the cab of the recently arrived train at Paddington on the fifth day of the General Strike.

RIGHT There are precious few pictures taken of work done during the General Strike, and it may have been that the company photographer was one of those who withdrew his labour. This rather grainy image shows volunteers loading goods into a lorry at Paddington.

BELOW RIGHT One of the most famous posters issued by the GWR during the strike.

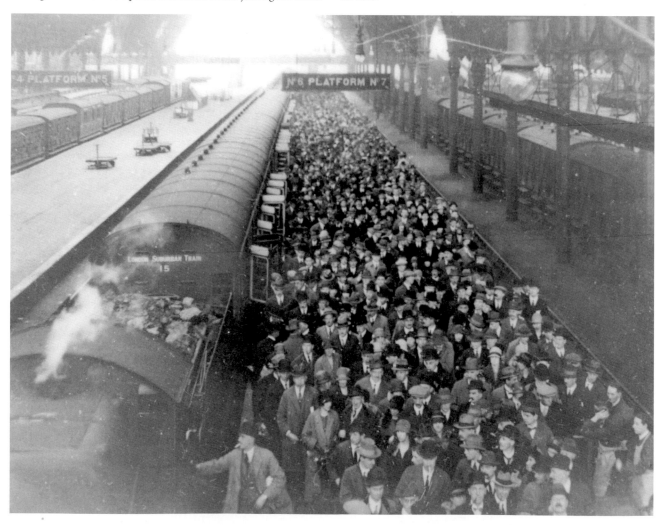

Great Western Railway
WHOM do YOU SERVE?

GREAT WESTERN RAILWAY

The Agreement of Service provides that each man will "abstain from any act that may injuriously affect the interests of the Company" and that "seven days' previous notice in writing of termination of service shall be given."

NOTICE TO THE STAFF

The National Union of Railwaymen have intimated that railwaymen have been asked to strike without notice tomorrow night. Each Great Western man has to decide his course of action but I appeal to all of you to hesitate before you break your contracts of service with the old Company before you inflict grave injury upon the Railway Industry and before you arouse ill feeling in the Railway service which will take years to remove.

Railway Companies and Railwaymen have demonstrated that they can settle their disputes by direct negotiations. The Mining Industry should be advised to do the same

Remember that your means of living and your personal interests are involved, and that Great Western men are trusted to be loyal to their conditions of service in the same manner as they expect the Company to carry out their obligations and agreements.

Felix J C Pole,
General Manager.

Paddington Station
May 2nd, 1926.

THE NATIONAL UNION OF RAILWAYMEN

Unity House,
Euston Road,
London, N.W. 1.
May 1st, 1926.

MINERS' CRISIS

Arising out of the dispute in the Coal Industry this Union in common with others affiliated to the Trades Union Congress has agreed to give its support to the Miners during the present lockout and further in accordance with the decision arrived at a Conference of Trades Union Executive Committees convened by the General Council of the Trades Union Congress it has been agreed to take steps in conjunction with the Transport Workers Union, to call upon our members to cease work on Monday next the 3rd instant

I am conveying this intimation to you in order that you may be cognisant of the fact that in ceasing work the men are acting upon the instructions of the National Union of Railwaymen

C. T. Cramp

Unity House,
Euston Road,
London, N.W. 1.
6th May, 1926.

MINERS' CRISIS

I desire to repeat on behalf of the N.U.R. what I said in yesterday's issue of the BRITISH WORKER

Members of our Union must handle no traffic of any kind. Food-stuffs or otherwise.

C. T. Cramp
National Union of Railwaymen

'titled ladies', who cared for the horses at depots. There were many more volunteers than work available, and it was estimated that the company used only around 40% of those who had offered their services during the strike.

Basic training was given to volunteer signalmen, guards and shunters at Paddington, and within hours of the strikes beginning, 60 volunteers were receiving training at the signalling school at Royal Oak. The following day they took a 'rigid' examination and, once passed, were sent to signalboxes in the London area. Two groups of more than 180 volunteers subsequently undertook the same training and were sent further afield. A similar process applied to shunters, goods and passenger guards, and the company's contingency plans also included 'appropriate emergency text-books for "lightning" courses of instruction'.[16] The efforts of the volunteers and 'loyal' staff were recorded in a typewritten 'Bulletin' which was produced daily. On 11 May, it reported that volunteers were 'settling down to their work and doing yeoman service. Paddington to-day is the home of democracy and the unusual sight may be seen of young men of all walks of society cheerfully unloading milk churns by the thousand.'[17]

The day before the strike began, a telegram was sent to all superintendents, requesting that they 'strain every nerve to see that milk traffic is dealt with' and asking them to make 'very special efforts in this direction'.[18] Other than on the first day, when there were large numbers of milk churns at stations but 'no prospect of moving them', the railway was able to transport increasing quantities of milk to the capital, the daily total increasing from 2,900 full churns on 5 May to well over 9,000 on the last day of the dispute. In general, however, freight traffic was badly hit during the strike, the highest number of trains run on any one day being 157, representing just 7.7% of the usual figure. In the Central Wales Division only 15 goods trains ran during the whole of the strike, and those trains that did run on the GWR network tended to be specials carrying foodstuffs such as bananas or margarine.

The company's *Strike Bulletin* provided its readers with a daily 'barometer' showing that it was able to operate an increasing number of passenger trains each day. It appears, however, that management accepted early in the strike that volunteer labour could run only the most basic services on the network and that to extend the timetable to anything like normal levels would have posed difficulties both operationally and in terms of safety. Nevertheless, after running only 194 trains across the network on the first day of the strike the company was able to run 1,517 by the ninth day of the dispute. These figures were, however, modest — a fact upon which the unions were quick to seize. The TUC issued its own propaganda, including a flyer, 'How the Gentlemen of England Man the Trains', which argued that, while the Government was giving the impression that it was 'business as usual' on the railways, they were actually 'practically at a standstill'.[19]

While the largest number of passenger trains was operated in the London area, away from Paddington the strike remained solid; GWR statistics reveal that during the dispute more than 80% of the 111,475 staff employed remained on strike until the last two days, when the percentage dropped to 78.8%. With almost 98% of footplate staff, 96% of guards and around 90%

of signalmen not at work, the task of running long-distance trains was difficult. Just how difficult was illustrated by a special passenger train from Cardiff to Paddington run on 8 May, which had a driver from Old Oak Common, a Bullo Pill fireman and a guard from Carmarthen. Even if a crew could be found, staff often had to be sent out to open signalboxes or level-crossing gates, riding on trains to do so. However, although there must have been unreported mishaps, there were no serious accidents on the railway during the strike. The most serious incident occurred on 8 May at Oswestry station, where a train ran through the buffer-stops, demolishing the end of the parcels office and leaving the leading carriage wedged inside it. There were no serious injuries amongst the 16 passengers, although a clerk riding on the train as guard was bruised and shaken.[20]

Those who remained at work had to contend with a fair amount of intimidation and violence; on 5 May police were called to Old Oak Common, where a large crowd had gathered outside the signalbox. There were numerous reports of stones having been thrown at trains and signalboxes, but no serious injuries appear to have been sustained; there were also a number of isolated reports of sabotage, such as the loosening of track bolts. A number of notices were issued by the General Manager on the subject of 'victimisation', the first claiming that 'the victim in this case was the Great Western Railway' and questioning why so many men should have left their work — something that passed 'all comprehension'. Continuing, Pole echoed the views of many, including Winston Churchill, arguing that the strike was a 'deep conspiracy against the state'.[21]

Until the strike there had been many on the GWR who thought that Pole, although a 'company man', still felt some sympathy with the rank-and-file worker, but his pronouncements as the dispute was played out seemed to dispel this. By the end of the first week some strikers were clearly having second thoughts, and a number began to return to work. The General Manager was in no mood for compromise, however, and issued a circular noting that 'men on strike who offer to return may be re-employed, providing that their services can be utilised in any capacity, but no man who is known to have taken a leading part in organising or carrying out the strike, nor any supervisor, is allowed to resume work without explicit instructions from this office'. Returning staff were also required to sign a document that reminded them that they were re-employed on the understanding they were 'not relieved of the consequences of having broken your contract of service with the Company'.[22] Not all strikers were taken back immediately, and the strike log for 11 May noted that, while 208 men had been reinstated, 56 had not.

From the second day of the strike the railway was able to keep the capital supplied with milk, and the number of churns carried gradually increased, so that by the last day of the strike more than 9,000 were transported.

In South Wales, reported Pole to the board on 21 May, 'practically the whole of the subordinate grades and a large proportion of the clerical and supervisory staff of the docks department withdrew their labour,' but staff who remained 'loyal' maintained essential services such as power and lock gates. Volunteers also operated tug boats, such as the *Earl* at Cardiff. There were no reports of disturbance or damage at ports, but this may well have been due to the fact that a Royal Navy submarine docked at Cardiff on Tuesday 4 May, to be joined two days later by a light cruiser. Some 160 officers and men landed at Newport on 5 May for 'protection' purposes, and the following day the destroyer HMS *Tetrarch* docked at Swansea.[23]

A week after the strike had begun, the General Manager felt confident enough to issue a notice to the volunteers and staff, telling them that he could state 'with confidence that railway services are improving rapidly each day'.[24] The company had even been able to run an Ocean Mail special from Plymouth, and the number of trains run had exceeded the 1,000 mark for the first time since the strike began. Other reports noted that the strike was still solid in some places, particularly Wales; on 11 May the superintendent of the Chester Division informed Paddington that no one had appeared for duty that morning. Elsewhere, however, staff began reporting for work; the *Strike Bulletin* for the following day noted that 'uneasiness prevails, as it is beginning to dawn on strikers that by their own rash act they are destroying their means of livelihood'.[25]

ABOVE The 'Bertie' and 'Trevor' pits of the Lewis Merthyr Colliery Co at Trehafod, as pictured in the *Great Western Railway Magazine*. Following the General Strike the miners were locked out for another six months before finally returning to work.

BELOW LEFT Another message to staff from the General Manager, issued before the end of the dispute.

The strike was finally called off by the TUC on 12 May. The NUR informed the company that a telegram had been sent to members, telling them: 'Trades Union Congress notifies strike called off. Members must present themselves for duty at once.' Pole was in no mood for compromise and had no intention of taking all the men back to work until their services were needed, and notices were posted at stations, reminding staff that the strike had been called off 'unconditionally' and that, while services would be restored as soon as possible, 'the injury to trade is believed to be so serious that for some time full pre-strike services will not be required'. Instructions were sent to reinstate signalmen first, but many other workers refused to sign the aforementioned document; when told by the unions on 13 May that their policy was 'all in or none in' the General Manager replied 'Then it is none in', and the strike continued.

Pole, as Chairman of the Railway Companies' Association, was determined to dictate terms, and the agreement finally signed by the railway unions on 14 May was a humiliating admission of defeat in which they had to admit that 'in calling a strike they committed a wrongful act against the Companies' and were forced to undertake 'not to again [*sic*] instruct their members to strike without previous negotiations'.[26] Back on the GWR, following the agreement a telegram was sent to superintendents, asking them to run a special passenger service on Saturday and Sunday that did not exceed 50% of the pre-strike timetable and to spend the weekend 'squaring up' goods yards.

In the weeks following the strike the ramifications of the dispute rumbled on; further negotiations with unions resulted

GREAT WESTERN RAILWAY.

VICTIMISATION.

The word Victimisation has often been used in connection with Strikes. In the experience of the Great Western Railway, it has usually been imported at the end of a Strike, the Trade Unions invariably asking that there should be no victimisation. The present strike not only differs from previous strikes in that it is not associated with any dispute or Labour question affecting the Company, but because of the fact that victimisation started with the strike, the victim in this case being the Great Western Railway Company. It is indeed true to say that the Country as a whole is being victimised by a strike which is the blackest spot in the history of Labour in this country. That thousands of men with no grievance against their employers should have been "instructed" to leave work, and that so many of them should have done so passes all comprehension. It can only be explained on the ground that there was a deep conspiracy against the State. Thank God such a conspiracy cannot succeed and can only result in the discrediting of its promoters and the disillusionment of those who have been used as pawns in the game.

F. Pole

General Manager.

PADDINGTON STATION,
May, 1926.

in the suspension of the guaranteed week until the financial position improved. There was much bad feeling regarding the way in which staff were reinstated, some men arguing that the strike had given supervisors the opportunity to settle old scores. Matters came to a head at Oxford in June, when a mass meeting of staff threatened to 'work to rule'. The response to the NUR from the General Manager was swift: 'Any man who resorts to a "go slow" policy will be dismissed.' The board was subsequently informed that 'the matter was evidently reconsidered by the men as the threat has not been given effect to'.[27]

The position in which the company now found itself was serious. Not only did business take some months to recover from the strike, but it was severely affected by the fact that the miners remained locked out, 'left alone in their struggle',[28] until the end of the year. Economies were needed, and these included reducing or cutting non-essential maintenance on buildings, lines and rolling stock and cutting expenditure on printing and advertising. Swindon Works remained on short time for the rest of the year, and further staff redundancies were made.

Aside from financial damage to the company there were serious ramifications for industrial relations. In editions of the *Great Western Railway Magazine* published in the months following the strike there were a number of articles written by 'loyal' staff, including one titled 'Afterthoughts of Striker' in which the author, R. F. Thurtle, argued that the strike was a 'moral mistake' and that the most important task was to 'assuage all soreness and dissolve all bitterness'.[29] Not all staff agreed, and bad feeling between strikers and those who had remained at work would linger for years; a bitter 'Open Letter to Sir Felix Pole' published by the Paddington branch of the NUR argued that his pleas for co-operation before the strike had been 'so much hypocritical trash'. It also ridiculed a GWR circular 'telling us that unless we speak to "scabs" we are liable to dismissal', arguing that 'No man who sells his soul and his self-respect to his enemies and betrays his comrades is entitled to the comradeship of a class-conscious worker.'[30]

A postcard photograph of coal being unloaded at Swindon and awaiting distribution in the town following the General Strike. Judging from the wheels, which look like those used on platform barrows, at least two of the handcarts had their origins in the railway works.

1 Great Western Railway: Minutes of Chief Officers' Conference Meeting held 15 July 1921

2 Great Western Railway: 'Economy & Co-operation — A Few Words to Great Western Employees' (GWR, Paddington, December 1921)

3 Cabinet papers, 21 February 1924 — National Archives: CAB/23/47

4 Cabinet papers, 6 June 1924 — National Archives: CAB/23/48

5 *Great Western Railway Magazine* March 1925, p89

6 Great Western Railway: Minutes of Chief Officers' Conference Meeting held 4 May 1925

7 Perkins, A.: *A Very British Strike* (Pan Books, 2006), p52

8 *Great Western Railway Magazine* January 1926, p1

9 *Great Western Railway Magazine* February 1926, p59

10 Home, G.: *Peeps at Great Railways: The Great Western Railway* (A. & C. Black, 1926), p65

11 *Great Western Railway Magazine* February 1926, p61

12 *Conditions in the Mining Industry — Speakers' Notes* (Trades Union Congress Publicity Committee, 1926) — Modern Records Centre collection, University of Warwick

13 Great Western Railway: *General Strike, May 1926* (General Manager's Office, Paddington, 1926), p10

14 Great Western Railway: 'Notice to Staff No 7765-5-26', issued 2 May 1926

15 Graves, R., & Hodge, A.: *The Long Week-End — A Social History of Great Britain, 1918–1939* (Hutchinson, 1940), p163

16   *Great Western Railway Magazine* June 1926, p235

17   Great Western Railway: *Strike Bulletin* 1926 — STEAM archive

18   Potts, C. R.: *The GWR and the General Strike* (Oakwood Press, 1996), p19

19   Flyer issued by the General Council of the Trades Union Congress, 1926 — STEAM archive

20   General Strike: Log of the Superintendent of the Line — National Archives: RAIL786

21   Great Western Railway: 'Notice to Staff: Victimisation', issued 5 May 1926

22   Great Western Railway: *General Strike, May 1926* (General Manager's Office, Paddington, 1926), p12

23   Great Western Railway: Minutes of Board Meeting held 21 May 1926

24   Great Western Railway: *General Strike, May 1926* (General Manager's Office, Paddington, 1926), p114

25   Great Western Railway: *Strike Bulletin* 12 May 1926 — STEAM archive

26   'Terms of Settlement, 14 May 1926', reprinted in *General Strike, May 1926* (General Manager's Office, Paddington, 1926)

27   Great Western Railway: Minutes of Board Meeting held 25 June 1926

28   Cook, A. J.: *The Nine Days* (Co-operative Printing Society, 1926), p23

29   *Great Western Railway Magazine* July 1926, p252

30   'Open Letter to Sir Felix Pole from the Paddington Railwaymen' (NUR, Paddington, 1926) — STEAM archive

CHAPTER 7

HIGH-WATER MARK

The year 1926 was an *annus horribilis* for the GWR, but in 1927 there was the prospect, at least, of better times. In a message in January, Sir Felix Pole told staff that the previous 12 months had been a 'black year' but that an agreement between coal owners and miners in South Wales signed on 30 November 1926 was a first step in reviving the prosperity of the industry. Although mining had recommenced in December, shipments from docks had been slow to restart because of an embargo on coal exports enforced by the Government. The Docks Department had been very badly affected, as it depended so much on the coal trade; there had been a decrease of 74% in coal traffic in 1926, and the consequent depression felt in the iron and steel industry and other allied trades made matters worse. Pits having remained at a standstill for more than six months, imports of pit wood and mining timber — regular business for the docks — were minimal. Exports of tinplate, steel and 'patent fuel' were also well down; the only positive news concerned an increase in the imports of oil — and also of foreign coal which, while good for business in the short term, did not bode well for the future of the British coal industry. Figures produced by the company early in 1927 confirmed the extremely poor position in which the docks found themselves; exports had dropped from just under 27 million tons in 1925 to 12 million tons in 1926, although imports had actually increased slightly, from 4,859,000 to 5,346,000 tons.

The Great Western had itself had to resort to imported coal in order to maintain services as supplies of Welsh coal dwindled. In July 1926, C. B. Collett estimated that the company had enough coal to last until the end of August,[1] but with the continuation of the miners' strike this was not enough, and in October it was reported that 742,953 tons had been purchased from Europe, South Africa and the USA.[2] In order to conserve coal, with effect from 12 July the GWR had reverted to its 'winter' timetable, supplemented by additional trains to meet holiday demand, but there was considerable pressure from the Government to reduce consumption still further as the winter approached.

RIGHT Delivering a GWR lunch basket at Paddington in 1929.

BELOW The scene at Hockley goods depot in Birmingham in April 1927, with examples of GWR Burford, Thornycroft and AEC lorries in evidence. *Philip Kelley collection*

By the spring of 1927 there were signs of improvement, the *Great Western Railway Magazine* reporting: 'Whilst traffic is generally considerably below that for the corresponding period last year, there is evidence of steady progress towards normal conditions … the trade of the country is improving, and it is for all of us to see that the Great Western gets its fair share.'[3] Conditions had eased sufficiently for negotiations to resume regarding the reinstatement of the 'guaranteed week' for staff, and agreement with unions had been reached on 16 February. This gave each employee guaranteed weekly earnings of not less than four days' pay at ordinary rate, rising to five days' pay in April, when all grades, including clerical and supervisory, had their guaranteed week restored.

Following the General Strike the GWR introduced revised conditions of service for its workforce. Beginning with the statement that any staff recruited should 'be able to read and write

with reasonable facility, and be generally intelligent', the terms and conditions also strengthened the employer's position in any future dispute, stipulating that staff must 'be loyal and obedient' and 'abstain from any act that may injuriously affect the interests of the Company'. Supervisory staff were also required to sign an additional declaration that they would do everything 'to promote the best interests of the Company' and they would not withdraw their service 'under any circumstances' without first giving the railway the requisite notice to terminate their engagement.[4]

With signs of improvement lifting the mood, the GWR took centre stage once more with the announcement that, following the introduction of its first new 'King'-class locomotive, in July 1927, it could once again boast that it had the most powerful locomotive in Great Britain. Sir Felix Pole had been stung by the announcement the previous August by the Southern Railway that its new express locomotive *Lord Nelson*, developing a

BELOW LEFT One of a series of photographs taken in the 'A' Erecting Shop at Swindon Works in 1927, illustrating the construction of the first of the 'King' class locomotives, *King George V*. The locomotive is about to be wheeled using one of the 100-ton cranes, capable of lifting complete locomotives when required.

RIGHT The *North Star* replica being craned off the ship on arrival in the United States, after its transatlantic journey in September 1927.

tractive effort of 33,500lb, was now the most powerful, eclipsing the GWR's 'Castle' class. It seemed, however, that any further development of express locomotives on the GWR was restricted by weight limits imposed by the Chief Civil Engineer. Collett, the Chief Mechanical Engineer, was moved to inform Pole: 'If I could have an axle load of 22½ tons, I would build you a very fine locomotive.' What then transpired illustrates some of the difficulties the General Manager had experienced, ever since taking up office, with the departmentalised and inward-looking structure of the railway. When Pole and Brocklebank, Chairman of the Locomotive Committee, discussed the matter with J. C. Lloyd, the Civil Engineer, they were informed that the maximum axle loading allowed on bridges was in fact 22 tons and had been so since 1903! Both men were 'astonished' at this revelation, as this fact had not been communicated to any other department, so when Lloyd told them that an axle load of 22½ tons would be acceptable, Collett was instructed to go ahead and build a new locomotive in readiness for the 1927 summer timetable.[5]

Addressing the board in July 1927, Pole was rather more diplomatic, noting that the outcome of co-operation between the CME and Chief Civil Engineer to build 'heavier engines to meet present-day traffic requirements' had been the construction of new locomotives and the completion of 'further bridge reconstructions and permanent-way alterations required' on 'the main line between Paddington and Plymouth, via Lavington, and between Paddington and Swindon'.[6]

The first 'King' was revealed to staff in the July 1927 edition of the *Great Western Railway Magazine*, Pole asserting that its introduction would 'deservedly arouse widespread interest' and reporting that many people had asked him if 'the GWR Company would surrender the honour of possessing the most powerful express passenger locomotive in the country', concluding: 'The answer is now given'.[7] Much has been written about the most famous locomotives built by the GWR, especially in relation to their design, construction and operation, and space does not permit more than the briefest mention of their attributes here.[8] Within a year W. G. Chapman had written another 'Book for Boys of All Ages', *The King of Railway Locomotives*, and in it he told the story of the design, arguing that its appearance was part of a 'progressive' policy being pursued by the company in order that it should remain at the 'forefront of locomotive construction' and continue to improve the average speeds of its 'crack' trains.[9]

Chapman described the 'King' as Britain's 'mightiest passenger locomotive', pointing out that its tractive effort, at 40,300lb, was 'considerably higher' than that of other locomotives currently being used, although the company in its publicity was rather more circumspect in making this claim than it had been with the 'Castles' some years earlier.[10] Weighing more than 135 tons, a 'King' was considerably heavier than a 'Castle'; a larger boiler with increased pressure of 250lb was required, with four cylinders arranged so that the inside pair drove the leading driving wheels and the outside the middle coupled wheels. One of the most unusual features of the locomotive was the leading bogie, which had outside bearings for the front axle and inside bearings for the trailing axle, allowing the whole assembly to clear the inside cylinders. The locomotive was also fitted with smaller driving wheels (6ft 6in rather than the 6ft 8½in of a 'Castle'), which, Chapman noted, gave better adhesion on gradients.

While the GWR's publicity department boasted about the appearance and power of the new locomotives, the most important factor for the company was their performance on the heaviest trains being run. A publicity leaflet asked: 'What are the advantages of these high-powered locomotives?' The answer, it concluded, could be found in the timetable, which showed that the 'Cornish Riviera Limited', previously timed to cover the 225¾ miles from London to Plymouth in 4 hours 7 minutes, was now scheduled to complete the journey in 4 hours exactly.[11] The greater power of the 'Kings' enabled them to lift much heavier trains over the steeply graded main line from Taunton to Plymouth; the maximum loading for a 'King' was 45 tons greater than that allowed for a 'Castles' and 128 tons greater than for a Churchward 'Star', with the result that fewer trains required double-heading.

The first locomotive, No 6000 *King George V*, ran trials and made publicity runs and appearances in June and July 1927, generating funds for the GWR Social & Educational Union. There was huge interest in the locomotive, and on 1 July at Paddington more than 3,000 people came to see it, with more turned away; it

then visited Exeter, Plymouth, Newton Abbot, Reading, Taunton and Swindon. All visitors were charged 6d; at Plymouth a local resident reportedly handed staff a 'treasury note' to enable a number of 'poor boys' from the town to view the locomotive.[12] It drew large crowds at Swindon, including many of those who had worked on its construction, 'though it may have simply been the cutting of a bolt', who brought families to inspect their work. Collett had been characteristically modest about his work on the 'King', praising staff and noting that they 'had worked together in a most admirable way for a number of years in the manner that I have heard you refer to so aptly in the phrase team-work'.

King George V worked the 'Cornish Riviera Limited' for the first time on 20 July, but its arrival in early summer had been scheduled so that it could make an appearance far away from the West of England. In 1925, whilst attending the Stockton & Darlington centenary celebrations, Pole had met Edward Hungerford, a prominent American railway enthusiast, and

following discussions it was agreed that the GWR would supply an 'English' locomotive for the centenary celebration of the Baltimore & Ohio Railroad, to be held in 1927. The decision to name the class after English kings had been taken once the possibility of an American appearance was confirmed; it had been rumoured that they were to be given the names of cathedrals, but a royal appendage was a greater attraction and publicity coup, so, once the approval of the King himself had been received, the first 20 locomotives were so named, in reverse order, starting with the reigning monarch.

On 3 August, No 6000 was shipped from Cardiff to appear as part of the Baltimore & Ohio Railroad's 'Fair of the Iron Horse', which ran from 24 September to 15 October. Visitors to the event were amazed at both the appearance and performance of the locomotive, which, despite being much smaller than its American counterparts, ran smoothly, with none of the black smoke that normally issued from native locomotives. Following a successful run from

Baltimore to Washington and Philadelphia it had been fitted with a brass bell, required for use on the main line; this was subsequently presented to the GWR, along with two commemorative medals, and it was decided that these should remain on the locomotive. Its triumphant return from North America in November received wide press coverage, *The Times* reporting that more than 2 million people had seen it during its trip.[13]

Another innovation announced in the month that *King George V* was unveiled was the 'Land Cruise'. This was the running of all-inclusive tours in Great Western territory by both road and rail. A leaflet issued to promote the venture claimed: 'At first sight the term "Land Cruise" seems an anomaly. Land cruises are a new venture as far as railways are concerned in this country, and those arranged by the GWR, and outlined in this folder, will send you adventuring by rail and road, leisurely wandering along the highways and byways … into regions that lie well off the beaten track.'[14] Initially three tours were announced, of which two took six days — one taking in the Forest of Dean, the Wye Valley,

FAR LEFT GWR staff at the Baltimore & Ohio Railroad's 'Fair of the Iron Horse'. In the background visitors are admiring the clean lines of the locomotive and queuing patiently to get onto the footplate.

BELOW LEFT A postcard view of the Wye Valley line, a branch running from Chepstow to Monmouth which must have struggled to generate much income — although, had it survived, it would now be a wonderful heritage line for tourists and enthusiasts.

RIGHT A publicity leaflet issued to accompany the start of the Land Cruise venture in 1927.
Great Western Trust collection

33840. SYMONDS YAT.

Malvern and 'Shakespeare Country', the other the Vale of White Horse, Lambourn and the Marlborough Downs, Cheddar, the Mendips and the Cotswolds; each cost 12 guineas, which included all transport, hotels, meals and entry to 'places of interest'. The third had a more ambitious itinerary. Starting at Fishguard, it included the Cambrian Coast, the Lleyn Peninsula, Snowdon and the Vale of Llangollen; it cost 25 guineas and was also run in the opposite direction. 'Select your cruise, take your tickets, and, beyond making any necessary arrangements regarding your luggage, you have no further trouble,' the leaflet concluded.

The Land Cruises proved popular enough for the railway to continue their operation the following year, despite their making a loss. In 1929, the GWR's publicity department produced a booklet written by a young traveller, Margaret Cross, whose charming first-hand account of a cruise through the Cotswolds, Shakespeare Country and the Wye Valley told of a trip with a party of only six, 'owing, probably, to the fact that the cruises are not yet well known'.[15] By 1934, however, *Holiday Haunts* was advertising a series of six-day Land Cruises, beginning each Monday between May and September and visiting variously the Wye Valley, Devon and Cornwall, Somerset and Devon, and North Wales. These 'all expense' tours offered 'maximum sightseeing without fatigue', the company argued.[16]

In parallel with work being done to develop express train services, Paddington was looking closely at ways in which it could generate business in the rural areas through which some of the Land Cruises were run, as well as smaller branch and cross-country routes elsewhere on the system. After the war the GWR revived the policy of opening 'halts' — small unstaffed stations built cheaply with wooden platforms and simple buildings or shelters. These stations were constructed to cater for steam railmotors or one- or two-coach trains but enabled the railway to put facilities where they were needed at a relatively low cost; in 1929, the company built no fewer than 25 — part of a scheme that saw 169 such stations opened between 1927 and 1934.

This development followed discussions in the wake of a report on branch lines that had been produced in March 1926 by the Assistant Superintendent of the Line. The report's terms of reference asked whether branch lines were being worked 'on the most economical lines' and whether the existing operation was capable of improvement. A total of 53 branches were inspected, and information gathered for receipts, maintenance, renewal and running costs. The conclusions reached clearly reflected the dilemma facing the railway; at the Grouping it had inherited a large number of branch lines, which, added to those that were already part of its network, made up a very mixed crop. Some, like the St Ives branch, with receipts in 1925 of £41,110 and expenses of £12,542, were profitable, but others, like the Eardisley line in Herefordshire, with expenses of over £5,000 against receipts of £2,512, clearly did not pay their way.

The report highlighted issues that would be reconsidered years later by Dr Beeching: many rural lines were expensive to maintain and included level crossings that required staff to operate them. It also noted that, although branch lines often ran close to main roads, stations were 'usually placed some distance from the villages and outskirts of towns', concluding wearily that, whilst this had not been important when the railways had enjoyed a 'virtual monopoly', the 'remote situation of stations is a severe handicap in securing and retaining the passenger-carrying business under present conditions'.[17] Often the level of staffing provided at stations along a branch was not justified by the level of traffic or receipts earned, and the report recommended replacing stationmasters with porters at smaller stations.

On the plus side, the report noted that in most cases the cost of operating branch lines compared favourably with that of main lines; it was 'paucity of traffic' rather than expensive methods of working that increased their costs. It was reluctantly concluded, however, that there were three unpalatable courses of action that the company could take to make real savings. These were closing lines, confining goods and passenger services to an eight-hour period during which passenger traffic was negligible, and turning passenger services over to road transport. Exercising any of these options on a branch would 'give rise to public protests and will raise a question of principle, *viz* whether the Company are under any obligation to continue to provide services which are proved to be unremunerative', the report noted. Where receipts were low, and there was no prospect of developing traffic, 'serious consideration' should be given to closing lines, although it was also suggested that rails should not be lifted for at least three years, in case 'prospects improved'. The idea of an eight-hour day, while superficially attractive, was fraught with difficulties, especially on branches with connections to main-line services — an example being the St Ives branch, on which the last train from London did not reach St Erth until 9.45pm.

The idea of transferring uneconomic services to road was recommended, the report noting that 'Road services foster travel and

encourage and develop inter-station areas not adequately tapped by branch lines'. The impact of road competition ran through the whole report, and the signs could not have been clearer; road competition had 'made serious inroads into the passenger-carrying businesses on branches', buses giving 'door to door service without a change or wait at a junction which travellers naturally prefer, and are prepared to pay higher fares to secure'. In addition, the bus journey was often much shorter than that on the railway. The only place where the company could successfully compete with road services for the short-distance passenger-carrying business, the report concluded pessimistically, was on the roads themselves.

The report's conclusions served only to confirm the GWR's increasing fears regarding the threat of road competition; since the war, which had shown the tremendous possibilities of road transport, railways no longer held a monopoly over goods or passenger business, and they had been slow to acknowledge the inevitability of change. The number of motor vehicles had grown rapidly, from 975,783 in 1922 to 1,888,726 five years later, and while the number of private cars had doubled in this period, the largest growth was in the numbers of buses and lorries.[18] The 'old order of things has changed', and 'motor transport has long since ceased to be a "new-fangled idea"', trumpeted the *Morris Owner Magazine* in 1926, noting that seldom was the motor van 'outpaced' by its 'four-footed road companion'.[19]

The establishment of the Ministry of Transport had seen schemes to improve and widen trunk routes, including the construction of the Great West Road, completed in 1925. Motor buses became more popular after 1918, replacing trams and

trolleybuses in cities, but their greatest impact was felt in country areas, where they competed directly with railways and often proved quicker and more convenient than rail. Just as worrying was the rise of road hauliers, as ex-servicemen returning from the war bought Army Surplus vehicles 'dumped on the market'[20] at knock-down prices and new haulage companies went into direct competition with railways like the GWR.

As early as 1921, the GWR Chairman had reminded shareholders of the competition from road traffic and also the fact that, in his view, it was being subsidised; railways had to provide and maintain their own track, whereas hauliers paid little for the upkeep of the roads. The irony of the fact that the railway was also contributing to the maintenance of that road network through local rates, costing the company well over £1.5 million a year, was not lost either.[21] The railway invested heavily in motor buses in the 1920s and in 1927 had carried more than 8 million passengers. A major obstacle to the railways competing directly with road hauliers and bus companies was a lack of clarity regarding the statutory powers required for them to run additional motor services under existing railway legislation. Fierce opposition from the road lobby had meant that any reference to further powers for developing road traffic was omitted from the Railways Act 1921.

Following the Grouping all four companies had considered a joint Bill to secure full 'road powers', but nothing was done; in correspondence with Herbert Walker, his counterpart at the Southern, in November 1926 Sir Felix Pole noted that the GWR had been operating road services since 1903 and that 'the right to do so has never been contested'. Promoting a Bill for extra powers, he argued, might weaken the railways' position, implying that they had been acting illegally. All the same, he agreed to a meeting of general managers to discuss the matter; the letter clearly prompted the memorandum titled 'Railways and Road Transport' which was presented to the GWR board in December, recommending the establishment of new road services to 'feed' railway business and combat road competition where it was 'attacking' the GWR.

Following the board meeting further meetings were convened by the Superintendent of the Line to discuss road competition. In a memorandum to Pole he identified a number of points that had emerged from the discussions; the 'menace' of increasing numbers of private cars had cost the company 'many thousands of local passengers he argued, leaving some stations 'more or less derelict' for passenger business. Worse still, bus companies, 'encouraged by their success in securing a large portion of local rail traffic', were now turning their attention to long-distance travel using 'high-powered luxurious cars [buses] that reproduced all the amenities of rail travel', including lavatory accommodation, meals and 'facilities for writing'. To fight back, he argued, the GWR should attack competitive services, even if the company

TOP A beautiful picture, taken at Slough in March 1929, of a new 22-seat bus provided for the Great Western's Oxford–Cheltenham service. The chassis was built by Gilford, and the coachwork was by Wycombe Motor Bodies Ltd. *Philip Kelley collection*

ABOVE A 1938 poster, issued jointly by all 'Big Four' railways, advertising the Country Lorry service. *Philip Kelley collection*

TOP RIGHT The railway also provided small wooden buildings to serve as halts for its omnibus services. This postcard photograph was taken on the opening of Coverack Road Halt in Cornwall, on 26 January 1928. *Philip Kelley collection*

made a loss for a few years, with the object of crippling rivals. He also recommended establishing new services on routes where other firms could be kept 'off the road'. As many stations were on the outskirts of town, the company should provide bus services from the town centre; it should also consider substituting bus services for branch-line trains, he argued. Finally, the company should acquire certain competitive road companies and enter into agreements with others if this would reduce competition or improve co-ordination between road and rail.[22]

Ultimately each of the 'Big Four' railway companies submitted a separate Bill to Parliament, and in January 1928 it was announced that a GWR's Bill had been deposited for the purpose of securing powers for 'road motor services'. A joint statement issued by the 'Big Four' in support of the new legislation explained that they were seeking powers to transport passengers and goods by road in areas served by them, arguing that in so doing they were aiming to 'secure the fullest measure of co-operation and co-ordination between road and rail transport'. They wished only to be 'entitled to the same free and unfettered use of public roads as enjoyed by others' and were 'not aiming at a monopoly of road traffic, and the powers they are seeking cannot be said to give it to them', it concluded.[23]

After all the talk at Paddington of fighting road competition by investing in new vehicles and opening up new routes, with the passing of the Great Western (Road Transport) Act in August 1928 the policy changed dramatically, and the company instead entered into discussions with a number of existing bus companies with a view to setting up joint ventures with them. Sir Felix Pole had been seriously ill during the committee stage of the Bill and discovered too late that a pledge had been given that railways would not expand and develop bus schemes but instead invest in road transport companies up to a 50% share. Pole thought this 'foolish' and 'ill-advised' but had little choice but to accede.[24]

Partnerships were now concluded with four existing regional bus operators, most notably the Western National Omnibus Co, which assumed responsibility for services run hitherto by the National Omnibus & Transport Co and other operators, including the GWR, in Cornwall, Devon and West Somerset, as well as parts of Gloucestershire and Wiltshire. The Western Welsh Omnibus Co (formerly South Wales Commercial Motors) took over services in South and West Wales that had been operated by the GWR and a number of smaller firms; Crosville Motor Services, based in Chester, took over independent and GWR operations in North and Mid Wales, while the Devon General Omnibus & Touring Co, the dominant operator in an around Exeter and Torbay, also ran services in the Okehampton and Sidmouth areas. The agreements concluded with these companies usually included a combination of cash and assets; the GWR sold to Western National 'vehicles, furniture and chattels' along with property and 'goodwill' for the sum of £180,000, to be paid in the form of 87,000 6% shares in the new operation.[25]

The years following the conclusion of these agreements saw a gradual reduction in wasteful competition, and the GWR bus fleet dwindled. The railway continued to make considerable use of road vehicles to support its goods business, however, and the number of motor lorries, which had increased steadily in the 1920s, continued to grow. The scale of the business is illustrated by statistics revealing that in 1927 the Road Transport Department shifted almost 5 million tons of goods and carried more than 20 million parcels. A railhead distribution service was developed, lorries being operated within a 20-mile radius from stations. Although goods could be delivered to any customer, the service was particularly successful when applied to consignments for regular customers. In 1927, new services to deliver tobacco to W. D. & H. O. Wills in Cardiff and Swansea and confectionery to Barker & Dobson in Cardiff were inaugurated. Returns from the railhead distribution service were nevertheless modest; in 1927,

the profit was only £2,293, which serves to illustrate how much ground the railways had lost to competitors.

The GWR also operated a 'Country Lorry' service, which acted as a feeder to the railway and provided direct competition with road haulage firms. By 1928, the Superintendent of Road Transport was able to report that the service was 'very nearly self-supporting and should in time prove a separate source of revenue'.[26] The introduction of country lorries led to the GWR absorbing independent cartage agencies and reducing costs, as well as to the withdrawal of horses at many stations; in 1927, seven horses were removed from stations such as Castle Cary and Dorchester, saving

ABOVE By the 1930, the GWR was transporting an increasing quantity of livestock by road. Taken in 1935, this picture features a Thornycroft with a body that could be fitted with an extra deck to carry sheep. *Philip Kelley collection*

RIGHT Great Western high summer: crowds of holidaymakers on Platform 1 at Paddington in August 1929, pictured five minutes before departure of the 'Cornish Riviera Limited' at 10.30am.

the railway more than £500. The railway pressed ahead with the introduction of more Country Lorry schemes, adding 24 in 1927 alone; this growth was 'to forestall any action' that bus companies might take in the future, when they had finished developing their passenger services, the Superintendent of the Line noted.[27]

1   Great Western Railway: Minutes of Chief Officers' Conference Meeting held 12 July 1926

2   Great Western Railway: Minutes of Chief Officers' Conference Meeting held 22 October 1926

3   *Great Western Railway Magazine* March 1927, p82

4   Great Western Railway: Minutes of Chief Officers' Conference Meeting held 31 January 1927, Appendix I

5   Pole, F. J. C: *His Book* (Town & Country Press, 1968), p87

6   Great Western Railway: Minutes of Board Meeting held 1 July 1927

7   *Great Western Railway Magazine* July 1927, p263

8   Nock, O. S.: *The GWR Stars, Castles and Kings*, Parts 1 and 2 (David & Charles, 1967)

9   Chapman, W. G.: *The King of Railway Locomotives* (GWR, 1928), p2

10   Holcroft, H.: *An Outline of Great Western Locomotive Practice* (Locomotive Publishing Co, 1957), p146

11   'The Power of the Kings' (GWR, Paddington, 1928) — Great Western Trust collection

12   *Great Western Railway Magazine* August 1927. p333

13   *The Times* 28 November 1927

14   Great Western Railway: *GWR Land Cruises* (GWR, Paddington, 1927) — Great Western Trust collection

15   Cross, M.: *Impressions of My Land Cruise* (GWR Paddington, 1929)

16   Great Western Railway: *Holiday Haunts* (GWR, Paddington, 1934)

17   Wilkinson, H. L.: *Report on Branch Lines* (GWR, Paddington, March 1926)

18   Mowat, C. L.: *Britain Between the Wars 1918–1940* (Methuen, 1955), p233

19   Gronback, F.: 'The Supremacy of Light Motor Transport', *Morris Owner Magazine* May 1926, p376

20   Great Western Railway: 'Memorandum in Regard to Railways and Road Transport' (General Manager's Office, Paddington, December 1926), p13

21   *Great Western Railway Magazine* March 1921, p58

22   Great Western Railway: *Road Motor Competition as affecting Passenger, Parcel and Miscellaneous Traffic* (GWR, Paddington, 22 July 1927), p5

23   'Railways and Road Transport' (statement on behalf of railway companies promoting bills in Parliament for powers to provide transport by road, January 1928)

24   Pole, *ibid*, p97

25   Copy of an agreement between the Great Western Railway and the Western National Omnibus Co, 17 April 1929 — P. Kelley collection

26   Great Western Railway: *Annual Report of the Superintendent of Road Transport for the Year 1927* (GWR, Paddington, 1928)

27   Great Western Railway: Minutes of Superintendents' Meeting held 11 July 1927

CHAPTER 8

RECONSTRUCTION

Despite the years 1927 and 1928 representing a high-point for the GWR, what Sir Felix Pole called a 'high-water mark of service';[1] it had made a steady recovery and was the only 'Big Four' company to have cemented its reputation since the Grouping. Its express trains and powerful locomotives had won the admiration not only of the travelling public but also of shareholders, who, despite the relatively poor performance of the railway, were still earning better dividends than their counterparts on other railways. The financial picture was, however, complicated and less positive, for what the company called the 'general trade depression' was still badly affecting its business, particularly in South Wales, where coal exports were poor and the railway's revenue from this business was down by £3 million in 1928. Reporting a loss for that year of almost £1 million and a dividend down from 7% to 5%, Viscount Churchill reminded shareholders that the overall loss had been kept to this figure only because of the 'praiseworthy' efforts of all staff, who in August 1928 had taken a 2½% pay cut.[2]

Early in 1929, there were signs of improvement; coal mines and blast furnaces in South Wales were reopened, and the company was able to report increased exports from the docks for the first time in months. The docks were badly affected by blizzards in

LEFT The refreshment cabin at Taunton station in 1928. As well as sticky buns priced at 11/2d each, passengers had the choice of a wide range of chocolates and sweets displayed in the glass cabinets on either side of the counter.

RIGHT Sir James Milne, who in 1929 succeeded Felix Pole as General Manager of the GWR.

February, however, with coal-tipping equipment out of use and freezing weather meaning that dock workers had to dig coal out of wagons by pickaxe. It took the docks several weeks to recover, staff working long hours to make up the backlog. The disappointing results for the docks generally had not been because of a lack of effort on the part of the GWR; considerable sums of money were spent renewing facilities and equipment. In 1928, the company acquired a large floating crane, capable of lifting loads of up to 125 tons, which could be used in all its South Wales ports.[3] Records show that in 1929, £30,913 was spent at Newport on the provision of nine 3-ton electric cranes, associated electrical equipment and the transferring of nine other hydraulic cranes and removal of obsolete cranes.[4] The previous year more than £25,000 had been spent connecting facilities at Barry Docks to mains electricity — a sum that included 'switchgear, cables and transformers, buildings, cable trenches and motors'.[5]

As well as re-equipping docks the company carried out a number of reviews to ensure that they were being run efficiently. A report issued in 1929 noted that steps had been taken to make changes to staffing and working arrangements. This involved the centralisation of facilities previously run at each dock such as dredging, building and dock maintenance; in the case of dredging this meant the loss of almost 100 staff. Recommendations were also made for the replacement of obsolete or ageing equipment, such as the aforementioned Lewis-Hunter cranes. The economies proposed reduced expenditure on maintenance by almost £100,000 compared with 1924, and overall costs by £436,817 — a decrease of 18%.[6] Timekeeping and productivity was also clearly an issue, the report noting that three time clerks had been replaced by clocking-in machines, saving more than £300 per year. Meanwhile an agreement with unions resulted in the establishment of a 'split-shift' system enabling day-and-night working to be introduced, speeding up the loading of coal.

July 1929 brought news of a most unexpected development; after spending more than 30 years in the service of the company and steering it through one of the most turbulent periods in its history, Sir Felix Pole announced that he was leaving to become Chairman of electrical company AEI. The sense of shock at Paddington was palpable, and the *Great Western Railway Magazine* reported that GWR employees had 'reacted with incredulity' at rumours that Pole would be going.[7] Unlike his predecessors, who had spent their whole lives working for the company and in some cases had died still in its service, Pole was doing the unthinkable and moving on. He told staff that there had been 'every indication,

and indeed personal desire, that my working life should end with the same excellent employers' but that 'the experience of many is that there is an over-riding "something" which intervenes when least expected'.

That 'something' had been an approach from Sir Guy Granet, previously Chairman of the LMS, who had asked Pole in 1928 if he had ever thought of leaving the GWR. Pole had initially replied: 'No and I shall never do so.' Granet then mentioned that a new electrical company was being set up, and that it was looking for a full-time chairman. Further approaches were made to Pole, and, as he noted later, 'while there was no immediate financial advantage … it was a fascinating idea to be the Chairman of a new company'.[8] Telling his chairman of the proposal, Pole offered to stay, but Churchill said that he would not stand in his way, and that it might be a good opportunity for James Milne, Pole's second-in-command. Churchill must have been disappointed, but as a leaving gift he sent Pole a silver ink stand, noting in a letter that he hoped it would remind him of the 'many happy hours we have spent trying to do our best for the dear old GWR'.[9]

There has been debate as to why Pole should have taken such a bold step. There is little doubt that, despite being a company man through and through, he found the GWR's innate conservatism hard to deal with, and some of the reforms he felt necessary, including the reorganisation of its operational structure, had been frustrated. In any event, he was leaving the railway at a high-point, and, as one writer has noted, given the darkening economic clouds on the horizon, the only way was down. It seems, however, that the chance to work in a new environment was simply too good to miss for the ambitious Pole.

Churchill had tried to persuade Pole to remain as a 'Consulting General Manager', but in the end it was agreed that the GWR would retain his services in a 'consultative capacity', allowing his successor, Milne, some space to establish his own role within the railway. With Milne's appointment the company maintained the tradition going back many years of recruiting from within for the General Manager's job. Milne, 46 years old on taking the top job, had begun his career at Swindon in 1904 and had climbed the promotion ladder, pausing only to spend three years working for the Ministry of Transport from 1919 to 1922. He had been Pole's principal assistant from 1922 and Assistant General Manager from 1924, so the transition to the role of General Manager was achieved with the minimum of difficulty.

Milne took up his new position at a time of great economic and political uncertainty; a new Labour Government had been elected in May 1929 amidst continuing gloom over unemployment. In June the General Manager reported discussions with the Lord Privy Seal, J. H. Thomas, during which he had stated that 'Government were anxious to proceed with schemes for the relief of unemployment on sound business lines and had decided to approach the great industries with a view to obtaining their co-operation'.[10] At a subsequent meeting general managers of the 'Big Four' suggested that Government advance them a loan of

£30 million, to be paid back over 30 years, with reduced interest payments initially. Thomas was quick to squash such suggestions, and what finally emerged was a scheme whereby the Government would guarantee and pay interest on capital raised by railways for approved improvement projects as part of the Development (Loans & Guarantees) Act of 1929.

The Great Western already had a long list of projects ready and so was quick to provide the Government with proposals for approval. Asked in a House of Commons debate in late December how much money had been sanctioned for use by the GWR, Thomas reported that schemes amounting to £4,860,000 had already been approved and orders worth more than £300,000 already placed.[11] A condition of approved schemes was that materials 'were required to be of British origin, and all manufactured articles of British manufacture'.[12] Reporting the approval of the first batch of schemes to the board, the General Manager estimated that all could be complete by the end of 1934, with the Government paying interest of £1,365,000 and the GWR £635,000 over a 15-year period.

Much investment focused on improving passenger traffic, through the rebuilding or enlargement of stations or the easing of bottlenecks on major routes. The first group of schemes included improvements at Paddington, with new longer platforms, a new parcels depot and passenger concourse, and the rebuilding of Bristol Temple Meads and Cardiff stations. A number of projects helped speed traffic on the West of England main route, namely the doubling of track in Cornwall, the provision of new 'cut-off' lines at Westbury and Frome and the quadrupling of the line between Cogload Junction and Taunton, along with station rebuilding at the latter. Other work included extensions to Swindon and Wolverhampton Works and new marshalling yards at Banbury and Severn Tunnel Junction. The reconstruction of a number of locomotive sheds, particularly in South Wales, was also planned, and in the following years the list of works would lengthen as other projects were added.

The initial proposals would, the company argued, provide employment for 200,000 'man months' and make some impact on unemployment figures, although the nature of work envisaged meant that it would take some time to make an appreciable difference. Few in Government believed that there would be any rapid reduction in the increasing levels of unemployment, and in a briefing in late October, Thomas told Cabinet colleagues that, however much money was 'lavished' on the railways, it would make little impression on the unemployment register that winter, arguing that a 'programme of £40 or £50 millions of capital works may sound impressive' but that, as industry paid £25 million every week in wages, Government assistance needed to be put in perspective.[13] The Wall Street Crash did not immediately affect the British economy, but as its consequences spread across the world, unemployment began to rise further, and the 'Roaring Twenties' gave way to the 'Threadbare Thirties'.[14]

Thomas noted that work on Government schemes could not start at once and that 'much of it was spread over months and years', and so it was with the Great Western; while some projects could start straight away, others required careful planning and development. Because of the relatively prolonged process undertaken to complete some of these schemes, for neatness

they will be considered as a group in this chapter rather than appear chronologically in later chapters. There is not space to list every project undertaken in the 1930s, but the sheer number clearly illustrates how much investment the railway needed.

One of the earliest schemes was the construction of cut-off lines at Westbury and Frome; plans were deposited for approval as early as 29 November 1929, which suggests that surveys and plans were already in existence, perhaps dating back to before 1914 when other cut-off lines were built on the West of England main line. The deposited plans noted land required and the owners affected; on the Frome line one Emily Jane Talbot was listed as having a 'house, garage, store, greenhouse, coalhouse, offices, well, garden and field' in the path of the line, and the Bishop of Bath and Wells and the Marquess of Bath a 'stream and field'.[15] The Westbury avoiding line

was only 2¼ miles long but diverted main-line expresses away from a busy junction; this and the two-mile Frome line were opened in March 1933 and saved a modest 3 minutes on the journey time but increased average speeds of express trains by 10mph. Part of the £220,000 cost included £5,063 for the removal and re-laying of the water troughs at Westbury — a contract carried out by the Locomotive Department, the work including the provision of a 'new water tank, including all necessary girders, joists and foundations'.[16]

The acceleration of West of England expresses was improved rather more dramatically by work undertaken at Taunton. The old station and the junction of the West of England line and that of the erstwhile Bristol & Exeter Railway had become hopelessly clogged and in need of renewal. Speaking in 1931, A. E. Hicks, the GWR's Superintendent for the Exeter Division, gave an upbeat and comprehensive account of improvements planned for Taunton; highlighting the congestion, he noted that on a busy Saturday in August there would be more than 124 down and 121 up trains passing through Taunton in 24 hours and that the line between Norton Fitzwarren and Cogload was so busy that it was necessary to divert trains onto a goods line with a 10mph speed limit, which was hardly ideal.[17]

The quadrupling of line between Cogload in the east and Norton Fitzwarren in the west began in the autumn of 1930, work on the seven-mile section including the rebuilding of 16 bridges and considerable earthworks. The most significant development was the construction of a 'fly-over' bridge at Cogload, replacing a double-line junction with the down Bristol line and entailing the construction of a 227-ton steel skew girder bridge. The line between Cogload Junction and Taunton was also quadrupled, the final section from Creech Junction to the station being completed by 13 December 1931. The station itself was completely transformed; by January 1932, the old roof had been removed, and a month later the two main up and down lines, together with up and down relief and island platforms, were in use. In addition to these new, longer platforms a modern booking hall was provided, and the footbridge replaced by a modern subway. The goods yard was also extended, and an enlarged goods shed was opened in February 1932, on allotment land acquired from the local GWR Garden Association.[18]

The work carried out at Paddington brought a resolution to a long-running debate about the future of the terminus, discussions about its enlargement having been ongoing since the early 1920s. In 1926, the General Manager had commissioned a report on its

LEFT With the extension of platforms beyond the Brunel trainsheds it was necessary to provide passengers with protection from the elements. Here, with the steel framing complete, work is well under way to finish the platform awnings.

BELOW A 1935 advertisement, showing the new glazing used in the refurbishment of Paddington station.

BOTTOM With the rebuilding of the Lawn as a passenger circulating area the company also provided this smart new arrivals indicator. It is 3.45 in the afternoon, and passengers are awaiting the arrival of trains from Torquay, Ilfracombe and Penzance.

LAYLIGHTS

ECLIPSE Patent Glazing Laylights and Lighting Boxes erected and completed at Paddington Station by

MELLOWES

WRITE FOR FULL PARTICULARS OF PRODUCTS TO
MELLOWES & COMPANY, LIMITED, SHEFFIELD & LONDON

future from the Civil Engineers' Department, but work on this was delayed because of the General Strike; finally completed early in 1929, it recommended a huge development which was 'a vision of Brunellian scale and thoroughness',[19] double the size of the existing structure. The old GWR Royal Hotel and most of the houses in Eastbourne Terrace were to be demolished, and three extra roof spans built. However, by the time the report was considered properly the moment for this grand scheme had passed; following the strike, revenue had started to drop, and there was clearly little appetite for such major investment. At a meeting in February 1929 attended by Sir Felix Pole, C. B. Collett and R. T. Nicholls, the Superintendent of the Line, it was noted that in view of the 'various factors involved … the time was not ripe for embarking upon the complete reconstruction of the station'.[20]

Nicholls argued further that Paddington station 'substantially meets present-day requirements' and that, if proposals for lengthening the platforms were adopted, 'there would appear to be no need to embark on any scheme for the entire reconstruction of the station for a good many years to come'. It was also felt that pressure on the station could be relieved by diverting trains to Bishops Road station. Suburban traffic, while nowhere near as substantial as that on the Southern, had been steadily increasing since the Great War; the number of season tickets issued in stations within a 40-mile radius had grown by 150% between 1924 and 1928, and at Reading the number actually sold had risen from 6,291 to 16,279 over the same period.[21] It was also decided to investigate the electrification of the line between London and Reading, working with Metropolitan and 'Underground' railways.

The steel structure of the new office block takes shape on the arrivals side of the station.
Great Western Railway Magazine

The building complete. The smart art-deco design
provided a real contrast with Brunel's Victorian station.
Great Western Railway Magazine

access to both the Underground and the hotel; the improvements also helped link the arrival and departure sides of the station. A new ticket office, refreshment room and other facilities were grouped around the Lawn, and the space was covered by a steel-framed glass roof. On either side of the Lawn the Great Western's principal architect, P. E. Culverhouse, designed two contrasting office blocks to house headquarters staff at Paddington. For some years lack of accommodation for administrative staff had been a problem; the minutes of a meeting held in 1923 reveal that more than 300 clerks were working in 22 different houses in nearby Eastbourne Terrace and James Street.[22] Although Sir Felix Pole had considered moving departments out of Paddington, the problem was finally solved by the provision of an eight-storey steel-framed office block in Eastbourne Terrace in a 'restrained classic style'[23] and, to the west of the Lawn, a more striking art-deco-style block.

ABOVE LEFT Work under way on the rebuilding of Bristol Temple Meads station in 1934.

LEFT A view of the extensive excavation and building work required to construct the new passenger subway at Bristol Temple Meads. Two of the large girders needed to support the track lie in the subway itself, awaiting lifting.

BELOW A slightly tatty piece of GWR paperwork that nevertheless tells an interesting story. The list of locomotives booked to leave Old Oak Common shed on 5 December 1932 includes three 'Kings', four 'Castles' and various 'Stars' and 'Halls', as well as a variety of suburban tank engines. The latter appear to have received little or no cleaning, in contrast with the larger types. *Author's collection*

FAR RIGHT A portrait of Percy Culverhouse, the GWR architect responsible for the design of many of the reconstruction schemes of the 1930s, including Paddington, Bristol and Cardiff. Born in 1871, he started his career at Paddington as a clerk, but by 1906 was architectural assistant to the Chief Civil Engineer. He died in 1953. *Author's collection*

Pole reported to the board in March 1929, confirming plans for large-scale reconstruction at Paddington had been shelved. The improvements that were finally carried out using Government funds were therefore a watered-down version of the 1929 scheme, without the major rebuilding this would have entailed. Six of the station's 11 platforms were lengthened to accommodate the longer trains now being operated, and, as these now extended beyond the trainshed, new canopies were built to provide passengers with shelter. The most important task was to free up the area known as the 'Lawn', situated behind the buffer-stops and the back of the Great Western Royal Hotel; this space was used as a loading area for the Parcels Department and was a crowded and unsightly prospect for passengers. The clearing of the area was achieved by building a new parcels depot in Bishops Road, at the west end of the station. A new subway was also built to link the depot to other platforms and reduce the cluttering of Paddington with barrows.

With the removal of the parcels depot the Lawn could be rebuilt as a 'commodious' and elegant concourse for passengers, giving

The remodelling of Bishops Road suburban station involved the construction of two island platforms which became part of the main station. This required extensive excavation, the goods office next to Bishops Road Bridge having to be supported whilst old brick supports were removed and new steel girders substituted. Upon completion of the work the name 'Bishops Road' was dropped, and the platforms were simply numbered 13 to 16. The total cost of the reconstruction at Paddington was estimated at £685,000, and much of the work was complete by 1934. Meanwhile a further £60,000 had been authorised by the Government in January 1930 for the installation of colour-light signalling between Paddington and Slough.

The rebuilding of Bristol Temple Meads station was one of a number of unemployment relief schemes undertaken in the city and when submitted by the GWR for approval in 1929 was estimated as costing over £1 million. Temple Meads had long been a bottleneck, even after the West of England main line was opened in 1906, and its facilities were in need of updating. Whilst the station approach and exterior of the 1876 station, with its overall roof, changed very little, the interior was much altered. By acquiring land to the south the GWR was able to increase the number of platforms from eight to 15, of which six were situated outside the old station roof; all were provided with new awnings and platform buildings housing waiting rooms and refreshment facilities, all faced with art-deco 'Carrara' tiles. All the main platforms were linked by a subway of 'unusual dimensions', 300ft long and 30ft wide, replacing a footbridge; two additional subways provided connections with other platforms, while a further subway served as a link to a new parcels depot that had been built nearby. A new booking office with seven ticket windows was provided, along with passenger waiting rooms and refreshment and dining rooms, which were described by a Ministry of Transport inspector in 1936 as 'noteworthy'.[24] A good deal of the cost of the project was incurred as a result of improvements to approach lines; two bridges at either end of the station were reconstructed, and numerous other bridges over roads in and around the station complex were rebuilt or replaced. It was reported that congestion at Temple Meads was 'materially reduced' by the construction of four running lines to the east and west of the station, quadrupling extending north to Filton Junction and south to beyond Parson Street station. New colour-light signalling, controlled by three new power signalboxes, was provided. The redevelopment scheme also included a new locomotive shed, built to replace an old Bristol & Exeter Railway structure; the new facilities comprised a standard-design straight shed with 10 roads, a large coal stage and two 65ft turntables.[25]

The redevelopment of station facilities at Cardiff had been a high priority for the Great Western in its renewal plans for South Wales, and the £800,000 project involved the complete rebuilding of Cardiff General and the adjacent Riverside station, the latter

becoming part of the main complex. Other features included the provision of longer and additional platforms, independent running lines (to speed through services) and new storage for carriage stock, as well as quadrupling of lines to the east and west of station. Elegant art-deco station buildings with a façade faced in Portland Stone were constructed, providing a large concourse housing a booking office, cloakrooms and luggage facilities. The island platforms, including four of 1,000ft in length, used for main-line traffic, were approached by a new 16ft subway, which necessitated the lowering of roads on the up and down sides of the station, the old subway now being used for parcels and luggage. Two platforms were built for Taff Vale traffic, and two on the site of the old Riverside station were provided to deal with Barry traffic. The quadrupling of lines through the main station involved the reconstruction of no fewer than 14 bridges as well as the removal of level crossings on the Radyr line. The locomotive depot at nearby Cardiff Canton was also improved, and, while the shed was retained, new coaling and watering facilities and a new 65ft turntable were provided. The existing carriage shed was converted into a fruit and milk depot, and a new 11-road carriage shed costing more than £40,000 was built, providing accommodation for 150 coaches.[26]

Mr. P. E. Culverhouse
Architect

The station at Swansea was another rebuilt under the Government scheme; hitherto it had had three platforms, of which the longest measured just 580ft, but improvements meant that the new facility had four 900ft platforms and a 600ft bay. 'The new Swansea High Street station buildings marked another step forward in the progress of station architecture,' wrote Richard Tourret, and the front of the station was said to be 'in the character of modern renaissance, giving the whole a dignified and pleasing appearance'.[27] An additional running line to Landore was also built, improving the operation of the terminus. Prior to the alterations main-line trains had been halted at Landore, where coaches were detached, before proceeding to High Street behind another locomotive; the new work meant that main-line trains could now run straight into the station to set down and pick up passengers. A vast amount of work was required during the reconstruction, for the station had been hemmed in by residential streets, and its expansion necessitated the compulsory purchase of property and the diversion of some roads.

Additional to the long list of major works carried out by the Great Western for unemployment relief was a series of locomotive-shed reconstructions undertaken in South Wales, at Landore, Pantyffynnon, Radyr and Treherbert. Employing materials typically used in the 1930s for light-engineering facilities in industrial estates, with roofs of sheet metal and walls that were half-brick and half-asbestos, these so-called 'Loan Act' depots were built to a standard pattern, with offices, stores and mess rooms along the side of the shed itself, and replaced inadequate pre-Grouping facilities; the old shed at Radyr could house only six locomotives, whereas its steel replacement was built to accommodate 24.

In January 1930, the General Manager was able to announce to the board that, amongst a number of additional schemes approved by Government, it had been agreed that the GWR's Automatic Train Control safety system should be extended to cover virtually all the company's main lines. Until now the mileage covered by the system had been just 372, and only 334 locomotives had been fitted with ATC equipment. New investment would enable well over 1,700 miles of track, including routes from Swindon to Plymouth, Weymouth, Oxford/High Wycombe and Hereford, to be covered and a further 200 locomotives equipped, at a cost of more than £200,000.[28]

LEFT An official picture of the rebuilding work at Cardiff General. The new concrete of the platforms is apparent, as are the new buildings on the island platforms. *Great Western Trust collection*

BELOW Building work is still much in evidence in this postcard view of Swansea High Street station. Note the running-in board propped up against a post, awaiting installation.

TOP RIGHT A view of the new locomotive shed at Radyr, recorded on 9 September 1931.

Board minutes continued to report new initiatives, including the construction of extra 20-ton coal wagons for South Wales collieries. Despite its best efforts, the GWR had failed to persuade colliery owners to acquire the larger wagons, and by the early 1930s the majority of them could not do so without financial assistance; however, as the company had already spent considerable sums of its own money re-equipping its docks to handle the 20-ton stock it was unlikely to recoup any of this investment until more were in use. In 1933, the Government sanctioned a proposal for the construction of 5,000 wagons, costing £1.1 million, and in March directors were told that arrangements had been agreed to hire these to colliery companies, with an option to purchase at the end of a 10-year period. Some 4,000 wagons were hired by two companies, Stephenson, Clarke & Co and Welsh Associated Collieries, the rest being shared by a further eight firms.[29] Continued investment in the docks was used to fund large schemes, notably the construction of a new lock at Swansea, which cost more than £1 million, and smaller projects, such as the installation of electric lighting and the replacement of cranes and other equipment.

1   *Great Western Railway Magazine* January 1929, p1

2   *Great Western Railway Magazine* April 1929, p140

3   *Great Western Railway Magazine* June 1928, p251

4   GWR allocation statements, CME Department No 362, 24.1.29 — STEAM archive

5   GWR allocation statements, CME Department No 362, 22.11.28 — STEAM archive

6   Great Western Railway: *Committee of Enquiry into Dock Costs — Second Interim Report* (GWR, March 1929) — National Archives: RAIL253/46

7   *Great Western Railway Magazine* July 1929, p251

8   Pole, F. J. C.: *His Book* (Town & Country Press, 1968), p176

9   *Ibid*, p176

10 Great Western Railway: Minutes of Board Meeting held 28 June 1929

11 House of Commons debate 24 December 1929, *Hansard* Vol 233, c2121W

12 Great Western Railway: Minutes of Board Meeting held 11 October 1929

13 Lord Privy Seal: 'Memorandum: Unemployment Policy', 23 October 1929 — National Archives: CAB/24/206

14 Attributed to Groucho Marx; see Graves, R., & Hodge, A.: *The Long Week-end* (Hutchinson, 1940), p247

15 Great Western Railway: *New Railways and Deviations: Railways* Nos 2 and 3 (GWR, 1929) — Somerset Heritage Centre

16 Great Western Railway: New Work Order No 2/2874: Westbury and Frome Deviation Lines (GWR Locomotive Department, August 1932) — STEAM archive

17 *Somerset County Gazette* 25 November 1930

18 See also Madge, R.: *Somerset's Railways* (Dovecote Press, 1981)

19 Brindle, S.: *Paddington Station — Its History and Architecture* (English Heritage, 2004), p63

20 Great Western Railway: Minutes of meeting held at Paddington, 6 February 1929 — National Archives: RAIL253/343

21 *Great Western Railway Magazine* April 1930, p134

22 Great Western Railway: Minutes of meeting held 26 November 1923 — National Archives: RAIL253/343

23 Brindle, *ibid*, p64

24 *Report of New Works at Bristol* (Ministry of Transport, 20 June 1936)

25 Tourret, R.: *GWR Engineering Work 1928–1938* (Tourret Publishing, 2003), p107

26 *Great Western Railway Magazine* March 1931, pp121-123

27 Tourret, *ibid*, p182

28 Great Western Railway: Minutes of Board Meeting held 24 January 1930

29 Great Western Railway: Minutes of Board Meeting held 24 March 1933

CHAPTER 9

GO GREAT WESTERN

A welcome inheritance for the Great Western in the 1920s and 1930s was the pioneering work done by the company in the years before the Great War in the field of advertising and publicity. Under James Inglis the GWR had been extremely active in publicising both its trains and the areas served by them, particularly the Cornish Riviera, and had laid the foundation for work done after the war. Following the appointment in 1921 of Felix Pole as General Manager the company once again began to expand and develop its publicity and advertising. Pole had worked closely with Inglis at Paddington and was very aware of the power of 'publicity and propaganda', as he called it. He later recorded that the GWR advertising department was already 'highly efficient'[1] by the time he took over in 1921, but it was not until 1924 that he made major changes, creating a Publicity Department which, although still part of the Superintendent of the Line's Department, had more autonomy and influence than the old advertising department.

To run the new department Pole appointed W. H. Fraser, a GWR stalwart with more than 30 years' experience in various departments of the railway. Fraser proved an able and energetic manager who pioneered many innovations and worked closely with Pole to raise the profile of the GWR. Following his retirement in 1931, he was succeeded by K. W. C. Grand, later to be General Manager of BR's Western Region. In 1934, the GWR took the bold step of creating a new post of Publicity Officer and employing Major M. J. Dewar, who since leaving the Army had worked entirely in marketing and publicity. Dewar took up his new position at a time when the gloom of the darkest days of the Depression was just beginning to lift and holiday traffic was beginning to pick up. Reviewing the 1934 edition of *Holiday Haunts*, the company magazine argued that the book should prove especially popular, as 'this year the national interest decisively indicates a British holiday for British holidaymakers'.[2]

Later in 1934, G. E. Orton, Commercial Assistant to the Superintendent of the Line and a colleague of Major Dewar, gave a revealing lecture to the London branch of the Lecture & Debating Society on Railway Publicity, in which he summarised

In order to provide pictures for the annual *Holiday Haunts* publication the GWR photographer roamed the territory served by the railway. Today the pictures serve to reveal a little about life in this era, as is apparent from this evocative image of Bodinnick, in Cornwall.

the scope and scale of what the GWR had achieved in recent years and intended to achieve in the future. He argued that the function of publicity was 'to make known to the population of the British Isles, and occasionally beyond, the various passenger and goods facilities of the railway' but that the vast range of services run by the company that could be advertised made this impracticable. It was, he continued, 'manifestly impossible' to advertise everything the GWR had to offer to the public and it could 'do no more than pick out what are considered to be the most attractive items after all the regular excursion arrangements have been advertised'.[3]

Orton divided the work of the Publicity Department into a number of important tasks. These included the advertising of train services, the promotion of what he called 'territory', namely 'sections of the country where we know that the amenities are such as to attract holidaymakers',[4] the production of travel literature, including books, posters, leaflets and so on, and 'prestige advertising' and press publicity.

The production of the summer and winter timetables for the Great Western was not the responsibility of the Publicity Department; the hours of work required to ensure that timings and connections were correct was carried out elsewhere at Paddington, in the Office of the Superintendent of the Line. The department was, however, responsible for timetable distribution via 'rail, post and hand' to important companies, ticket agencies, hotels, clubs and societies, and libraries, as well as railway stations on the GWR and elsewhere. Timetables were also supplied to all incoming ocean liners and sent abroad to agencies in Europe and the United States.

While the company did undertake limited promotion of its core services in newspapers, it spent far more on advertising its special excursions every year. In the 1930s, the GWR ran more than 25,000 special trains annually for a huge variety of activities and events. Orton estimated that the railway produced several million handbills and 250,000 letterpress posters a year to promote excursions and cheap tickets, and between the wars the GWR had regular contracts with around 250 local newspapers for advertisements, usually on a weekly basis. The management of this business was a large operation, with staff at Paddington co-ordinating the production of handbills, usually printed locally, the issue of posters, and the production of announcements to the local press.[5] A standardised template for letterpress excursion posters was introduced in 1922 in an effort to combat the poor impression of stations 'liberally bespattered' with posters of differing layouts and typefaces. Copying the style of theatre posters, the company adopted a standard border, heading and 'Winchester Bold' typeface to achieve a 'general effect of uniformity on station hoardings'.[6] A later variation was used following the introduction in the early 1930s of the GWR monogram roundel. Another form of poster advertising that was used extensively was the hand-written type, especially convenient for trains run at short notice. Commercial companies specialising in this work were employed in various traffic divisions to produce in only a few hours 'posters which by their originality in colour and design and by virtue of special positions assigned to them attract attention as no ordinary letterpress poster can'.[7]

The sheer number of excursions run by the railway is impressive; a report in a local Bristol newspaper giving details of trains run over the August bank holiday weekend in 1935 illustrates the numbers of passengers involved. Reporting a record rush by Bristol holidaymakers on a weekend of warm and sunny weather, it noted that many trains had to be run in triplicate to

ABOVE LEFT A row of GWR locomotives ready for use on excursion trains, each with a number hanging from the smokebox. Nearest the camera is 'Saint' No 2934 *Butleigh Court*.

FAR LEFT When this pamphlet issued by the GWR in 1938 is folded out it reveals a charming portrait of a Cornish fishing village. *Great Western Trust collection*

LEFT A 1931 GWR handbill advertising excursions to Ashley Hill, the nearest station to the Memorial Ground, home of Bristol Rugby Club. *Author's collection*

cope with the numbers; in total the GWR carried more than 100,000 passengers that weekend, including 35,000 to Weston-super-Mare, 13,000 to Weymouth — which the paper described as the 'Naples of England' — and a further 13,000 to the Bristol Channel resort of Severn Beach.[8]

As well as excursions to holiday resorts the railway ran special trains for all manner of events, including theatrical performances, horse races and sports fixtures, especially football and rugby matches. In 1922, the *Great Western Railway Magazine* reported the kind of enterprise the railway undertook to generate income; Cardiff City FC played out a 1-1 draw against Tottenham Hotspur in the fourth round of the FA Cup on 4 March, and, in anticipation of a possible draw, staff were ready to give out to supporters, as they left the ground, handbills advertising excursions for the replay the following Thursday — a game that would ultimately be lost by Cardiff.[9] The scale of services run for sporting events was further illustrated in 1927, when it was reported that for the Rugby International between Wales and Scotland on 5 February nearly 40,000 excursion passengers arrived at Cardiff stations, including 800 from LMS and LNER special trains from Glasgow and Edinburgh.[10]

The Great Western was fortunate that its network served some of the most scenic parts of South West and Southern England, and following the Grouping its lines also reached deep into Wales and the Cambrian Coast. 'Health-giving air and beautiful scenery are perhaps most important of all, and in these qualities Britain, and particularly "Great Western Land", is undeniably rich,' claimed the company's publicity in 1932; much of the material issued, whether posters, books, leaflets or handbills, portrayed a traditional and pastoral view of what it called 'Old England'. 'Old England is crumbling about our ears,' wrote S. P. B. Mais in the 1928 edition of *The Cornish Riviera*; it was 'a sorry business trying to find any trace of it in the Home Counties', he continued as he recounted the story of the Royal Duchy and its landscape, legends and history.[11] This image, reinforced by books and leaflets on topics like the 'Shakespeare Country', was, Alan Bennett has noted, in sharp contrast to the company's role as a modern railway which also served the highly industrialised areas of South Wales and the Midlands.[12]

Following the Great War the GWR continued to develop the 'Holiday Line' and 'Ocean Coast' imagery it had begun to exploit under James Inglis; 'The greatest curative power in the world is ocean air,' it claimed in 1925, asserting that 'every one of the numerous resorts along the thousand miles of ocean coast served by the GWR enjoys the genial Atlantic breezes laden with health-giving properties'.[13] Much attention was, of course, paid to the attractions of the Cornish Riviera and 'Glorious Devon', but the coasts of South and West Wales were also heavily promoted.

BELOW LEFT The cover of the 1930 edition of *Holiday Haunts*. Only about 20% of these guides were bought by passengers at stations, most copies being sold through the book trade.

BELOW CENTRE *Smiling Somerset*, published by the GWR in 1931, was written by Maxwell Fraser, editor of *Holiday Haunts*. *Great Western Trust collection*

BELOW RIGHT Besides this 1933 title the GWR published similar guides covering the Cambrian Coast, the Chilterns, Devon, Pembrokeshire and the Wye Valley.

RIGHT Happy holidaymakers enjoying a sunny afternoon at Plymouth Lido. This had opened in 1928 and had been further extended in 1930 and 1933.

Between the wars, however, the nature of the Great Western's boast that it was the 'Nation's Holiday Line' changed; a holiday away from home, prior to 1914 seen by many as a luxury, was by 1939 something millions could aspire to and afford, even if it required careful planning and saving. Despite attempts during the 1920s and 1930s to make paid holidays a right proving unsuccessful, many employers increasingly saw them as a boost to productivity, and by the outbreak of World War 2 more than 11 million Britons enjoyed this privilege.[14] Although older, more affluent passengers still used the GWR to travel to rather more staid and traditional resorts like Torquay to take the sea air, holidaymakers increasingly came to sample some of the growing number of attractions provided for them at resorts that invested heavily between the wars. The company itself noted the 'carefree democracy' of popular family locations such as Barry Island, Paignton and Porthcawl, Weymouth and Weston-super-Mare; the 1936 edition of *Holiday Haunts* described Barry Island as 'a seaside resort where it is impossible to be dull for a single moment' and extolled its facilities, which included 'beautiful public gardens, miniature golf course, open-air dancing floors, cafés, dance halls, cinemas and the largest open-air swimming pool'.[15] The GWR worked closely with resorts and local councils, sharing advertising costs and promoting tourism and holidaymaking by developing links with the press at home and abroad.

The most obvious way in which the Great Western promoted both its own services and the territory it served was through the annual production of *Holiday Haunts*; although this was not the first publication to be produced by the company, its appearance in 1906 marked the beginning of a long series, interrupted only by the two world wars. After the first of these conflicts publication resumed in 1921, and Burdett-Wilson notes that the book's content and appearance were largely the same as they had been before the war. The first edition was nevertheless very popular, selling out its first print run of 20,000 within a month and necessitating a further 20,000 reprint, which also sold out. The 1927 edition marked the 21st anniversary of its first appearance, the company boasting that it was now 'bigger, brighter and more replete with information than ever before' and that circulation had reached 175,000 copies.[16]

It was not until 1929 that real change became apparent, when *Holiday Haunts* appeared with a colour cover featuring a 'red-costumed bathing beauty'[17] rather than its traditional design featuring the company coat of arms. The following year the book was completely revised by Miss Maxwell Fraser, the daughter of W. H. Fraser. The old arrangement of listing each county alphabetically was replaced by a new layout whereby seven regional sections were included, each divided by county. This new format made the book easier to use and also reinforced the GWR's idea of regional identity,

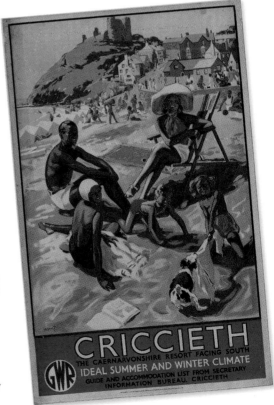

LEFT The last edition of *Camping & Rambling Holidays* published by the GWR before World War 2. *Great Western Trust collection*

RIGHT This 1937 poster of Criccieth by Alfred Lambart illustrates the close links between the railway and the town councils serving holiday resorts.

with sections such as the 'Cornish Riviera', 'Glorious Devon' and 'Somerset, Dorset and the Channel Islands'. In an article in the company magazine in 1930, Fraser noted that 'every word has been completely rewritten', a process that had taken from April to December 1929 to complete.[18]

Notwithstanding the revisions to its layout the basic premise of *Holiday Haunts* remained lists of accommodation 'for holiday-makers and travellers generally', featuring everything from expensive hotels to modest boarding houses provided for each county, along with advertisements, often selected with the assistance of local stationmasters. The degree of work required to collate and check material for the book, which by the early 1930s had grown to more than 1,000 pages, meant that it took many months to complete. From 1928, the book was printed by Butler & Tanner at Frome, where Publicity Department staff were based during the production process. In the 1930s, around 250 tons of paper was used annually to create *Holiday Haunts*, and although the print run was reduced during the Depression, by 1938 it had risen again, to 172,000. To boost interest in the book in 1933 the GWR ran a series of 'Holiday Haunts' express excursions from Paddington, Birmingham and Bristol to selected seaside locations on the network, cheap tickets being offered to allow holidaymakers to make short visits to resorts to select accommodation for their holiday later in the year.

Maxwell Fraser also found time to write a number of well-researched and popular books for the Great Western. Along with author and journalist S. P. B. Mais she was responsible for new editions of the company's best-known publications, notably *The Cornish Riviera*, *Glorious Devon* and *Somerset*. Despite selling extraordinarily well, the original editions of these books, written before the Great War by A. M. Broadley, were, by the late 1920s, rather dated. New editions, by Mais, of *The Cornish Riviera* and *Glorious Devon*, published in 1928, sold out their 20,000 print runs within six months. The books were true travel guides, and *The Cornish Riviera* featured no advertising material for the company apart from its name on the title page and a very small paragraph about its activities on page 161. Fraser produced a new volume *Southern Ireland* in 1932, and in 1934 the book *Somerset*, in which she described the county as being the 'Cinderella' of the West Country, arguing that its charm was quiet and unobtrusive in comparison to the 'flaming beauty' of Cornwall and Devon.

ROAD-RAIL CONTAINERS
DOOR
TO
DOOR
TRANSPORT
BY
GWR

In the 1930s, the GWR made great efforts to generate income from its road business. This leaflet features stylish art-deco-style sans serif lettering but a less convincing portrayal of the locomotive and rolling stock. *Philip Kelley collection*

The railway also produced a number of slimmer books, among them *Winter in the West*, published in 1929. Written by S. P. B. Mais, this extolled the virtues of taking a holiday in the West Country out of season and was clearly aimed at the more well-heeled traveller who had 'got into the groove of accepting August as his holiday month', noting that the winter visitor to the West Country might still wish to swim in the sea, warmed as it was by the Gulf Stream, play golf or 'ride to hounds six days a week'. The attractions of resorts such as Torquay, Minehead and Falmouth, which in January, Mais contended, shared the temperature of Madrid, Florence or Constantinople, were described, along with the facilities to be enjoyed at the company's Tregenna Castle Hotel at St Ives, which offered special winter terms of 4½ guineas a week.[19] In 1935, *Winter Resorts*, a similar volume by Maxwell Fraser, told much the same story but emphasised, in an echo of the prewar 'See Your Own Country First' campaign, the fact that British holidaymakers need not travel abroad to enjoy a mild climate in winter.

'The joyous army of campers-out has increased by leaps and bounds of late years,' reported a GWR publication in 1926; between the two world wars, in addition to the growth in seaside holidays, there was a corresponding growth of interest in the outdoors, camping and rambling becoming very popular. The GWR produced an annual publication, *Camping*, which provided not only practical hints and advice but also details of camp sites and special fares for campers; 'such holidays as these fill the stifled lungs of the city-dwellers with clean, fresh air ... those whose fetish is convention will do well to avoid a camping holiday', argued the company's booklet on the subject, which provided help for 'campers-out with the choice of site and accessibility to the railway'.[20] The railway also produced a series of well-received books for hikers and ramblers, many written by Hugh Page, Secretary of the North Finchley Rambling Club. It was his first volume, *The Chiltern Country*, that was given to passengers travelling on the first hikers' 'mystery trains', run from Paddington on Good Friday and Easter Sunday 1932. A cheap fare of 3s 6d was offered, but, reported the *Great Western Railway Magazine*, climatic conditions were 'not encouraging'; despite this, passenger numbers were adequate, and the refreshment department was happy, on account of a 'brisk trade' in snack boxes sold to ramblers, at 1s each.

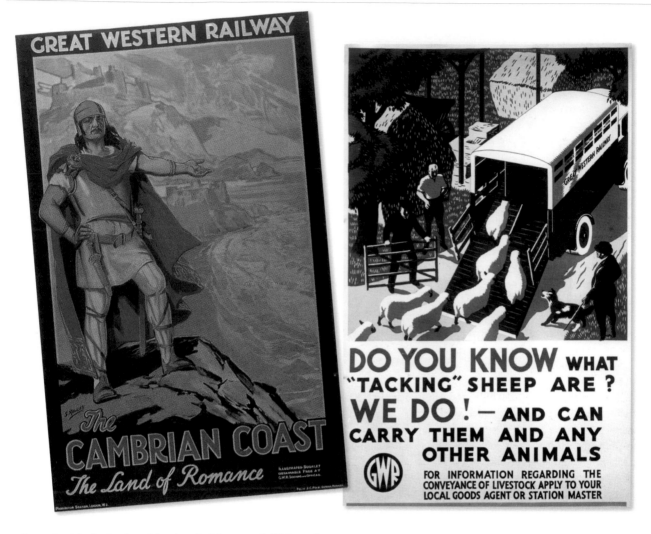

ABOVE LEFT While later posters promoting the Cambrian Coast concentrated on its beaches and resorts, this 1920s poster by S. C. Rowles evokes the region's Celtic past. *Great Western Trust collection*

ABOVE The image in this 1936 poster was inspired by a number of official photographs, including one reproduced in Chapter 7 of this book.

RIGHT The GWR roundel as applied in transfer form to the company's carriage stock.

In contrast to the books celebrating the history and folklore of the territory it served by the railway the Great Western produced others reflecting and celebrating its technological achievements; the series of books produced 'for boys of all ages' proved very popular, selling thousands of copies and enabling the GWR to boast of its achievements. Beginning in 1923 with *The 10.30 Limited*, the series went on to include six further titles — *Caerphilly Castle*, *The Cheltenham Flyer*, *The King of Railway Locomotives*, *'Twixt Rail and Sea*, *Track Topics* and *The Royal Road*. All included a mix of history, technology and outright public relations for the company and cost only a shilling. All sold well, the first four selling 130,000 copies.[21] Another steady seller was *Engines' Names and Numbers*, which grew from a rather drab and dull 24-page book listing the GWR locomotive fleet to a rather more attractive publication that by the 1930s included a colour cover and ran to more than 100 pages.

There is simply not space here to describe all the publications issued by the GWR between the wars, nor the plethora of free 'folders' (what would now be called leaflets) published on many subjects. These ranged from specific areas served by the railway, most notably Cornwall, Devon, Somerset and Wales, the Wye Valley, Isles of Scilly, Malvern Hills and the 'Glorious Thames', to more general subjects such as golf courses and bowling greens; others, such as 'The Joy of the Journey', produced in 1926, argued that 'even in this enlightened twentieth century there are folks who appear to regard holiday travel as a necessary but uncomfortable prelude to their enjoyment' and that, using the Great Western, 'Travel … can be, and is to the initiated, a true and essential part of the journey'.[22]

A further publicity venture was the provision of 'Lantern Lectures', which consisted of sets of lantern slides, along with accompanying notes that could be borrowed by clubs and societies and individuals. By the 1930s, there were more than 100 sets, numbering over 8,000 slides in all; most covered territory served by the GWR, including, naturally, the Cornish Riviera but also 'Shakespeare Country' and Oxford. The latter ran to 107 slides and was divided into two lectures; after an initial 53-slide tour of the city, including views of the castle and colleges such as Keble, Brasenose, Merton and Corpus Christi, the accompanying booklet assured those hardy souls present at the lecture that there was 'still much ground to be covered of equal importance in historical literary, antiquarian and architectural interest' in the second part![23]

In his memoirs Sir Felix Pole recounts a conversation with the president of an American railroad, who asked him: 'Do you mean to tell me that you make the public purchase your advertising?'[24] Pole was rightly proud of the success of the company's publications and another innovation, the highly successful series of jigsaw puzzles issued by the GWR between 1923 and 1937. The 44 designs, manufactured by the Chad Valley Co, featured railway subjects, including locomotives such as *Caerphilly Castle* and *King George V*, scenic views of locations on the railway and historic scenes, and most sold for 2s 6d, their cost price. Pole argued that, while the railway made little profit, it gained valuable publicity. An article in the December 1933 issue of the company magazine highlighted the level of jigsaw sales, reporting that sales for the whole range amounted to well over 650,000 in the course of a decade, the first design, 'Caerphilly Castle', having sold more than 77,000 since its introduction.[25] The GWR also collaborated with the Chad Valley Co to produce a board game, 'Race to the Ocean Coast', which appeared in 1930, although it appears not to have enjoyed the same appeal as the jigsaws and was discontinued within a few years.

G. E. Orton told GWR staff in 1934 that posters were 'a form of advertising that perhaps appeals more to the imagination than any other,' and 'one that has made a considerable advance in the past few years',[26] arguing that the public had been 'educated to expect these works of art to adorn our stations, but apart altogether from their ornamental utility, there is no doubt that publicity of this kind has assisted materially to build up the reputation of certain holiday areas and resorts'. In the years after the Grouping the poster designs produced by the company were lacking 'both imagination and style',[27] in sharp contrast to some of the travel literature it had issued. There appears to have been some scepticism at Paddington regarding the value of poster advertising, and matters did not really improve until after Fraser's retirement in 1931.

Under Grand (and, later, Dewar) poster design improved dramatically, Orton noting that 'we have broken away from conventional designs and employed artists who have given us the

latest fashion in poster art'. This comment may have been a reference to the commissioning of six posters of Devon and Cornwall by Edward McKnight Kauffer, an artist influenced by European art of the early 20th century and whose pictures were more abstract than many of the more traditional posters produced hitherto by the company. Not all reaction to these striking designs was favourable, from within the railway or outside, but posters produced in the years up to the outbreak of war in 1939 increased both in number and variety, and as well as using other artists, such as Claude Buckle and Ronald Lampitt, the company made a discovery amongst its own staff. Charles Mayo was responsible in 1939 for perhaps the most famous of GWR posters, 'Speed to the West', a striking image of *King George V* on a West of England express.

The change to more modern and adventurous poster designs followed a conscious effort by the Publicity Department to introduce a more contemporary look to what we would now call the 'corporate image' of the GWR. While the railway continued to use the more traditional 'Cheltenham' typeface on advertising material, it made increasing use of Gill Sans, a typeface introduced only in 1928, a spare and 'trustworthy' font in both pictorial and print forms.[28] The year 1931 also marked the appearance of the new art-deco GWR monogram which was to 'take the place of the words [*sic*] GWR and other combinations and abbreviations', according the company magazine, which noted that it would appear on items such as 'antimacassars, carpets, posters, handbills, stationery, cups and saucers, road motor vehicles and uniform buttons'.[29]

In addition to the marketing and publicity material it published or produced in the 1920s and 1930s, the GWR spent a good deal of time and money on public relations — what Sir Felix Pole had called 'propaganda'. Examples of some of this work have already been described, such as the press coverage generated by the visit of *King George V* to the United States; Pole employed the services of George E. Beer, formerly News Editor at *The Times*, whose role was to keep the Great Western name and its achievements to the fore. Pole also utilised what he called a team of 'budding journalists' already employed by the company, largely at Paddington; they were encouraged to write and were supplied with photographs and information so that they could provide copy for newspapers and journals. Pole and his successor worked hard to maintain good relations with the press, at national, regional and local levels, inviting reporters to all manner of special events, inaugural runs and tours of company facilities; constituting a good example of this kind of work were the tours of dock facilities in South Wales that were organised by the GWR in the 1920s and 1930s to raise their profile to potential customers at home and abroad.

The final aspect of the GWR publicity machine during the period was the company magazine itself. Felix Pole had been well aware of its potential since editing it himself in the years before the Great War and encouraged its new editor, Edward Hadley, appointed in 1919, to develop it further. The *Great Western Railway Magazine* was an important communication tool for the General Manager, and during his reign Pole's monthly column was used to highlight the financial performance of the company and at times to lecture staff on such subjects like courtesy to customers and the need for economy. The magazine also included a number of important regular features, most notably the 'Safety Movement', a campaign, begun before the Great War, that aimed to reduce the number of accidents suffered by staff. 'Freedom from Accident' competitions were reported, along with examples of good and bad working practices.

Between the two world wars circulation of the staff magazine rose to more than 40,000 copies a month, and there is little doubt that its high readership reflected the fact that it was a true staff journal, reporting the activities of employees outside working hours too. In

A specially posed picture used by the company in the *Great Western Railway Magazine* as part of its 'Safety Movement' campaign. The young member of staff about to be hit by the wagon door is wearing a smart white bow tie, in contrast to his scruffy uniform.

1922, the Great Western Social & Educational Union was formed, following the demise after the war of the GWR Temperance Union; its objectives were 'to encourage sports and pastimes, to form choirs and orchestras, provide occasions and pursuits that would interest and educate its members',[30] and its activities were heavily featured in the magazine, among them sporting competitions, arts and crafts and 'fur and feather', as well as horticultural, musical and theatrical events. In the years following the Grouping, branches of the union were opened all over the network, some, like that at Swindon, occupying large buildings; other, smaller groups occupied more modest premises, such as converted railway carriages. The union also ran the staff 'Helping Hand' fund, used to provide support to GWR employees 'suffering distress brought about by lengthy illness and bereavement'.[31]

1   Pole, F. J. C.: *His Book* (Town & Country Press, 1968), p83

2   *Great Western Railway Magazine* March 1932, p111

3   Orton, G. E.: 'Railway Publicity' (GWR [London] Lecture & Debating Society, 18 October 1934), p3

4   *Ibid*, p3

5   Burdett-Wilson, R.: *Go Great Western — A History of GWR Publicity* (David & Charles, 1970), p45

6   *Great Western Railway Magazine* February 1931, p74

7   Orton, *ibid*, p8

8   *Bristol Evening Post* 3 August 1935

9   *Great Western Railway Magazine* April 1922, p148

10   *Great Western Railway Magazine* April 1927, p151

11   Mais, S. P. B.: *The Cornish Riviera* (Great Western Railway, 1928), p7

12   Bennett. A.: 'The Railway Writers: GWR Creative Identity', *Backtrack* August 1999, p428

13   Great Western Railway: 'The Ocean Coast' (GWR, 1925) — Great Western Trust collection

14   Pugh, M.: *We Danced All Night — A Social History of Britain between the Wars* (Vintage Books, 2009), p234

15   Great Western Railway: *Holiday Haunts* (GWR, Paddington, 1936), p834

16   *Great Western Railway Magazine* March 1927, p111

17   Burdett-Wilson, *ibid*, p115

18   *Great Western Railway Magazine* March 1930, p101

19   Mais, S. P. B.: *Winter in the West* (Great Western Railway, 1929)

20   Great Western Railway: *Camping Holidays* (GWR, Paddington, 1929)

21   Burdett-Wilson, *ibid*, p88

22   Great Western Railway: 'The Joy of the Journey' (GWR, 1926) — Great Western Trust collection

23   Great Western Railway: *A Lantern Lecture: Oxford, the City of Dreaming Spires* Part 1 (GWR, undated) — Great Western Trust collection

24   Pole, *ibid*, p84

25   *Great Western Railway Magazine* December 1933, p530

26   Orton, *ibid*, p7

27   Cole, B., & Durack, R.: *Railway Posters 1923–1947* (National Railway Museum) 1992,, p9

28   Garfield, S.: *Just My Type — A Book about Fonts* (Profile Books, 2010), p50

29   *Great Western Railway Magazine* September 1934, p387

30   *Great Western Railway Magazine* January 1923, p36

31   Great Western Railway: *Swindon Works and its Part in Great Western History* (GWR, 1935)

CHAPTER 10

SPEED AND STYLE

No 6017 *King Edward IV* in charge of a Birmingham express in 1930. This picture was used as the basis of a jigsaw puzzle issued by the Victory company.

While the effects of the Great Depression that followed the Wall Street Crash were felt more keenly in Germany and the United States than in Britain, its consequences were still serious to those most directly affected, whether they were unemployed miners and their families in South Wales or companies like the GWR. Although Government money was enabling the company to re-equip and rebuild its network, its financial position was still difficult in the early 1930s, and it was the workforce that once again bore the brunt of economies made during the period. In March 1931, following an acrimonious public debate between unions and railway companies, a compulsory 2½% pay cut had been imposed along with reductions in overtime and bank holiday pay rates. The President of the NUR argued that, despite sacrifices made by railway staff 'to appease the greed of the railway directors … wolves as they are, once having tasted blood they could not stop until we were drained dry'.[1]

The railways, for their part, argued that conditions were as bad as they had ever been, and, with their 'backs against the wall', as one commentator put it, a wage cut was inevitable, the alternative being redundancies. However, as Adrian Vaughan records, GWR directors were excluded from any drop in remuneration, and, while the wage cut saved the company well over £650,000, staff were, not surprisingly, unhappy at this turn of events.[2] The 'Big Four' companies made another collective attempt to reduce wages even further at the end of 1931, proposing a 10% cut; this particular measure was not carried out, but not until 1934, by which time conditions had eased somewhat, were wages restored, and then only following a threat of strike action by the unions.

Retrenchment by the Great Western in the early 1930s did at least enable it to fare better than the other 'Big Four' companies, and the foundations laid by Pole in the preceding decade meant that it was better placed to emerge stronger; staff were asked to maintain a regime of strict economy, described by the General Manager as a 'self-preservation campaign' for the railway.[3] Shareholders also had to endure much-reduced yields from their investment, the company paying a 3% dividend every year from 1930 to 1936; even these dividends were made possible only by dipping into reserves, as evidenced by the Chairman's report of 1934, which noted that £710,000 had been needed from the contingency fund that year.

In these difficult times, even though the GWR was in a less profitable position than previously, James Milne tried to emulate his predecessor, Felix Pole, in pursuing new ventures that provided some positive publicity for the company. The development of the new 'King' class and its introduction on accelerated 'Cornish Riviera Limited' trains had been a high-point for the GWR at the end of the 1920s. When new rolling stock was introduced on the company's most famous express in July 1929, the company magazine had reported that its appearance had been met with 'general approbation'. Fittingly, the first new train had been waved

off by Milne and Chief Mechanical Engineer C. B. Collett, who had ceremonially rung the bell of *King George V*, the locomotive rostered to deliver the train to its West Country destination.

Half an hour after the new express had left Paddington's Platform 1, another new service had departed for Torquay; this was the inaugural run of the 'Torquay Pullman', a train that ran non-stop to Newton Abbot in 3 hours 25 minutes, arriving in Torquay after a journey of 3 hours 40 minutes. Sir Felix Pole recalled that the Pullman Company had 'made overtures' to the GWR on a number of occasions but that it was not until 1929 that negotiations between the two companies finally took place. Initially the company ran special Pullman boat trains from Plymouth to Paddington, boasting in an advertising leaflet that by landing at Plymouth overseas travellers could 'make the journey in a sixty-miles-an-hour express train instead of prolonging the sea voyage'. The 'time-saving "boon" the route affords is apparent', argued the company. For passengers with a 'reasonable' amount of luggage, first-class Pullman tickets cost 61s — 10s more than normal boat-train services.[4] In 1930, however, Pullman stock was

withdrawn both from boat trains and from the 'Torbay Pullman' service; Pole recalled that, for some reason, Viscount Churchill was 'really not in favour of the innovation' and that, as a result, 'the service was not given a proper chance to succeed',[5] although it may be that the Chairman resented the GWR's having to pay a surcharge to the Pullman Company for the use of its rolling stock.

In the 1930s, the GWR's reputation continued to be bolstered by the successful operation of its most famous named expresses: the 'Cornish Riviera Limited', the 'Cheltenham Flyer', the 'Torbay Express' and 'Torbay Limited' and, latterly, the 'Bristolian'. Although the GWR could no longer boast that the 'Cornish Riviera Limited' was the longest non-stop service in the world — a record it eventually lost to both the LMS and LNER — the train remained the company's premier express and in the summer months was extremely well used, necessitating the introduction in 1935 of a sister service, the 'Cornishman', which left Paddington five minutes after the 'Limited'. On busy summer Saturdays another relief train left at 10.25am, to cope with additional holidaymakers.

To the regular traveller on the GWR it may have seemed that the company appeared content to run express trains like the 'Limited' in much the same way as it had done for years, providing a reliable, comfortable and relatively profitable service. The Collett-designed locomotives that hauled the trains were, to some, beginning to look a little outmoded in comparison to the Gresley Pacifics being operated on the LNER, but in 1932 the GWR was able to score a significant public relations coup when a new record for the 'Cheltenham Flyer' was achieved. On 6 June the train, hauled by No 5006 *Tregenna Castle*, covered the stretch between Swindon and Paddington in 56 minutes 47 seconds — an average speed of 81.7mph. 'Such a journey speed has never been equalled by steam, so far as railway records go' boasted the company, and the record would not be beaten for some years.[6] It should be remembered that the name 'Cheltenham Flyer' was not the official title of the service; it was recorded in timetables as the 'Cheltenham Spa Express', although it was the more informal name that was used as the title of a book published by the company and in its own staff magazine!

Normal timings for the service were slower than the record run of *Tregenna Castle*, but in October 1932, in announcing its new winter timetable, the GWR reduced the timing of the train from 67 to 65 minutes from Swindon. The journey from Cheltenham to Swindon via Gloucester and Stroud was a fairly leisurely affair, so the company's continuing boast that the 'Cheltenham Flyer' was the 'world's fastest train' could be applied only to the Swindon–Paddington section and was based on average rather than maximum speeds. From 1932, passengers were given a special souvenir luggage label, and a special headboard (now preserved at the STEAM Museum in Swindon) was produced for publicity purposes.

Although the 'Torbay Pullman' had run for only a year, the group of resorts known collectively as the 'English Riviera' were still well served by fast trains from the capital. 'The advantages of Torquay stand out like the quills on a porcupine,' wrote S. P. B. Mais in 1932, noting the resort could be reached from London in 3½ hours.[7] Before 1914, the 'Torbay Express' had left Paddington at 11.50, running non-stop to Exeter, *en route* releasing at Taunton no fewer than four slip coaches for Ilfracombe. The departure was subsequently moved to 12 noon — a time the train retained even with the introduction of 'clock-face' departures in 1924. Unusually, the departure time for the London-bound service was also noon, although adverse gradients meant that it took 15 minutes longer.

ABOVE LEFT The short-lived 'Torbay Pullman' service, pictured passing Twyford box in 1929. The overall effect is rather spoiled by an additional GWR carriage attached to the rear of the train.

LEFT The cover of a GWR leaflet produced to advertise Pullman boat-train services in 1929. The time-saving service was a 'boon', it argued.
Great Western Trust collection

Between the wars the service was accelerated to run at an average speed of almost 60mph and from Paddington to Torquay was hauled by a 'King' or 'Castle' class locomotive, which would be replaced by lesser motive power for the remainder of the journey to Paignton, Churston and ultimately, on a single-track section of line, Kingswear.

For passengers the experience of travelling on the Great Western gradually improved in the 1920s and 1930s, especially as increased investment in the 1930s enabled the company to build better and more up-to-date rolling stock. Following Churchward's retirement his successor, Collett, introduced carriages that had steel instead of coach-built wooden sides, which gave them a rather more modern look. As this stock, which included new articulated trains, was introduced, older stock was relegated to cross-country and minor lines, on which the travelling experience was less pleasant, gas-lit non-corridor clerestory carriages being still in evidence. The new train provided in 1929 for the 'Cornish Riviera Limited' consisted of flush-sided steel-construction 61ft carriages built as big as the loading-gauge would permit, which whilst making them spacious also restricted their route availability. In 1931, following the abandonment of Pullman services, Swindon produced eight of the most luxurious carriages ever to be used on the railway, with the exception of the Royal Train; the 'Super

Saloons', named after members of the Royal Family, were designed specifically for use on boat trains from Plymouth, with fares carrying an extra premium above that of first class.

For the more well-heeled passenger a number of other developments made travel rather more pleasant. The first was the large-scale introduction of electric (rather than gas) lighting in trains. This was not a cheap process; in 1927, the Chief Officers noted a plan from the CME to convert 12 gas-lit dining cars and two buffet cars to electric lighting which would cost £4,501, along with a more ambitious scheme to convert a further 202 passenger carriages 'when they pass through shops for overhaul'.[8] This modernisation continued throughout the 1930s, although the introduction of more modern stock fitted from new with electric lighting made life easier for passengers. The company also made strenuous efforts to bring more restaurant cars into service, especially for third-class passengers, in 1934 introducing the 'buffet car', which looked very different from the old-fashioned dining cars of the 1920s. It also built two 'quick snack' carriages that featured an art-deco-style counter running almost the entire length of the carriage, passengers sitting on bar stools to take refreshment. Another innovation in the 1930s was the construction of what the company called 'excursion stock'; these were 'open' carriages (without corridors), passenger seating being arranged either side of a central gangway — an

arrangement familiar to travellers today but at that time rather less popular. However, in view of the huge amount of business done by the GWR in the running of excursions, their production was a logical development.

It is perhaps not surprising that, given both the modernisation of the GWR carriage fleet and the assimilation and withdrawal of older coaching stock from absorbed pre-Grouping railways, the Carriage & Wagon Department at Swindon was faced with a good deal of work to scrap or dispose of old rolling stock. Many older and time-expired carriage bodies were sold to private individuals or clubs for use as holiday homes, sheds, livestock accommodation or sports pavilions, but the GWR also introduced a novel and popular use for others as part of its promotion of the railway as a 'holiday line'. The LNER had introduced a number of 'Camp Coaches' in 1933, and, spurred on by this development, the Great Western launched its own scheme the following year, providing coaches at 19 locations all over the network, from Fowey, in Cornwall, to Rhayader, deep in Mid-Wales. The following year a further 20 were added, 15 more in 1936 and another 15 before the outbreak of war in 1939; the total of 69 was lower than that for the other 'Big Four' companies, which had embraced the idea enthusiastically, although the GWR did try to maintain an air of exclusivity and sophistication for its camp coaches, which were

LEFT A well-known posed publicity photograph used to promote the 'World's Fastest Train', the 'Cheltenham Flyer'. The wooden headboard mounted on the front of the locomotive is now in the collection of the STEAM Museum in Swindon.

BELOW The special luggage label issued to passengers on the 'Cheltenham Flyer' service after 1932.

ABOVE RIGHT Like a character from a 1930s Hollywood movie, a passenger peeps around the door of a new GWR 'excursion' carriage. The 'passengers' were usually Great Western employees.

aimed at a 'discerning clientele' wanting 'a quiet vacation away from the crowds'.[9] Swindon Works undertook the conversion of old wooden-bodied carriages to incorporate a kitchen, dining area and sleeping compartments. At £3 per week the camp coach was a relatively cheap alternative to the boarding house or 'bed and breakfast' and proved popular with holidaymakers.

In January 1931, the Government published the final report of a Royal Commission on transport. Two earlier reports had dealt largely with road traffic issues, but the third made recommendations about railways, noting that they were 'far from having been rendered obsolete by newer forms of transport'.[10] One of its main recommendations was that rail services should be speeded up and made more convenient, and while the GWR began to lose ground to the LMS and LNER in terms of speed records and non-stop runs, throughout the 1930s it managed to operate a good number of fast services across its network, being second only to the LMS in terms of the mileage worked by trains running at an average speed of 58mph or above.[11]

While its steam locomotives might have still been influenced by the standard locomotive policy laid down by Churchward almost 20 years previously, in 1933 the GWR showed that it could embrace new technology by announcing that it had purchased a diesel railcar from AEC in Southall. The streamlined design caused a sensation; 'In appearance, the car is not unlike a huge seaplane float surmounted by a series of flush-fitting observation windows which merge at each end into a control cabin,' wrote a

correspondent in the company magazine. The 'heavy oil' railcar was displayed at the Commercial Motor Show at Olympia in November and placed in traffic the following month on services in the Thames Valley. The railcar design utilised technology borrowed from commercial vehicles, including a pre-selective gearbox and other standard road-chassis parts. It was hoped that the streamlining and relatively low weight of 20 tons would make the railcar cheap to run, but the single 121bhp engine proved to be underpowered, although after some teething problems the prototype covered more than 61,000 miles in service.

The GWR was sufficiently impressed by the success of railcar No 1 to order another six from AEC early in 1934; these had two engines, which gave them an impressive top speed of over 80mph. Whilst later railcars were designed for use on branch lines, the early examples were intended for fast services on cross-country routes such as Birmingham–Cardiff and so were fitted with toilets; Nos 2-4 also had a buffet bar, limiting accommodation to 44 passengers. When the first three of the new batch were delivered in July 1934, they were used on an inaugural press trip from London to Birmingham and thence to Newport and Cardiff. In a speech given at a lunch in Cardiff, K. W. C. Grand, whilst admitting that it might appear strange that the GWR was using a diesel-powered railcar to run to and from the centre of the Welsh coalfield, argued that fast trains between Cardiff and Birmingham had been regarded as a necessity for some time but that 'the number of passengers did not justify an addition to steam services, particularly in existing economic circumstances'.[12] The railcars were economic to run, he continued, as they required only one man on the footplate, and having the engines under the floor made it possible to use

almost all the space for passenger accommodation. On the press trip the railcar reached a top speed of 73mph, whilst achieving an average of more than 53mph. 'Even at maximum speed there was remarkably little vibration or noise,' reported the *Great Western Railway Magazine*, adding, reassuringly, that 'conversation could be carried on with ease'.[13] The New Work Order issued by the company to record the purchase of the six vehicles reveals that AEC was to maintain them for the first year of service, excluding tyres and bodywork, for a payment of 1¾d per mile. For each car the chassis cost £3,500, the bodywork £2,791.[14]

The Birmingham–Cardiff service began on 9 July 1934 with morning and late-afternoon departures aimed at business passengers; these services were well patronised, and the remaining three railcars, with bodywork by the Gloucester Railway Carriage & Wagon Co, were introduced in the summer of 1935. These were subsequently used on services between Paddington, Hereford, Worcester and Birmingham. Following their introduction a number of other variants continued to appear until the 1940s, among them No 17, an express parcels van. In 1938, the company decided to produce its own designs at Swindon, using AEC engines and transmission, but whilst these were striking in appearance, they lacked the art-deco elegance of their predecessors. These were intended for use on branch lines, on which speeds and traffic levels were lower, so the streamlining of the earlier designs was deemed unnecessary; the value of railcars for lightly loaded services to small stations and halts was now fully appreciated by the management at Paddington.

Unlike the LMS, which had embraced the use of diesel locomotives for shunting in goods yards, the GWR was slow to adopt them. A Fowler 0-4-0 diesel-electric shunter had been purchased for use at Swindon Works in 1933, but it was another two years before another appeared, this time a Hawthorn Leslie 0-6-0 diesel-electric shunter, which worked at Acton Yard. No further purchases were made before World War 2, shunting continuing to be performed in the main by the hundreds of GWR tank engines in service on the railway.

At the same time as it was looking towards the future with the adoption of diesel traction, the GWR took a bolder step (for the movement of passengers, at least) by launching its own air services. Following the war, when aircraft had played a key role, civil aviation had grown only slowly, despite efforts to promote 'air-mindedness' through record-breaking and solo flights like those of Alan Cobham and, most famously, Amy Johnson. Long-distance air travel was slow and expensive and largely the province of the rich and famous, but in March 1933, the GWR approached Imperial Airlines with a proposal to make use of the air powers the company had been granted in 1930 alongside those of road transport. Mr Stanley Collett from the GWR Solicitors Department wrote to Colonel Burchall at Imperial, stating that 'for

ABOVE LEFT One of the special 'Super Saloons', often described as the most luxurious carriages to be built by the company, constructed at Swindon to replace the Pullman stock. A number of these grand coaches have been preserved on heritage railways.

LEFT A list of camping coaches, as reproduced in *Holiday Haunts*.

BELOW Another posed photograph, this time featuring one of the Great Western's new 'quick snack' buffet cars introduced in 1934. A box of Huntley & Palmers biscuits, produced (in Reading) for the company, sits atop the bar.

RIGHT The interior of one of the camping coaches so modified by the GWR. The picture was probably taken at the Carriage Works at Swindon, judging by the view from the coach window.

the moment it is undoubtedly Sir James Milne's desire to conduct a purely Great Western experiment and that the company wished to operate a service from Cardiff to Torquay — an area that was 100% Great Western. The route was chosen to demonstrate the advantages of air travel at the time, enabling passengers to travel quickly between two areas separated by some difficult geography which would entail a long trip by rail.

Collett admitted that the proposal was a 'rather a big order', but noted that urgency was required because 'report has it that the other railway companies are about to enter the field and I am particularly anxious that the Great Western should be the first'.[15] Replying on 27 March, Burchall poured cold water on the idea, noting that 'only in exceptional cases can an air service, at the present state of development of aviation, hope to operate without a subsidy'. Milne was not to be deterred, and on 28 March he told Imperial Airways that he was prepared to conduct an experiment on the lines discussed and that he 'particularly desired to inaugurate the service before Easter'. Imperial agreed to operate the service on behalf of the company, using a four-seater Westland Wessex aircraft turned out in Great Western colours, the paint and transfers having been supplied by the GWR. Imperial also supplied air and ground crews to maintain the service, being paid 2s 3d per mile by the company to do so.

The new air service began on 12 April and operated between Cardiff and Haldon, the airfield serving Torquay and Plymouth; two trips were operated per day in each direction, with a flight time of 1 hour 20 minutes — much quicker than spending a large part of the day on the train. Milne clearly saw the service as an experiment, telling the board at the end of April that 'it must be recognised that at the present stage such services are unlikely to prove remunerative' but that he thought the company 'might test public demand'.[16] Westland was keen to maximise publicity from the new services, and when sending the manufacturer copies of GWR advertising material Collett stressed: 'It is early days yet to form an opinion of the patronage of the service, but the first week was not too bad, and

we shall now have to wait and see whether it "catches on" when we get nearer to the regular holiday period.'[17] Flights were extended to Birmingham from 22 May, and the operation of the whole service extended from 12 to 30 September. The return fare of £6 was not cheap, and, given that the aircraft could accommodate only four passengers, the experiment was not profitable, but the GWR had learned a great deal from it.

In 1934, the Great Western joined with the other 'Big Four' railways to set up their own airline, Railway Air Services, with capital of £50,000, in collaboration with Imperial Airways. Wing Commander A. H. Measures was appointed Superintendent in May 1934, having been selected from well over 200 applicants. Measures began by carrying out inspections of the services; at the end of May he travelled on the newly extended Plymouth–Liverpool service, noting that 'generally speaking it was being operated very satisfactorily' and that the flight passed 'without incident'. He did, however, report that 'the pilot flew with the cockpit door open', which must have been rather unnerving for passengers! The primitive nature of early air travel is illustrated by the fact that if there were no passengers to pick up at Haldon a white sheet would be laid out on the runway. At Plymouth passengers checked in for their flight at North Road station and were then taken by taxi to the aerodrome. Measures also reported that there was no RAS sign at the station to advertise the service, nor any advertising at the aerodrome. On arrival in Liverpool the Superintendent was also unimpressed by the appearance of the aircraft engineer, who was 'attending his duties dressed in a dirty pair of trousers and a sports coat'.[18]

Measures' greatest concern was over passenger numbers, which he described as 'very disappointing', recommending that 'an active publicity scheme be instituted throughout the areas served by this route';[19] when hotel porters in Plymouth and Birmingham had been asked about RAS, 'none had heard of the services being run by the Company'. Posters and leaflets were soon produced, but matters were not helped by delays in obtaining new aircraft; plans for introducing an accelerated service on the Plymouth–Liverpool

LEFT Pictured shortly after construction, railcar No 11 shows off its sleek lines at Bristol Temple Meads in 1936.

ABOVE RIGHT An aerial photograph of Haldon Aerodrome, taken on the day of the inauguration of the first GWR air service in 1933. The GWR's Westland Wessex (G-AAGW) is in the foreground. This airfield served Teignmouth.

RIGHT The cramped passenger compartment of the De Havilland Dragon Rapide, used extensively by the Railway Air Services operation from 1934.

FAR RIGHT The ground crew stand proudly in front of the three-engined Wessex, whilst behind it a fuel bowser stands close to the hangar. This six-seat aircraft was introduced by the Westland company in 1929.

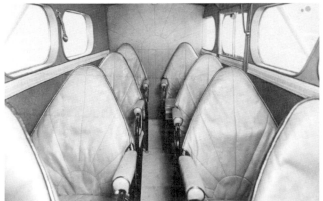

route and introducing a new Bristol–Southampton service were delayed by the fact that De Havilland could not deliver new, larger Dragon Rapide aircraft until late in August 1934. A standard Dragon was, however, loaned to RAS on 25 July, enabling the company to run a shuttle service between Birmingham and Southampton or Bristol and Cardiff. Fares were still expensive, and the company had to work hard to gain extra publicity for the new services, asking various correspondents for a 'write-up' of the new route. An article in *The Times* of 22 June 1934 noted that a passenger who chose to fly from Plymouth to Cardiff could do so in 40 minutes instead of spending 3½ hours on the train. The company wrote to the *Times* correspondent, thanking him for his help whilst noting that he had 'not been too fortunate with the weather' and had endured rather a bumpy flight.

An article in the *Great Western Railway Magazine* in 1936 described some of the delights of domestic air travel between the wars, recording that there were two main disadvantages of flight, the first being noise so loud that conversation consisted of 'shouting'. The second was air sickness, passengers experiencing a feeling similar to that of 'a springy bus on a bad road'; bowls were provided under seats for emergencies, it added, helpfully. Despite this — and the fact that flights cost two and a half times that of third-class travel on the railway — the writer concluded that 'most people who have tried flying aver that whenever possible they will always travel by air in preference to land or sea'.[20]

By 1937, RAS was operating a weekday service between May and September linking Bristol, Cardiff, Exeter and Plymouth, while the GWR and the Southern Railway were jointly operating a weekday service between Liverpool, Birmingham, Cheltenham, Bristol, Southampton, Ryde and Brighton, as well as a Sunday

A cleverly framed portrait of the GWR steamship *St David* at Fishguard Harbour in May 1937.

service between Cardiff, Bristol, Southampton, Ryde and Brighton. The LMS and LNER were less enthusiastic about the air travel experiment, and in 1938 the GWR and the SR set up their own joint air company, which continued to run services until the operation of domestic flights was curtailed by the outbreak of war in 1939.

It remains only to give a brief summary of the Great Western marine fleet during the period; by the Grouping the company owned nine large steamships and a similar number of smaller vessels. All were by this time becoming rather old, the most modern being the *Waterford*, built in 1912, and the four turbine steamers built between 1906 and 1908 for the Fishguard route; others, like the *Pembroke*, dated back to the 1880s. Two new ships, the *St Helier* and *St Julien*, were brought into service in 1925 for use on Channel Island services, and two new cargo vessels, *Roebuck* and *Sambur*, were also launched that year. In 1929, the SS *St Patrick*, which had served as a relief boat for both Irish and Channel Island services, was badly damaged by fire, and a replacement of the same name was commissioned the following year. Replacements for the *St Andrew* and the *St David*, used on Fishguard–Rosslare sailings, were placed in service in April 1932.[21] With the addition in 1934 of a new ship carrying the company name and the upgrading of tender ships at Plymouth to service Ocean Mail traffic the GWR fleet was complete. By 1939, the profitability of the operation had improved significantly from the loss-making position in which it had found itself in the 1920s. With the outbreak of hostilities the fleet took on a new and vital role as part of the war effort.

1   *Bristol Times & Mirror* 24 November 1930
2   Vaughan, A.: *The Great Western at Work, 1921–1939* (PSL Books, 1993), p157
3   *Great Western Railway Magazine* November 1932, p420
4   Great Western Railway: 'GWR of England — Pullman from Plymouth' (GWR, Paddington, 1929) — Great Western Trust collection
5   Pole, F. J. C.: *His Book* (Town & Country Press, 1968), p157
6   *Great Western Railway Magazine* June 1932, p154
7   Mais, S. P. B.: *Winter in the West* (Great Western Railway, 1932), p6
8   Great Western Railway: Minutes of Chief Officers' Conference Meeting held 2 May 1927
9   Fenton, M.: *Camp Coach Holidays on the GWR* (Wild Swan Publications, 1999)
10 *Great Western Railway Magazine* February 1931, p57
11 Nock, O. S.: *A History of the Great Western Railway* (Ian Allan, 1967), p140
12 *Great Western Railway Magazine* August 1934, p347
13 *Ibid*
14 Great Western Railway: New Work Order No 1609 (GWR CME Department, 3 August 1934) — STEAM archive
15 [Collett, S. B.:] letter dated 24 March 1933 — National Archives: RAIL258/210
16 [Collett, S. B.:] letter dated 28 April 1933 — National Archives: RAIL258/210
17 [Collett, S. B.:] letter dated 22 April 1933 — National Archives: RAIL258/210
18 Railway Air Services Ltd: Correspondence file — National Archives: RAIL258/510
19 Railway Air Services Ltd: Report dated 1 June 1934 — National Archives: RAIL258/210
20 *Great Western Railway Magazine* July 1936, p320
21 *Great Western Railway Magazine* May 1932, p139

CHAPTER 11

THE CENTENARY

The Great Western Railway was the only 'Big Four' company able to celebrate its 100th birthday by virtue of an unbroken history that stretched back to 1835. Although there had been events staged by the LNER and LMS to mark the centenaries of the Stockton & Darlington and Liverpool & Manchester railways, one might have assumed that the chance for the GWR to celebrate its centenary in style was an ideal opportunity for the company to strike a blow against its 'Big Four' rivals and also to publicise its services to the travelling public at a time when both private car ownership and bus and coach travel were increasing rapidly.

In the event, the celebrations organised by the Great Western were far more low-key than might have been expected for a railway well used to making the most of its publicity machine to promote itself and its services. The truth was that the company was in no real position to emulate its rivals in staging elaborate and expensive events like the 1925 Stockton & Darlington celebrations, at which, in addition to a large exhibition at Faverdale Wagon Works, the LNER had also staged a cavalcade of more than 50 locomotives featuring relics like *Locomotion* and also current designs like Gresley's A1 Pacific. The GWR had participated in the event, supplying a number of its locomotives, and five years later had dispatched No 6029 *King Stephen* north to take part in celebrations marking the centenary of the Liverpool & Manchester Railway.

As early as 1932, a memorandum concerning the company centenary was prepared by D. F. Levien, who worked in the

GWR Record Office at Paddington and noted that it would seem entirely proper the company should 'celebrate the centenary of their own railway, more especially as unlike other pioneer lines which have lost their identity by reason of amalgamation or absorption, the GWR company has remained through the periods in the public eye as … an object of intense and human interest'[1] Levien suggested that the railway should stage what he called a 'Popular Event' and argued that such an event as a centenary celebration would be 'attended by wide public support'. His suggestions for the week-long event included a 'pageant' of historic locomotives and rolling stock with GWR Social & Educational Union and Dramatic & Operatic Society members in costume 'visualising a centenary of railway progress' and separate displays of models and other smaller relics, as well as refreshment and toilet facilities. It was intended that there would be an admission charge for the event, but it was not thought that this would pay the costs of the celebration; 'The advertisement would be invaluable and so long as the organisation was sound, the public would not be slow to take advantage of seeing a spectacle of this nature, so long as the railway fare was kept down to a really attractive figure,' Levien concluded.[2]

Clearly the choice of site for a celebration would greatly affect the success or failure of the event; it should 'be as near the Metropolis as possible', Levien suggested, close to the railway, so that connecting sidings could be laid easily and cheaply, and in a location that would also bring the company passenger revenue. Maidenhead, destination of the GWR's first passenger trains, run in 1838, would have been the best location, but its position on an embankment ruled it out. A number of sites in the London area were inspected, including Shepherd's Bush coal depot, Kensington Warwick Road goods depot, Old Oak Common, Park Royal, Greenford Triangle and Hayes, but none was really large enough for a celebration on the scale envisaged. Potential sites at Didcot and Newbury Racecourse were also discussed, but these were deemed too far from the capital.

There was no shortage of ideas for the proposed centenary event, but the difficulty lay in the cost; Levien had noted that the LNER's directors had provided over £10,000 towards the Stockton & Darlington celebrations in 1925, but estimated that any GWR celebration might cost at least £15,000. He then wrote a gloomy summary of the current economic situation facing the country and, more particularly, the railway itself. Faced with these 'depressing factors', Levien wondered 'whether it is prudent in the existing circumstances to be considering the question of incurring expenditure on a celebration of any kind until, maybe, there is a clearer indication of a return to better times'.[3] Submitting his report to the Company Secretary, F. R. Davis, he also suggested that it might be advisable to postpone any celebrations until 1938, which would have been the centenary of the running of the first trains on the GWR.

ABOVE Viscount Horne, who succeeded Churchill as Company Chairman in 1935, retaining the position until the railway was nationalised.

FAR LEFT Passengers wait at Paddington in August 1935. Two large hoardings advertise *The Times'* GWR Centenary supplement to travellers crossing the Lawn to their trains.

In 1934, the Great Western had suffered the loss of one of its greatest supporters and a man who had witnessed a great deal of its history. Viscount Churchill died suddenly on 3 January, having been Chairman since 1908 and worked with five general managers. His recollections of the growth, changes and turmoil experienced by the GWR over more than 25 years would have enriched any centenary celebration, and his death from pneumonia at the age of 69 came as a shock to many GWR staff. The 'duty of a railway chairman' was to 'guide a great organisation in safe financial courses and to encourage initiative and progressive spirit in its staff,' reported *The Times*, adding that the GWR of future years would be a monument to Churchill's chairmanship.[4]

By the time James Milne wrote his first monthly report of 1935 in the *Great Western Railway Magazine* he was able to note that business had improved somewhat over the previous year, but he reminded staff that further efforts were required before company

ABOVE An official photograph taken to record the final overhaul of record-breaking Churchward 4-4-0 *City of Truro* before it was dispatched in 1930 to York for exhibition in the city's railway museum.

RIGHT The scene inside 'A' Shop at Swindon Works on 16 June 1927, during the construction of the first batch of 'King' class locomotives. The picture, by the company photographer, was titled 'Comparison of chimneys' and features a 'King' chimney, the tall chimney of *North Star* and another unidentified example from an earlier design.

finances could be 'regarded with satisfaction'. Despite the tough trading conditions it faced, the company had continued to pay shareholders a dividend of 3% every year since 1930, something it could afford only by drawing large sums of money from its reserves. In 1933, these drawings had amounted to £1,350,000, a huge sum; it seems, therefore, that the £15,000 cost of a centenary event on the scale proposed some years earlier proved too much for the directors, and it is not surprising that the GWR's 100th anniversary turned out to be a rather more low-key affair than might have been expected.

Nevertheless, preparations were made to celebrate the anniversary; an announcement in the *GWR Magazine* at the end of 1934 also illustrates just how much attitudes to railway heritage have changed in the last 75 years. In advance of the centenary the editor reported that the company 'desires to discover, to the greatest extent possible, the existing relics, of any kind, of the early years of either the original GWR or the railways that have been absorbed by or amalgamated with it'.[5] From a modern perspective it seems incredible that the company should have had to resort to asking its staff to search for items of historic interest, but many managers and staff were keen to move on from the era of Brunel and the broad gauge and were intent on looking forward rather than back. Levien had noted in his memorandum that the LNER had a distinct advantage over the GWR, as it 'already had a lot of original rolling stock and locomotives and a museum'.

It may also be that the Great Western was keen to avoid a repeat of the embarrassing situation it had faced when trying to retrieve surviving parts of the broad-gauge 2-2-2 *North Star* in 1924 when scrabbling to provide early relics for the Stockton & Darlington celebrations the following year. The resulting locomotive, built by apprentices, incorporated some original parts found at Swindon Works or rescued from private individuals but was largely a replica. The lack of sentiment felt by management about company heritage which had led to *North Star* and *Lord of the Isles* being scrapped in the first place in 1906 had diminished to some extent, the General Manager in 1925 noting that it was 'much regretted' that these broad-gauge relics had not been preserved.[6] Despite this statement, however, by 1935, Swindon had ruthlessly scrapped, rebuilt or sold many of the oldest pre-Grouping locomotives acquired by the company a decade before, which left the GWR with only the *North Star* replica, the South Devon locomotive *Tiny*, part of an old broad-gauge coach preserved in Plymouth, Churchward 4-4-0 *City of Truro* and examples of 'old time' signals, kept at Reading.

ABOVE A Drawing Office print of the clumsily streamlined *Manorbier Castle* outside Swindon Works in July 1935. The addition of an excursion-number bracket on the buffer beam would scarcely have helped its aerodynamics.

RIGHT Fifty '57xx' pannier tanks were to be built in 1935. Here an example of the class is in charge of the Taunton Division weed-killing train.

Sir Robert Horne, the new Company Chairman, speaking at the GWR's Annual General Meeting in February 1935, reminded shareholders that they were heirs to a system that 'absorbs our interest and commands our loyalty'. He was upbeat about the company's prospects in the coming year and hoped that the centenary would mark an improvement in its fortunes. It was clear, however, that any substantial investment would be directed towards measures that would improve the profitability of the company rather than in celebrating its heritage.

In the following months there were numerous announcements designed to emphasise the 'Progress' element of the '100 Years of Progress' slogan adopted for the 100th anniversary. Early in 1935, the year's locomotive and rolling stock build programme was announced, involving an investment of almost £1 million. It was hoped that 95 locomotives would be built, 10 'Castles' and 15 'Halls' being augmented by well over 50 0-6-0 pannier tanks. The Carriage & Wagon Works at Swindon would also have a busy year, a welcome development after a lean period, being required to build

211 carriages and 2,486 wagons. The *GWR Magazine* reminded its readers that this investment would have an important effect both on the employees at the works and on their 30,000 dependants living in the railway town.

Another announcement designed to raise the company profile followed in April 1935, when the GWR showed off its first streamlined locomotive, a heavily modified 'King' 4-6-0, No 6014 *King Henry VII*. 'Streamlining is becoming more and more insisted on by all forms of transport,' noted the Publicity Department, citing contemporary Schneider Trophy seaplanes and Sir Malcolm Campbell's *Bluebird* and also noting that reducing 'head-on' air resistance made energy available for more useful purposes, requiring less fuel. In May a picture of No 5005 *Manorbier Castle*, similarly treated as a streamlined locomotive, appeared in the company magazine, having been modified at the same time as No.6014. The merits of this initiative have been debated at some length by enthusiasts over the years, but the Great Western's efforts appear crude and almost comical in comparison when compared to the LNER's properly streamlined Gresley 'A4' Pacific *Silver Link* which did not appear until September 1937. The experiment was not a success, and the streamlining was gradually removed, little trace remaining by 1939. Hugh Freebury, an apprentice in 'A' Shop while the streamlining was being fitted, remembered that there had been 'great attempts made at secrecy' during the work but thought that the locomotive was 'grotesquely adorned almost beyond recognition', concluding that it 'looked to us exactly what it was — a bodged up job'.[7]

The company also capitalised on another significant anniversary in 1935. The Silver Jubilee of King George V and Queen Mary was the occasion for national celebrations, and on 6 May, a national holiday, the GWR ran hundreds of excursion trains, many to the capital. Elaborate preparations had been made to cope with the traffic, commuter and business trains being suspended, and only a limited goods timetable run; 'all shunting engines will be cancelled unless ordered specially,' noted a memorandum from the Superintendent of the Line's Office.[8]

The railway also ran a number of special trains conveying troops to London for the royal celebrations, including one from Tidworth to Paddington on 5 May that transported nearly 200 military personnel from the '3rd Hussars, 9th Lancers and 4th Dragoon Guards', along with their riding horses and chargers. The weather that weekend was fine, and after the event the Birmingham Divisional Superintendent reported that 'traffic was heavy for London, but otherwise only moderately heavy on the Saturday', but it was, he noted, so heavy the following day that two additional trains were provided to carry over 2,000 passengers to London.[9] It was also reported that in the company's hotels special menus were offered, composed entirely of what the GWR Hotels Department called 'Empire dishes'. Receipts were up by more than £133,000 during the month, and Great Western employees were even given a day off with pay for good measure. The increased business generated during the Jubilee celebrations was an encouraging start to the company's summer season.

The 1935 edition of the ever-popular *Holiday Haunts* guide was published as a 'Centenary Number' with what the company magazine called a 'dignified' specially designed cover printed in chocolate, cream and gold. As well as containing the usual mix of advertisements and information on holiday resorts on the GWR network it included a brief historical introduction to the company to mark its 100th anniversary. The original text for this had been written by Maxwell Fraser, editor of *Holiday Haunts* and author of a number of other travel books for the GWR. It was clearly not quite what the company wanted, for when a draft copy was sent to Levien in August 1934 for comment by the Company Secretary, the latter replied diplomatically that he would 'prefer to suppress my views on this article but would undertake to produce something worthy of the occasion if the secretary wishes it',[10] and it was his revised copy that finally appeared in the 1,024-page *Holiday Haunts* for 1935.

The publication of *Holiday Haunts* was followed by an announcement regarding the company's summer train service for 1935. The existing timetable was augmented by no fewer than 1,128 extra weekday and Sunday trains and featured more '60mph expresses' and services worked by streamlined railcars, as well as additional business trains between larger towns, and cross-country services linking the industrial Midlands and the North with the holiday resorts of the West and South West, using through carriages, between such distant locations as Aberdeen and Penzance.

Part of this ambitious new timetable was an additional train to bolster its most famous express, the 'Cornish Riviera Limited'. Heavy traffic in previous summers had severely taxed the carrying capacity of the train, and to meet increased passenger demands a companion express was introduced. The down 'Cornishman' left

BELOW Thirties elegance — the new 'Quick Snack' bar at Paddington station.

RIGHT Morris cars awaiting export at the Great Western Docks at Swansea in March 1935.

BELOW RIGHT A poster advertising the GWR house-removal service, reproduced in a centenary publication in 1935.

Paddington at 10.35am each weekday, five minutes after the 'Limited', to cater for passengers travelling to intermediate destinations, such as Weymouth, Plymouth, Newquay, St Erth and Helston, finally reaching Penzance at 5.07pm.

The company used its centenary in 1935 as an excuse to introduce two 13-coach rakes of brand-new corridor stock for use on the 'Cornish Riviera Limited'. Replacing the carriages provided by the GWR to mark the train's silver jubilee in 1929, what became known as the 'Centenary' stock was built to a very high standard and was what *The Times* called a 'triumph of British workmanship', the 60ft carriages being every bit as well equipped and luxurious as Pullman cars or the stock used by the LMS and the LNER on their premium expresses. In a departure from previous Great Western practice there were only two recessed end doors on each side, with two 'spacious vestibules', and large drop windows in each compartment.

With the majority of its investment directed towards the working railway, the Great Western decided that most of its centenary-related publicity activities should be timed to coincide with the 100th anniversary of the passing of the original GWR Act of Parliament on 31 August 1835. On this date *The Times* published a special supplement, marking the centenary of the founding of the company and including articles on its history as well as extensive coverage of many of the new initiatives it was now pursuing, such as air services and diesel railcars. The text for the supplement was provided by the ever-scrupulous Levien, who delivered his material in late June. Surviving correspondence suggests that the GWR had to pay *The Times* £750 for the supplement, equivalent to the cost of a full-page advertisement in the newspaper.

A memorandum dated 22 August noted that the railway was obtaining from *The Times* '49,000 copies of the GWR Centenary Supplement, the major portion of which are intended for distribution amongst the staff'. These, along with copies of a special Centenary edition of the company magazine, were stored at Paddington in readiness for distribution, but it appears that they did not prove quite as popular as the company had anticipated, for in April 1937, Levien would be moved to write to the Stores Superintendent at Swindon, noting that 'we have about 40,000 copies of the *Times* GWR Supplement together with about 12,000 copies of the Centenary number of the *GWR Magazine* which are to be treated as waste paper';[11] the 15 tons of scrap paper would be pulped a month later. *The Times'* supplement was also produced as a book, although the GWR had no financial commitment to its production; given the significance of the anniversary it was surprising that only one other book was published by the company in 1935, although the choice of title at least revealed that the management at Paddington had not lost their sense of humour. *Railway Ribaldry*, by W. Heath Robinson, was a 100-page book of cartoons featuring significant events in the history of the railway and sold well, costing only a shilling per copy.

On 31 August 1935, a Saturday, the Great Western ran a special train from Paddington, this leaving the capital at 10am and taking exactly two hours to speed down Brunel's old GWR main line to Bristol. A special lunch was held at the Great Hall of the University of Bristol, and in his speech to the assembled dignitaries the Company Chairman, Viscount Horne, announced another publicity coup for the Great Western. The occasion of the company's centenary would be marked by the introduction of a brand-new express, the 'Bristolian'. This new train would appear in timetables in September and would run non-stop from Paddington to Bristol Temple Meads in 1 hour 45 minutes, an improvement of 15 minutes on any previous train between the two cities. Horne told the gathering: 'We are not out to do any stunting. We could

expedite these times if we wished to make a public demonstration, but we wish only to give times which will be the ordinary running schedule of our trains.'[12]

J. H. Thomas, by then a government minister, it was reported, began his speech in 'jocular vein'. Noting that he had accepted his invitation to this lunch as 'ample apology for the sweated conditions when they first employed me and paid me seven bob a week,' he concluded by wondering: 'What other country in the world would invite all classes and creeds, with one, responding for the guests, a representative of the Government but once also fireman and engine driver?' Guests at the lunch were then whisked back to the capital at 4.30pm, the new time for the 'Bristolian', behind No 6000 *King George V*, the train comprising six special saloons and a buffet car. Once introduced, the 'Bristolian' was one of the quickest on the network, second only to the 'Cheltenham Flyer', but, for all the favourable publicity that had been generated, a lack of investment meant that the new train was not provided with any special new carriage stock. Its timing, particularly its 11am departure from Paddington, also reflected some conservatism and a lack of understanding at Paddington, for few business travellers with appointments in Bristol would wish to leave the capital so late.

Before returning to London, guests at the Bristol lunch were also treated to a showing of a special centenary film, *The Romance of a Railway*. Much of the filming had been done at the Merton Park studios, under the direction of Charles Creighton, and the *GWR Magazine* reported, 'Well-known artistes have impersonated famous personalities connected at various times with the Great Western Railway.' The first meeting of the GWR in 1833 was re-enacted at the Merchants' Hall in Bristol, members of the Society of Merchant Venturers and directors, management and staff from the railway and Bristol City Council acting as extras.

A larger and more elaborate set piece re-creating the arrival of the first GWR service at Maidenhead in 1838 was filmed at a much less glamorous location — waste ground to the west of 'A' Shop at Swindon Works. Filming took place on 4 April 1935, and the *North Star* replica (propelled by a diesel shunter placed out of shot) was pressed into service, burning cotton waste placed in the smokebox completing the effect. The track was mixed gauge, as the carriages and locomotive tender were standard-gauge replicas used in the Liverpool & Manchester Railway celebrations, but using clever camera angles the deception was quite convincing. The actors playing the crowd and passengers were members of the Great Western (London) and Swindon Operatic societies, who were commended for their performances — even if one rather spoiled the historical accuracy of the piece by looking at his wrist-watch in one scene! Intercut with these

A 'King' 4-6-0 heads the 'Cornish Riviera Limited' along the Devon coast in 1935. The train comprises the new 1935-built Centenary stock that replaced the stock built for the service in 1929.

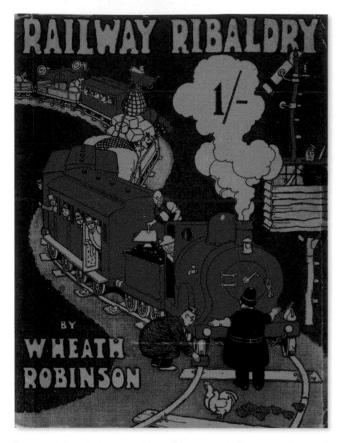

historical interludes were 'cleverly contrived glimpses of several resorts served by the railway, and of traffic operations', reported the *GWR Magazine*, as well as a lengthy sequence filmed at Swindon Works.[13]

The centenary was also celebrated by a BBC radio programme, broadcast on 30 August 1935, which told the story of the Great Western through a journey from Paddington to Penzance. The two narrators, Mr V. C. Clinton-Baddeley and Mr Robert Speight, were able to interview a variety of Great Western staff about the railway past and present. A retired guard, H. J. New, reminisced over the broad gauge, while W. H. Bickham, who had been Mayor of Swindon in 1934, was interviewed about the works and town, as well as the relative merits of the 'Castle' and 'King' class locomotives. The infamous story of the refreshment rooms at Swindon was followed by a discussion with F. H. Shephard, a chef on the 'Torbay Express', who told listeners just how he cooked meals in a small kitchen at high speed! The broadcast also featured a recording of the pumps in the Severn Tunnel, giving some idea of the work required to keep the tunnel dry 24 hours a day. More Great Western employees told the story of the railway in the West Country, the programme ending with a whispered 'good night' from Mr Froude, a retired guard from Penzance — a conclusion described by one national newspaper as 'a touch of genius'.

The end to the Great Western's centenary celebrations was marked by a grand banquet held at the Grosvenor House Hotel in London on 30 October 1935. This lavish event was attended by more than 1,100 guests, including the Prince of Wales and mayors and lord mayors of towns and cities served by the Great Western. Also present were some rank-and-file staff, although many were from trade unions, pension and provident societies and the St John Ambulance Association. The menu included fillet of sole and caviar, accompanied by Harvey's 'Bristol Milk' sherry, Liebfraumilch wine and 40-year-old Courvoisier brandy.[14] After the meal the Prince of Wales gave a witty speech praising the achievements of railways and reminding guests that his grandmother, Queen Victoria, had first travelled by train on the GWR in 1842, which entitled the railway to call itself the 'Royal Road'. He concluded that, on its 100th birthday, the company 'was entitled to have its own trumpet blown, and I am very happy to give it a hearty and resounding blast'. Each of the diners was presented with a cigar, cigarette and match container in the form of the broad-gauge locomotive *Lord of the Isles*. An invoice dated 29 October 1935 from a local printer recorded that the cost of these, the wrapping of the cigars and the provision of strawboard boxes in which to take the containers home amounted to £155.[15]

No doubt the 1,100 guests attending the centenary banquet enjoyed the experience, but there is no avoiding the fact that it ended what had been a rather disappointing celebration of 100 years of Great Western history. There had been little chance for railway enthusiasts or the public at large to mark the anniversary, and the difficult trading conditions endured by the railway at the time clearly took their toll. As if that were not enough, earlier in the month the LNER had taken a decisive step forward by launching its 'Silver Jubilee' express service from King's Cross to Newcastle, and during a trial run of the train undertaken in late September one of Gresley's new streamlined 'A4' Pacifics, *Silver Link*, had achieved a top speed of 112.5mph, scoring an important public relations coup.

100 YEARS OF PROGRESS
1835 — 1935
GWR

1   Great Western Railway: Centenary Celebrations File — National Archives: RAIL253/720

2   *Ibid*

3   *Ibid*

4   *The Times* 4 January 1934, p12

5   *Great Western Railway Magazine* December 1934, p552

6   *Great Western Railway Magazine* January 1925, p1

7   Freebury, H.: *Great Western Apprentice* (Wiltshire Museums Service, 1985), pp123-124

8   Great Western Railway: 'Silver Jubilee Arrangements, 1935' — National Archives: RAIL253/457

9   Great Western Railway: Centenary Celebrations File — National Archives: RAIL253/720

10   *Ibid*

11   *Ibid*

12   *Bristol Daily Herald* 3 September 1935

13   See: Bryan, T.: *North Star — A Tale of Two Locomotives* (Thamesdown Museum Service, 1989)

14   'Banquet to Commemorate the Centenary of the Great Western Railway' (menu card), 30 October 1935 — STEAM archive

15   Great Western Railway: Centenary Celebrations File — National Archives: RAIL253/720

CHAPTER 12

SWINDON WORKS

Writing about Swindon a few years after the Grouping, the author Gordon Home described the 'long roofs of the works, with engines in every state of repair and standing on the sidings in the foreground, as the train leaves Swindon on its westward journey'.[1] Many of the locomotives awaiting repair were 'without paint, and to the ignorant their rusty appearance seems to suggest that they are fit for nothing but the scrap-heap,' he continued. His vivid account of the complex, including the 'hot' shops, where 'the strange orange-coloured glow from the molten metal' lit up 'the muscular arms and keen faces of the foundry-men as they ladle out the molten liquid,' was an evocative portrait of a place that had grown dramatically since its establishment almost a century before. The 310-acre site had been extensively modernised before 1914 and was well equipped to undertake the wide variety of tasks given by the War Department during the conflict.

The effects of the war on the workshops were much the same as those suffered elsewhere on the GWR; there were backlogs of maintenance and repairs, and staff who had enlisted returned only slowly after the signing of the Armistice. The war had interrupted the completion of the last major development in the Locomotive Works, this being an extension to the 'A' Erecting Shop, a huge building, covering more than 11 acres, that Churchward had planned for the construction and maintenance of his new locomotive fleet. Despite Churchward's recommendation, the GWR board had initially been unwilling to approve such a large scheme and commissioned a report by Sir William Plender, who after some deliberation agreed that the extension could go ahead.

Work progressed slowly during the war due to shortages of men and materials, and, as the new building was completed, sections were used for storage. With peace, work could begin on the completion and commissioning of the new workshops; the wheel shop was opened first, in March 1920, to be followed by the main erecting shop, the boiler shop section not being fully in use until 1923. Money had been drawn down at regular intervals, and the whole complex would cost the company £433,853 — a sum which encompassed not only the new building but also cranes, traversers, sidings and machinery.[2] Although the cost was high, it gave the company the resources to build and repair its locomotives for the next two decades. The board was asked for another large sum in 1920 when proposals for a new gasworks were submitted; as the size and complexity of the factory had increased, so had demand for gas, and a larger facility was required. The new retort house and additional gas holders were to cost well over £300,000, the biggest single request ever made to the board. After some debate the request was finally approved in July 1920, and the new gas works was completed two years later.

These developments put the works in a good position to move forward, but the poor state of the economy following the signing of the Armistice meant that returning to prewar conditions was not a straightforward process. The changed labour market had also affected relations between staff and management at Swindon; in January 1919, working hours for workshop staff were reduced from 54 to 47 per week, the first such change since 1870. Staff now worked from 8am to 5.30pm each weekday and from 7.30am to 12 noon on Saturdays. A company memorandum noted: 'If overtime is required, 30 minutes are allowed for tea and then 2 hours worked from 6pm to 8pm.'[3] Although discipline in the workshops was still strict, the rise of trade unionism and changing attitudes were a step too far for the old guard, particularly G. J. Churchward. Describing him as a man of 'high integrity and genial disposition' and his career as 'busy, arduous and valuable', the *Great Western Railway Magazine* reported a gathering at the Mechanics' Institute to mark his retirement in 1921;[4] a large collection had been made by the staff, but typically Churchward declined to accept all the money, keeping enough for some new fishing tackle but putting the rest into a trust fund to provide prizes for engineering students at Swindon Technical School.

C. B. Collett was, the company magazine reported, a worthy successor to Churchward and had paid 'close attention to the labour question, more particularly as affecting railway workshops,' adding that 'his intimate knowledge of this matter should prove of exceptional value alike to the management and the workers'. This telling phrase gives some hint of why Collett, instead of William Stanier, was chosen to lead the Chief Mechanical Engineer's Department. Although Stanier was a talented locomotive engineer in the mould of Churchward (and had been expected by many to get the top job), Collett's valuable experience as Locomotive Works Manager from 1912 to 1919 and background in production and manufacturing meant that he was ideally placed to steer the department through what was to be a difficult period.

The fleet of standard Churchward locomotives already in operation meant that, initially at least, Collett could deal with the other difficulties facing the railway, of which the most serious was a lack of new work for both the Locomotive Works and the Carriage & Wagon Works. After the completion of Churchward's pioneering '47xx' 2-8-0 in 1919, the board did not authorise any orders for new locomotives for almost three years, and apart from dealing with a number of ex-ROD locomotives returned from war service, staff had to be content with repair and maintenance work. Staff were put on short time on a number of occasions, and overtime working was also curtailed; in January 1922, a circular from Stanier to foremen announced, 'It is unfortunately necessary to revert to short time in all the shops in the locomotive works.' There was to be no work on Saturday mornings, men losing four and a half hours' pay, and night-shift workers suffered a similar cut. Workers in the carriage shops were also affected, the only new work available being the refurbishment of ambulance trains used during the war.

FAR LEFT Behind the doors of the tunnel entrance to the works at Swindon thousands are hard at work. Meanwhile a few men wait outside the factory, hoping for some temporary employment.

BELOW C. B. Collett, Chief Mechanical Engineer of the GWR from 1921 to 1941. Sometimes cool and aloof, and as a result never as well liked by the men, Collett delegated many of the civic duties expected of the post to his second-in-command, William Stanier.

With the Grouping in 1922/3, Collett had to manage the enormous task of amalgamating and assimilating the locomotive departments of the various railways that were now part of the enlarged GWR, as well as dealing with their locomotives and rolling stock. One of his first acts was to 'rationalise' the main works inherited from the various Welsh railways, at Barry, Cardiff, Caerphilly and Oswestry, repair and maintenance being henceforth concentrated at the erstwhile Rhymney Railway's works at Caerphilly. The existing works here had been opened as recently as 1901, and with the addition of a modern erecting shop and further reorganisation Caerphilly became the centre for the repair and overhaul of locomotives used in Wales.

The modernisation of Caerphilly would take some years, the work not being completed until 1926, so in the meantime Swindon bore the brunt of assessing and overhauling what the company called 'foreign' locomotives. More than 900 of these were added to the GWR locomotive roster in 1923, of which more than 700 came from six constituent railways. By the high standards expected by Churchward and Collett some of the locomotives arriving at Swindon must have presented a sorry sight; many were in a poor condition, but, as Alan Peck pointed out, while the company would have liked to scrap large numbers of non-standard designs, to have done so would have led to a shortage of motive power at a time when it lacked the capital necessary to build replacements.[5]

As an interim measure many locomotives passing through the works were 'Westernised' by the substitution of standard Swindon parts where practicable, which meant the replacement of boilers with standard GWR types. Three existing boiler designs were adapted for this purpose, and in many cases locomotive performance was dramatically improved; the process also included the fitting of new cabs, chimneys and the distinctive GWR safety-valve cover. Locomotives were also renumbered and fitted with standard cast numberplates; a circular issued in 1923 included the instruction that 'when constituent locomotives are repaired at Swindon, GWR numbers should be stamped on all parts'.[6] As finances improved, and new standard designs were built, older constituent locomotives were withdrawn and scrapped or sold. The January 1932 issue of the *Great Western Railway Magazine* listed the locomotives condemned the previous year, among them two that had been inherited from the Alexandra Docks company, three from the Cambrian Railways, four from the Taff Vale Railway, four from the Brecon & Merthyr and no fewer than 30 from the Barry Railway, these last including 16 0-6-2 tank engines.

ABOVE LEFT A Rhondda & Swansea Bay Kitson 0-6-2 tank engine after rebuilding by the GWR. The transformation included a new boiler, cab, tanks and safety-valve cover.

LEFT A works-grey official portrait of No 6685, one of the batch of '56xx' 0-6-2 tank engines built by the Armstrong Whitworth company.

The withdrawal of these locomotives was a result of the introduction of the '56xx' 0-6-2 class, a genuine piece of pragmatism by Collett. Many South Wales railways had utilised the 0-6-2 wheel arrangement, finding it ideal for their 'pit to port' coal trains. Collett therefore designed a locomotive closely based on the most successful of these, the Rhymney 'M' and 'R' classes, fitting it with a standard boiler and side tanks. The 62-ton '56xx' was powerful and well suited to hauling heavy coal trains in the Welsh valleys, the first 50 examples being completed in 1924/5, to be followed by a further 150 built by the GWR and Armstrong Whitworth in the years 1926-8.

By 1923, the erecting shops were busy again. The programme, as noted by the Works Manager in February, included the production of further Churchward standard designs, such as '42xx' 2-8-0 tank engines, '43xx' 2-6-0s and '45xx' 2-6-2 tanks.[7] The most significant new work was Lot 224, an order for 10 new four-cylinder express locomotives; these were the first of the 'Castle' class, described in Chapter 5. The completion of the first, No 4073 *Caerphilly Castle*, was not without its difficulties, and by March 1923 the Drawing Office had still not been able to issue a full list of parts to workshop managers and foremen to enable them to manufacture the parts required for the new locomotive. At the same time staff were also working on the construction of two new locomotives for the Vale of Rheidol Railway, which the GWR had absorbed as part of the Cambrian network. A circular issued in late June noted that, to ensure that No 4073 was completed on time and that the two narrow-gauge locomotives were also built quickly, three gangs were to work in the Erecting Shop during the 'Trip' holiday, when the rest of the workforce would be away.[8]

Caerphilly Castle made its debut in August 1923, and a further nine of the class had been built by 28 April 1924, when the works was included in a royal visit to Swindon by King George V and Queen Mary. The three-hour visit caused huge excitement in both the town and the works, and naturally extensive preparations were made beforehand, as surviving correspondence reveals. Collett had asked the Stores Department to supply decorations, and on 1 April it was reported that 48 Union Jacks, 49 ordinary flags, 50 lengths of streamers and various quantities of bunting, in different colours, were in stock.[9]

On the day, after arriving in Swindon at 2.10pm the Royal party travelled through the town, pausing at the Cenotaph to lay a wreath, before spending time at the Victoria Hospital. From there the King and Queen drove back to the Railway Village, where they met staff from the Medical Fund Hospital; before the visit its interior had been repainted by the GWR, while the Works Manager had been asked by Collett some days previously to 'remove a heap of rubbish from the Accident Hospital garden'.[10] The Royal party spent 90 minutes touring the works, visiting the carriage shops, saw mill, and foundry before entering 'A' Shop, where they inspected the locomotive test plant, the erecting shop and the wheel shop, on the way meeting a group of 76 staff veterans, each with more than 50 years' GWR service. The most notable event occurred at the end of the visit, when, instead of joining the Royal Train to depart for Windsor, as anticipated in the programme, the King and Queen boarded the footplate of No 4082 *Windsor Castle*, His Majesty taking the controls for the short trip to Swindon Junction.[11] This unannounced alteration to the programme was due in no small part to General Manager Sir Felix Pole, who was always quick to spot a chance for good press coverage.

In a speech delivered at a Swindon Corporation banquet on 3 November 1924, Pole noted that in the past year the company had paid out £3 million in wages to staff. 'It must have been a nice little contribution to the prosperity of Swindon and its trade,' he remarked; the total employed by the Great Western in the town was 15,946, prompting him to conclude that, with their wives and children, 'that is quite a little army'.[12] Staff numbers had increased, and Pole hoped they would continue to do so, although he did not think it 'desirable' to get to the stage where redundancies would have to take place, as they had done before.

In 1925, 73 new locomotives were built at Swindon, repair work increased significantly, and the steady recovery extended to the Carriage & Wagon Works, where more than 4,500 carriages and 15,000 wagons had been repaired.

This mood of optimism would be dashed in 1926 by the General Strike, and the consequences of the coal stoppage that followed were felt strongly in the works, as short-time working was once again enforced. Men worked from Tuesday to Friday, and the night shift worked from 10pm to 8am on Tuesday, Wednesday and Thursday each week. For some months after the strike the usual free passes issued to workers were also suspended, except for those required for 'Company business'.[13] However, whilst relations between workers and management must have been strained in the aftermath of the dispute, the annual Trip Holiday went ahead as usual between 5 and 13 July, although few Swindon families would have been able to afford to travel far.

The year 1926 also saw the end of an old Swindon tradition — the employment of 'office boys' employed to run errands around the factory. There had been complaints about their behaviour for

BELOW The surviving part of Brunel's original 1846 engine house, before it was swept away in 1929 to make room for an extension to the 'B' and 'R' shops.

RIGHT The Royal visit to Swindon in 1924. The party passing a number of pre-Grouping locomotives includes the GWR's Chairman, Viscount Churchill, walking with King George V. General Manager Felix Pole can be seen right at the back of the group, talking to a reporter.

BELOW RIGHT Queen Mary and C. B. Collett share a joke as they walk across the GWR main line from the Carriage Works to the Locomotive Works.

some years, and in a 1922 circular the Works Manager had told staff that his attention was 'constantly being drawn to the slackness that prevails amongst the office boys employed in the works' and that they should ask their chief shop clerk 'to take the lads in hand with a view to improving matters'.[14] A new system of 'messenger lads' reporting directly to the Locomotive Works Manager's Office was set up in August 1926 to prevent the 'loitering' of which many in the factory complained.

Despite the difficulties suffered by the GWR as a result of the General Strike and the ensuing slump, the works continued to produce new locomotives and rolling stock. The new 'King' class raised the profile of the factory further, and in 1927 organised public tours of the works began. Sir Felix Pole noted in his memoirs that the idea arose from a remark by Gordon Selfridge Jr, who in an address delivered to the GWR Lecture & Debating Society had urged him: 'You have just sent one of your engines to America and people are talking about it. Don't you think a large number of people would like to see where it was built?'[15] Thus was born a tradition, beloved of schoolboys and trainspotters, that was to continue on Wednesday afternoons until the 1980s.

The Great Western was also able to use money from the 1929 Development (Loans and Guarantees) Act to finance a number of projects at Swindon Works. Amongst the initial list submitted by the company was a request for £65,000 for the 'rearrangement of locomotive shops' which involved the extension of the 'B' Repair

Shop, close to the main line. One consequence of this work was the demolition of the works' earliest buildings, which had constituted Brunel's original running shed. A more substantial project was the construction of No 24 Shop in the Carriage Works; occupying 7½ acres, the building was situated on a piece of land north of the existing Carriage & Wagon complex and close to the old Wilts & Berks Canal, which had been acquired by the railway from Swindon Corporation in 1925 in exchange for the GWR Park in the Railway Village.

Opened in 1930, 24 Shop was the last major development on the works site before World War 2; used for carriage repairs and painting, it had 28 tracks and could accommodate 250 coaches. Next door was another new facility — the Carriage Disinfecting Plant (or 'Bug House', as the men called it), which was built for the destruction of vermin and bacteria in coaches and other vehicles. Inside the building was a steel cylinder 85ft long and of 16ft 6in diameter, complete with rails, which could be sealed with an air-

tight door. Creating a vacuum and raising the temperature to 49°C for six hours eradicated vermin, and, in the case of vehicles exposed to infectious diseases, formaldehyde gas was used to disinfect everything inside the carriage, including cushions, bolsters and rugs.[16]

A further scheme, costing £73,000, involved the creation of a new 'Concentration Yard' at the west end of the works. A contemporary guide to the works noted that it had been laid out with a view to 'considerable economies' resulting from the handling of all scrap, including 'the cutting up of condemned locomotives, boilers, tenders etc'.[17] The 'C' Shop building housed shearing machines and cutting equipment; in the yard Goliath cranes were provided, including one with a large drop-ball for smashing large castings. The yard was situated on 'built up' land created by the tipping of ashes and cinders from the many furnaces and boilers on the works site, and it would be a very busy place after 1930 as 'absorbed' and older GWR locomotives were scrapped, having been replaced by new Collett designs.

Despite the provision of Government money to modernise parts of the works, the effects of the Depression were felt strongly by the company and the workforce. The slump, particularly in the coal trade and the docks, caused a reduction in income, notably from goods traffic. This in turn meant a sharp reduction in wagon repairs and construction, and short time was introduced again from August 1930. Business was so bad that the new 24 Shop, completed earlier in the year, remained half-empty until trade picked up. Short time and lay-offs would continue for

ABOVE LEFT A snowy photograph showing work proceeding on the construction of 24 Shop in the Carriage & Wagon Works in February 1932. The cottage, a relic of the old Wilts & Berks Canal that ran in the cutting in front of the new workshop, appears still to be occupied.

LEFT The interior of the 'Bug House', officially the Carriage Disinfecting Plant. *Author's collection*

BELOW Collett 'Hall' 4-6-0 No 5919 *Worsley Hall*, photographed at Swindon in 1931 on account of its new experimental eight-wheel tender. Subsequently this tender would be attached to various other 'Halls' and 'Castles' until withdrawn in the 1960s.

the next few years, the total complement of staff at the works dropping to 10,000 from the 14,000 employed in the early 1920s. Hugh Freebury, describing his apprenticeship in the works in the 1930s, remembered the stress and anxiety felt by people in Swindon during the Depression. Rumours would often circulate around the factory and town to the effect that men were to be 'let go' in the next week or fortnight, making it a very uncertain time for staff and their families.[18] The Great Western Medical Fund Society, which provided health care for workers through a weekly contribution from their wages, reported in 1932 that membership was down by 4,000 and that to cope with 'the extraordinary situation created by the large scale dismissals of members from the GWR and to prevent distress' the Society had decided to allow unemployed workers to retain membership, provided they could make contributions.[19]

As the 1920s drew to a close, the ambitious build programme was continuing apace, despite the continuing drop in revenue suffered by the Great Western, the construction of new locomotives being made possible by drawings from company reserves. K. J. Cook recalled, 'In the late 1920s and 1930s, when revenue was low, the renewal fund was in a very healthy position, and with prices stable at that time it gave us considerable assistance in meeting our commitments.'[20] With most of the work done on re-boilering and refurbishment of absorbed locomotives, Collett was able to turn his attention back to producing designs to replace ageing pre-1914 locomotives large and small. In 1924, 'Saint' 4-6-0 No 2925 *Saint Martin* had been modified by fitting 6ft (instead of 6ft 8in) driving wheels, and this locomotive ran around the system for four years before its excellent performance as a mixed-traffic design led to the creation of the 'Hall' class. An initial order for 80 locomotives, placed in 1927, was fulfilled by the end of 1930, and a further 249 examples of this basic design would be built over the course of the next 20 years.

There has been much debate over the conservative locomotive policy pursued by Collett, particularly in the 1930s. There is little doubt that he was content to refine the standard locomotive policy laid down by Churchward, and the departure of Stanier in 1931 to become CME of the LMS was a severe blow. Collett was, however, able to make good use of the 'Renewal' fund during what were undeniably stringent times. In the period 1936-9, some 80 mixed-traffic 'Grange' 4-6-0 locomotives were built using the wheels, motion and tenders of withdrawn '43xx' 2-6-0s, and 20 smaller 'Manors' were produced in the same manner. Both classes were reliable and well liked, the 'Manors' being used extensively on Cambrian lines.

Another ingenious 'renewal' was undertaken when Works Manager K. J. Cook saw two elderly 4-4-0s, a 'Duke' built in 1896 and a 1903-built 'Bulldog', next to each other inside the works. By combining the frames of the 'Bulldog' with cab, boiler and smokebox fittings from the 'Duke' a new locomotive was

created. After some months in traffic the solitary locomotive was deemed a success, so the entire 'Duke' class was so treated in the period 1936-9. The resultant locomotives were named after earls, these including a number of GWR directors. However, despite the clever recycling of parts, the locomotives still looked antiquated, and it was reported that many distinguished earls were less than amused to find their names on such ancient locomotives. The names were subsequently removed and given to 'Castle' class locomotives, many believing that Collett, a man who hated pomposity, had deliberately chosen to name the rebuilds in this manner.

Despite 'renewing' larger passenger locomotives, the GWR still had many old tank locomotives in use for shunting and branch-line work. These were in urgent need of replacement, and the appearance in 1929 of the first of the ubiquitous '57xx' pannier tanks allowed many older and less powerful locomotives to be withdrawn.[21] The '48xx' (later '14xx') 0-4-2 tank engines introduced three years later were designed to work lighter push-

BELOW William Stanier, Collett's assistant until his move in 1931 to become Chief Mechanical Engineer of the LMS.

RIGHT The scene at the new GWR Laundry at Swindon, not long after opening. The ladies are working on the ironing machine, which is pressing towels for use in hotels, stations and buffet cars.

BELOW RIGHT The Mechanics' Institute at Swindon following its rebuilding after the serious fire of 1930. Large posters advertise Saturday-night dances and a new drama production at the Playhouse Theatre.

pull trains on branch lines, and their success led to the eventual phasing out of the steam railmotors which, as Cook noted, were 'rather a trouble in the works', as the steam boiler and bogie had to be overhauled in the locomotive shops and the carriage section taken separately to the Carriage Works for repair.[22]

G. J. Churchward, who had been such an influence on Collett's work and on Swindon and the GWR as a whole, died in tragic circumstances in December 1933, being run down and killed by the 10.20am Paddington–Fishguard express as it passed through Swindon, close to the works. It appeared that he had noticed a loose rail joint on the track close to Newburn House, the GWR property he had lived in since his retirement in 1922. Having never married, Churchward had continued to be a regular visitor to the works, and his death came as a huge shock to the workforce and the town as a whole.

Although life for GWR workers was difficult between the wars, they could rely on a number of organisations to provide vital services and facilities. The Medical Fund and the Mechanics' Institute were both independent bodies, but from time to time they benefited from financial assistance from the company. The GWR Hospital in Emlyn Square was extended in 1926 with the assistance of a £4,000 loan from the GWR, although the company had a vested interest in supporting the hospital, as, according to

the Medical Fund Surgeon, under the Factories Act 'the hospital's primary function is the treatment of accidents occurring in the works'.[23] Accidents were still common in the works, and, although St John Ambulance-trained workers were very capable, on occasions Medical Fund doctors were called into the Factory to give emergency treatment.

The Medical Fund provided a vital and high-quality healthcare service for staff and their families, and its annual reports reveal that it dealt with a wide variety of ailments. In 1931, the Dental Department performed 16,457 extractions but only 2,035 fillings. The Fund also provided a funeral service for members and even in this period members could still hire a horse-drawn 'Shillibeer' for funerals, and in 1931, it was in service 143 times, although the increased use of the Whitworth Road cemetery, several miles from the Railway Village, led to the acquisition of a 'motor hearse'.

The Mechanics' Institute building in the centre of the Railway Village continued to be a hive of activity, and the Playhouse Theatre, situated within, staged musical events and touring productions. Disaster struck on Christmas Eve 1930, when the centre of the building was badly damaged by fire; the Institute was saved, but the theatre had to be completely rebuilt, with a rather ugly brick 'fly-tower' added which enabled larger theatrical productions to be staged in later years but did little for the aesthetics of the building.

The Institute continued to run two major events in the Swindon calendar, of which the Children's Fête, in Faringdon Road Park, had been held since 1866 and attracted thousands of children from railway families. In 1939, entertainment included 'The Great Blondini, King of the High Wire', Punch & Judy and other fairground attractions, while the main highlight was a piece of fruit cake, made every year to the same secret recipe, supplied at 3d per slice with tea.[24]

The other annual event organised by the Institute was the Trip Holiday. An article in the company magazine in August 1933 reported that the 'town was depleted of half its population' in a few hours on the night of 13 July and early the next morning, when staff and families left for their annual holiday. The exodus of a staggering 27,416 people required 31 special trains, 24 of which carried more than 23,000. The arrangements, which always began early in the year, were described in the press as 'a piece of organisation without equal in the world of transport'.[25] Holidays were unpaid until 1938, but most workers tried to get away with their families, even for a short break, and although Weymouth and Weston-super-Mare were always the most popular resorts for Swindon trippers, more intrepid travellers visited places like Blackpool and even Scotland using the free tickets issued to them by the company. Whatever the destination, it helped provide a welcome diversion for staff, especially in the worst years of the Depression.[26]

BELOW This Drawing Office print from Swindon Works was produced to illustrate 'Trip Friday' — the day before the great exodus to holiday destinations. Stead & Simpson is offering 'Bargains for Trip', and the town is full of shoppers, although the weather is none too promising, judging from the wet road.

TOP FAR RIGHT Eager trippers make their way along the sidings next to Swindon Works on Trip morning in July 1934.

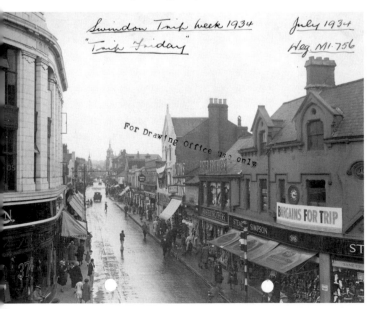

1   Home, G.: *Peeps at Great Railways: The Great Western Railway* (A. & C. Black, 1926), p46

2   Peck, A. S.: *The Great Western at Swindon Works* (Oxford Publishing Co, 1983), p188

3   GWR Locomotive, Carriage & Wagon Department, Swindon: Memorandum No 2621, 1 January 1919

4   *Great Western Railway Magazine* January 1922, p23

5   Peck, *ibid*, p197

6   GWR Locomotive Department, Swindon: Circular No 2874, 1 June 1923

7   GWR Locomotive Department, Swindon: Circular No 2859, 23 February 1923

8   GWR Locomotive Department, Swindon: Circular No 2882, 28 June 1923

9   Great Western Railway: Royal Visit Correspondence, Swindon Works, 1924 — Peck Collection, STEAM archive

10 *Ibid*

11 'Visit of Their Majesties the King and Queen to Swindon, 28 April 1924' (official programme)

12 *Swindon Evening Advertiser* 7 November 1924

13 GWR Works Manager, Swindon: Circular, 27 May 1926

14 GWR Works Manager, Swindon: Circular, 31 August 1922

15 Pole, F. J. C.: *His Book* (Town & Country Press, 1968), p92

16 *Great Western Railway Magazine* January 1933, p71

17 Great Western Railway: *Swindon Works and its part in Great Western History* (GWR, 1935), p33

18 Freebury, H.: *Great Western Apprentice* (Wiltshire Museums Service, 1985), p96

19 GWR Medical Fund: Annual Report for 1932

20 Cook, K. J.: *Swindon Steam 1921–1951* (Ian Allan, 1974), p114

21 *Ibid*, p84

22 *Ibid*, p89

23 GWR Medical Fund: Annual Report for 1926

24 Cockbill, T.: *Our Swindon in 1939* (Quill Press, 1989)

25 *Great Western Railway Magazine* August 1933, p336

26 For further details see Matheson, R.: *Trip — The Annual Holiday for GWR's Swindon Works* (History Press, 2006)

CHAPTER 13

PRELUDE TO WAR

After all the positive publicity the company had gained during its centenary in 1935, the turn of the year brought unwelcome and tragic headlines. On 15 January 1936, Driver Ernest Starr and Fireman J. H. Cozens were in charge of No 6007 *King William III* on the up sleeper service, which had left Penzance at 9pm the previous evening. Shortly after 5am on this foggy morning, as the train reached Shrivenham, five miles east of Swindon, it collided with a brake van and four loaded wagons that had become separated from a 53-wagon coal train from Aberdare. The signalman at Shrivenham

box had accepted the express without realising that the coal train had become divided due to a broken coupling, and the express train ploughed into the brake van and wagons at around 55mph, derailing the 'King' and its leading carriages. Driver Starr was killed, as was a female passenger in the leading coach of the express; 10 other passengers were seriously injured.

The signalmen at Shrivenham and the next box at Ashbury Crossing had both failed to check the tail lights of the goods train and so had no idea that the last few wagons were blocking the main line. The guard of the coal train was also at fault, assuming that it had come to a halt at a loop further up the line. He told the Railway Inspector who investigated the crash that, after the train had come to a halt, 'a glance to the rear … showed to my horror an express approaching on me'. He had time only to wave his lamp in the direction of the sleeper service, by which time it was too late. While the Ministry of Transport report concluded that the accident was due in some part to the failure of the wagon coupling, the Inspector noted that the main cause was 'not the outcome of forgetfulness, incapacity, or overwork, but of failure on the part of two signalmen to perform a simple and fundamental duty, together with lack of zeal and alertness on the part of a guard'.[1]

The guard, along with the two signalmen, were dismissed as a result of their errors, while the locomotive was taken back to Swindon Works for examination and eventual rebuilding. The death of the passenger on the sleeper was the first fatality on the GWR for 20 years; 'The regrettable accident brings into relief the remarkable immunity from mishap that hitherto has been experience by Great Western passenger trains,' noted the company magazine, also praising the bravery of Driver Starr, who remained on the footplate and, when released from the wreckage, fatally injured, still had his hand on the brake.[2]

Only a few days later the GWR had to deal with another sombre occasion — the funeral of King George V, who had died at Sandringham on 20 January. In its account of the funeral arrangements eight days later the *Great Western Railway Magazine* reported that at Paddington 'an unaccustomed quietness pervaded the station'. The new king, Edward VIII, presented a 'tired, sad but regal feature,' it continued.[3] In addition to the funeral train, hauled by No 4082 *Windsor Castle*, the company ran five special trains to Windsor for dignitaries. The new monarch was honoured by the GWR some weeks later No 6029 *King Stephen* had its nameplates removed and was renamed *King Edward VIII*. However, 1936 became known as the 'Year of Three Kings' when on 10 December, Edward abdicated so that he could marry twice-divorced American socialite Wallis Simpson, and his brother became king. No 6028 *King Henry II* was duly renamed *King George VI* in January 1937, No 6029 retaining its new name, despite the abdication.

In an attempt to obliterate the humiliating events of the abdication from the public consciousness, no expense was spared for the coronation of the new king in May 1937, which is estimated to have cost more than £500,000 — two and a half times that of his father. Visitors arriving in London found many of its main stations transformed. The Great Western, 'realising that the work of nature can often delight the eye better than the hand of man, and perhaps

inspired by the name of the Lawn … decorated that part of the station with magnificent red, white, and blue flowering plants and ferns, some in hanging baskets and others clustered around the tops of pillars,' reported *The Railway Gazette*.[4]

Visitors to Paddington in 1937 would have also noted that the Great Western Royal Hotel, largely unaltered for almost 80 years, had finally been modernised after some years of building work linked to the reconstruction of the terminus itself. The interior had been extensively updated, and the exterior cleaned, removing years of soot and grime. By filling in basements at the front a new entrance road for taxis had been created, while the old *porte-cochère* had been removed. 'No longer will dear old ladies with flowers approach the hotel porter and inquire for a particular ward mistaking it for St Mary's Hospital,' reported the company magazine.[5] In the West Country two of the company's other hotels had already been modernised by 1936; the Tregenna Castle Hotel at St Ives, described in *Holiday Haunts* as a 'charming mansion', had been converted into 'one of the most comfortable hotels in the provinces', while the Manor House Hotel at Moretonhampstead provided the visitor 'with the latest comforts known to hotel science', including new garage accommodation for cars — a sure sign of the changing times.[6]

ABOVE LEFT The exterior of the Great Western Royal Hotel at Paddington, photographed after its refurbishment. To the left was a new block of offices provided for GWR headquarters staff in Westbourne Terrace.

RIGHT A refreshment trolley at Paddington, photographed in 1937.

For Drawing Office use only.

THE ROYAL COAT OF ARMS AS FIXED

FOR FUNERAL TRAIN OF KING GEORGE V.

NEW ED 20.1

PHOTOD 28 1 3

At its Annual General Meeting in 1937 the Chairman, Viscount Horne, noted that in the past five years the company had experienced 'one of the worst periods of trade depression ever known in this country'. Although he thought business would revive, he reported that the 'continued recourse to reserves' for investment in the railway had caused the company a 'good deal of anxiety'. More positive, however, was the fact that this was the first year since 1930 that earnings had been sufficient to cover payment of the 3% dividend to shareholders without dipping into those reserves.[7] There was certainly some optimism as trade generally began to improve. The year 1936 had been a record one for Swindon Works, which turned out 149 new and reconstructed locomotives, including 15 'Castles', eight 'Halls', 20 'Granges', eight 'Earls' and, effectively, a new 'King', a replacement No 6007 having been constructed after the Shrivenham accident, using some components salvaged from the original. The works also turned out more than 80 tank engines, while more than 1,000 locomotives had undergone heavy repairs, a further 1,100 having received light repairs. It was also a busy year for the Carriage & Wagon Works, which had built 393 carriages — another record.

Amongst the output of the Carriage & Wagon Works were 10 milk-tank trucks and more than 40 milk vans. By the 1930s, the transportation of milk by rail was changing significantly with the gradual phasing-out of milk churns, and increasingly the GWR was supplying the capital with milk in glass-lined tank wagons; the milk was transported by road from farms to creameries and then, once processed, to London in express trains hauled by 'Hall' or even 'Castle'class locomotives. In 1927, four-wheeled tank wagons had been introduced with a capacity of 3,000 gallons, compared with the wagons used to convey churns which could hold only 1,156 gallons. In 1933, larger, six-wheeled wagons were introduced; in addition, flat wagons were built that could accommodate road tankers as well.

Although coal played a significant part in generating income for the company, the Goods Department handled a wide variety of other loads; in 1936, it argued that it had made 'cheapness, rapidity and convenience in freight transportation its specialised study' and that 'it will be found that the Company can arrange a rapid, safe and cheap method of transportation for all classes of freight traffic'.[8] As well as continuing to carry staples like milk and foodstuffs, the GWR continued to advertise its express goods services, which carried products such as fruit, vegetables, meat and other perishable items. Goods dispatched in the evening would, the GWR assured customers, be 'delivered to the London and provincial markets in the early hours of the next morning to ensure that the best prices are secured for commodities'.[9] The speed and regularity of these vacuum-braked express services were 'unsurpassed elsewhere in the world,' the company boasted in 1936.

Many of these regular trains were named — a 'term of affection', the Goods Department argued, 'something that enhances the mere duty to ensure prompt dispatch and the elimination of all possible delays'.[10] The GWR had pioneered the 'Green Arrow' service, which guaranteed the delivery of urgent consignments of goods in 1929. The idea had been suggested by Felix Pole, but other 'Big Four' managers were nervous that such an idea might be too risky. Pole decided that the GWR would go ahead on its own. Despite the reservations of the Goods Manager, the scheme was a success, and in 1933 the other companies finally adopted similar schemes.[11] In 1935, no fewer than 135,821 'Green Arrow' consignments were handled by the company.

One particular perishable traffic that developed between the wars was broccoli. Although this had been carried in small quantities prior to 1914, by the 1930s it was a significant, albeit seasonal, source of income. In 1928 just over 13,000 tons of

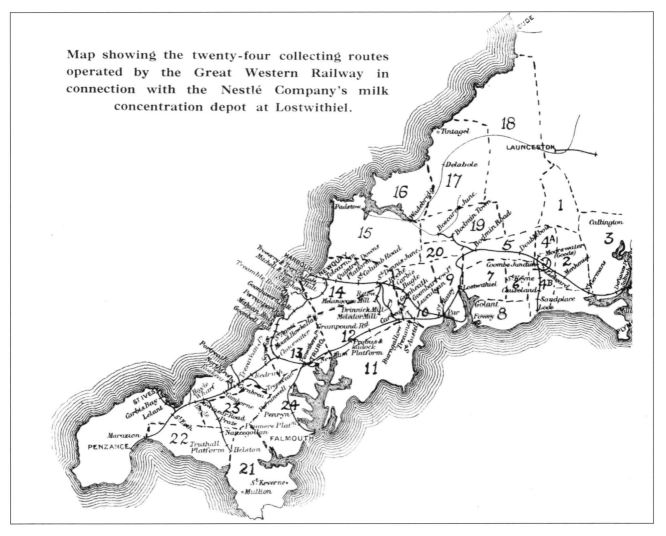

Map showing the twenty-four collecting routes operated by the Great Western Railway in connection with the Nestlé Company's milk concentration depot at Lostwithiel.

broccoli was moved by the GWR but this figure grew steadily so that by the late 1930's the quantities being transported from Devon and Cornwall were setting new records, with a total of 41,474 tons being shifted in 1938 alone . A year later more than 22,000 wagons were being used for Cornish broccoli alone, and the rise in demand had required sidings and loading docks to be enlarged at a number of stations.

The railway was forced to work very hard to generate new goods business, especially in the 1930s, in order to compete with road transport. One innovation was the introduction of 'road-rail' containers that could be carried both by lorries and by railway wagons. The GWR argued that the lorry was 'in effect a giant packing case into which goods may be packed at the sender's premises' and provided large numbers of different sizes capable of carrying all manner of loads, from bicycles to builders' materials. Linked to these developments, the company also established its own household removal service. This experience, it recognised, 'even in the most favourable circumstances, may be troublesome, but the anxieties attendant upon such occasions disappear if the whole of the work is entrusted to the removal experts of the GWR'.[12] A special container was utilised, and the service included the packing and transit of furniture and belongings while passengers travelled by train to their new home on discounted tickets.

In 1937, goods revenue, excluding coal, had been £9,493,000 — £405,000 more than in 1936; these encouraging figures were due to a steady revival of industry along with the growth of industrial and factory developments. The year saw the opening of 52 new factories in areas served by the Great Western, 21 of them in South Wales. Most of these ventures were in light industry, some, like the industrial estate at Treforest, benefiting from Government funding. There were also other developments around Bristol, Birmingham and Liverpool, as well as nearer London, where the GWR promoted sites at Hayes, Park Royal, Perivale and Slough. It also provided assistance to companies looking to relocate, maintaining a register of suitable sites; if seeking a location for a new factory 'you will be well advised to consult the company's Chief Goods Manager on the subject,' a GWR publication concluded. To boost traffic further, the railway also offered competitive costs for connecting factories to the network and providing private sidings. Traffic Committee minutes in the 1930s note many examples of companies applying for connections; in 1935, Courtaulds at Bridgwater paid the GWR £4,365 for private siding access, and in

the same year a new siding at Tavistock for the local gas company was authorised at a cost of £415.[13]

In tandem with increased goods traffic the Road Motor Department continued to grow. With the its former omnibus services now in the hands of companies like Western National, the GWR concentrated instead on modernising its cartage and delivery fleet. The policy of replacing horses with motor vehicles continued, and in 1934 it was reported that the company had ordered 396 motor vehicles, at a cost of £156,500. This order was one of a number placed in the 1930s to try to complete the motorisation of cartage fleets at Paddington, Smithfield and South Lambeth, and, increasingly, mechanical 'horses' replaced the flesh-and-blood variety.[14] The rise in parcels traffic and other ventures, such as the Country Lorry service and the household removal scheme, also required more lorries and vans. The Great Western's efforts probably came too late to regain business already lost to independent road hauliers, but they nevertheless generated valuable income and positive publicity.

By 1937, most of the major improvement schemes on the GWR had been completed, but a number of important projects still remained to be tackled. In October of that year the Traffic Committee sanctioned the expenditure required to rebuild the station at Leamington Spa. The scheme included longer and wider platforms, a stylish new art-deco station building and new station approach roads. The old station retained some parts of the original 1853 structure and had grown very shabby and

LEFT An unidentified 'Castle' races along the seafront between Dawlish and Teignmouth with a West of England express in the 1930s.

ABOVE The introduction of milk tanks in the 1930s led to the gradual phasing-out of churns such as these, pictured with GWR staff at Highbridge in 1928. *Philip Kelley collection*

outdated. Two contracts were required, the first to create a new forecourt, build retaining walls and excavate a new subway under the railway. The second, undertaken by Holliday & Greenwood, was a £35,353 contract to build the three-storey steel-framed station building. Faced with Portland stone, the elegant structure housed the booking hall and parcels office on the ground floor and, at platform level, a refreshment room, a bookstall, toilets and the stationmaster's office. Despite the disruption, the station remained open while the work was in progess, this finally being completed in 1939. The new station matched the sophisticated spa town of Leamington, and, to complete the work, the Corporation presented the GWR with a new clock for the booking hall.[15]

At the GWR's Annual General Meeting in February 1938, Viscount Horne informed shareholders that 1937 had been the best year experienced by the company since 1930, trade at the docks showing decided improvement, with coal exports up by 3 million tons. The general situation looked brighter, with industrial production and retail sales at record levels and even iron, steel and coal production improved. He was also able to report that the

company's contingency fund amounted to a healthy £3,166,448. Despite a reduction in trade in the second half of the year, the Chairman told the meeting that there were still 'good reasons for anticipating a further improvement in our business'. However, the worsening situation in Europe was clearly on the minds of many, as it was becoming apparent that Adolf Hitler had ambitions beyond the postwar recovery of Germany, and Horne noted that 'no man would be so imprudent as to predict what troubles may emerge in the near future from the clash of rulers or the rivalries of nations'.[16] Evidence of growing international tension could also be gleaned from the company magazine, which from 1935 carried increasing number of small articles and photographs featuring GWR Territorial Army and Royal Engineering units.

During the meeting the Chairman had specifically mentioned the impact of increasing commodity prices on the GWR. The rising price of coal was of particular concern, as, for every shilling it rose, the company's annual fuel bill increased by £100,000. The announcement early in 1938 that the GWR had asked the engineering firm of Merz & McLellan to investigate the electrification of part of its network is not so surprising in this context, although the choice of lines to be electrified was less obvious. The consultant engineers were asked to look at the West of England main line from Taunton to Penzance, the Kingswear and Newquay branch lines, and a number of other goods lines in Cornwall. This was not the first time that the company had considered electrification; in the early 1920s, it had commissioned

ABOVE The use of containers revolutionised the GWR cartage business. Two are seen here being used as part of the company's household removal service in 1936. *Philip Kelley collection*

LEFT A page from a GWR leaflet advertising weekly season tickets for holidaymakers in 1938. *Great Western Trust collection*

TOP RIGHT The new Parcels Department at Paddington, built as part of the station's reconstruction and pictured here in November 1938. *Philip Kelley collection*

BOTTOM RIGHT An architect's sketch of the proposed station building at Leamington Spa, taken from the May 1937 issue of the *Great Western Railway Magazine*.

reports on the feasibility of introducing electric traction to both the South Wales valleys and on main-line routes from London to Bristol and from London to Birmingham.[17] None of these schemes had been considered economically viable, and the new proposals also showed only modest savings, of around £100,000 per year, after a capital outlay of more than £4 million. The report by Merz & McLellan was discussed at a board meeting in March 1939, and after hearing the views of the General Manager, James Milne, the directors agreed 'that no further action should be taken on the matter'.[18]

By the summer of 1938, the economic recovery appeared to have stalled; coal exports were down by 16%, and in September it was reported that GWR revenues were down by £818,000 — results that meant that no interim dividend would be paid to shareholders, a worrying development. Trade was particularly bad in South Wales, where, despite efforts by Government and industry, coal mining and iron and steel production were struggling, and unemployment was extremely high. The GWR played a key part in trying to resuscitate the coal industry in South Wales, Viscount Horne for some years chairing a committee seeking to improve business in the area. Nevertheless, many commentators, notably J. B. Priestley, highlighted the increasingly sharp contrast between the relative prosperity of the Home Counties and suburbia with the Welsh mining villages, where poverty and deprivation was the norm.[19] One writer noted after the war that the 'squalor associated with technical achievement, wide exploitation and unemployment' was much in evidence and that the towns and villages were 'for the greater part

mean, drab creations each with its terraces of *papier mâché* houses piled higgledy-piggledy on the gashed mountainside'.[20]

The increasingly tense situation in Europe in the summer of 1938 led many to realise that another war was extremely likely, and at the end of September the Munich Crisis precipitated a national emergency which involved the evacuation of parts of the civilian population from London by special trains and the transfer of patients from major hospitals, to allow them to escape possible air raids. The Great Western initiated a pre-planned programme over three days, which on the first day involved the evacuation of children from London schools and on the two succeeding days clearing the remainder of the 'refugees'. The GWR ran more than 200 trains over the period, destinations including 30 stations in the provinces where, it was thought, there would be little risk of air attack. Similar arrangements were also organised for children in Birmingham. In addition, the railway ran 40 hospital trains accommodating stretcher cases.[21]

For some days immediately preceding the Munich Agreement, signed on 30 September 1938, there were busy scenes at Paddington as a result of a considerable exodus to the West of England and South Wales by people who wanted to get out of London. As it had done during the Great War, the railway also ran a large number of special trains in relation to the mobilisation of the fleet and the movement of military personnel. Following Neville Chamberlain's return from Munich and the promise of 'peace in our time' the tension was reduced, and those who had fled to the country travelled back, making for further busy days at the London terminus. The whole operation had run very smoothly, and management at Paddington learned much that would come in useful a year later, when war was actually declared.

The vital work undertaken by railways during the national emergency proved a useful tool in a national campaign waged by the 'Big Four' railways several months after the crisis. 'The Railways Ask for a Square Deal' was the headline of the campaign for the removal of outdated legislation which prevented them from competing on equal terms with their road competitors. The difficult economic situation had affected the GWR badly, but others, notably the LNER, were in even worse difficulties, and the railways jointly argued that their viability and very existence were at stake. The campaign used posters, leaflets, newspaper advertisements and included speeches by prominent supporters and railway chairmen. 'The time-honoured shackles which fetter the railways alone and well-nigh strangle their traffic must go, and they must go before it is too late,' argued the railways.[22] The press campaign appeared to have worked, and there was a good deal of sympathy from newspapers such as *The Times*, which asked readers: 'Dare we let the railways die? Can any means of transport other than railways evacuate in 48 hours London's millions, Birmingham's million, Liverpool's million, and millions from other danger zones?[23] The Minister of Transport appeared to agree, referring the matter to the Transport Advisory Council in the spring of 1939. Legislation to relax some of the restrictions on railways was ready to be enacted, but the outbreak of World War 2 and the creation of the Railway Executive Committee prevented the introduction of the Bill.

By the time shareholders had assembled for the company's Annual General Meeting in March 1939, both the economic and the diplomatic situation had deteriorated further. Viscount Horne reminded the meeting that 1938 had been a 'year of prolonged tension and unrelieved anxiety', with the 'happy anticipations of 1937 destroyed'. The year had gone from bad to worse,

One of a number of posters and hoardings erected at major stations by the 'Big Four' railways as part of their campaign for the lifting of some of the restrictions imposed on them by legislation. The publicity campaign was generally a success, but the war overtook any progress in implementing changes conceded by Government.

ABOVE A postcard view of Collett-designed 0-4-2T No 4805 stabled next to 2-6-2T No 5521 outside Swindon Works in February 1938. Although a relatively new design, the '48xx' was considered by many to look somewhat dated, its appearance harking back to the Edwardian era. *Author's collection*

BELOW The scene at Paddington in September 1938, when, as a result of the international tension generated by the Munich Crisis, the GWR carried out an evacuation that was a forerunner of a more wide-ranging exercise undertaken out when war broke out the following year.

international trade being down 10%. Industry could not 'thrive in apprehension and uncertainty', he argued, and the GWR could not attribute all its problems to the threat of war. Indeed, the company had benefited to some extent from the process of rearmament, carrying building materials and supplies to new shadow-factory sites and opening up new sidings for military traffic. In December 1937, the Traffic Committee approved two new War Department schemes: sidings facilities at Bridgend costing £16,100, and lines at Corsham and Thingley costing £4,520.[24]

However, the Chairman believed that, while the GWR might have had some benefit from War Department projects, rearmament as a whole had not had a huge influence on the general trade of the country. The annual income of £5,043,753 was the lowest net figure achieved by the GWR since 1933 and would have been worse still had there not been economies, notably the curtailment of the rolling-stock renewal programme, the impact of which was to precipitate a further round of lay-offs at Swindon.

As 1937 progressed, and the 'scenic ride to catastrophe' predicted by George Orwell continued, the Civil Defence and Air Raid precautions planned by the company for some years were prepared and tested. That year, the Great Western, along with the other 'Big Four' railways, London Transport and the

Home Office, had been part of a group discussing air-raid precautions for railways, which, the Government realised, were especially vulnerable to air attack. The measures needed to protect railways and their staff were estimated as costing more than £3 million — a sum the Government eventually agreed to pay. In 1937 a circular headed 'Air Raid Precautions' was issued to all staff, informing them that arrangements were being put in place for the protection of company personnel and property. Within a year, as thoughts turned to when (rather than if) there would be a war, the GWR convened its own ARP committee, which drew up detailed plans, and training schools were established in Bristol, Birmingham, Cardiff, Newport, Plymouth and Swindon to provide instruction for staff, particularly on anti-gas measures.

Reporting to the board, the General Manager identified a number of further ARP measures that needed to be addressed, including the protection of control centres, signalboxes and telephone exchanges from blast damage, the provision of additional civil engineering supplies for use in an emergency, and the provision of protective clothing and fire-fighting equipment. These measures and further expenditure on lighting would, he estimated, cost £500,000, while another £200,000 would be required for training company staff in air raid precautions. The board approved this expenditure in January 1939, money being drawn both from reserves and from the contingency fund.[25]

The most testing task facing the railway was the reduction of lighting levels in stations, depots and yards. It was clearly impossible, for both operational and safety reasons, to impose a total blackout, and there was much experimentation in terms of screening signal, yard and station lights and providing lower-wattage bulbs where practical. A major test of blackout measures at Paddington and Old Oak Common was carried out on 28 and 29 January 1939, with enough success to allow the GWR to plan and install measures for the coming conflict.

The preparations made by the GWR and its staff in the months and years before the outbreak of war on 3 September 1939 meant that, when the time came, it was in a high state of readiness for the conflict, and well-rehearsed plans for air-raid precautions and the evacuation of the civilian population could be quickly put into effect. In October 1939, James Milne told staff that, in the previous few months, 'we fully shared a general hope that a way would be found to prevent the catastrophe of a European war'. Unfortunately, he concluded, 'despite the nation's fervent wishes and our Government's best endeavours, war has come'.[26] After more than 20 years of tumultuous change for the GWR, the railway was now faced with an even bigger challenge — another world war.

1 *Report on the collision of an express passenger train at Shrivenham* (Ministry of Transport, 25 February 1936)
2 *Great Western Railway Magazine* February 1936, p71
3 *Ibid*, pp61-64
4 *The Railway Gazette* 21 May 1937, p977
5 *Great Western Railway Magazine* May 1937, p177
6 Great Western Railway: *Holiday Haunts* (GWR, 1936), p278
7 *Great Western Railway Magazine* February 1937, p104
8 Great Western Railway: *Guide to Economical Transport* (GWR, Paddington, 1936), p5
9 *Ibid*, p22
10 *Ibid*, p23
11 Pole, F. J. C.: *His Book* (Town & Country Press, 1968)
12 Great Western Railway: *Guide to Economical Transport* (GWR, Paddington, 1936), p20
13 Great Western Railway: Minutes of Traffic Committee Meeting held 30 May 1935
14 *Great Western Railway Magazine* September 1934, p390
15 Gibbons, W. G.: *Royal Leamington Spa: Images from the Past* (Jones-Sands Publishing, 1995), p91
16 *Great Western Railway Magazine* March 1938, p99
17 Great Western Railway: Minutes of Board Meeting held 1 May 1925
18 Great Western Railway: Minutes of Board Meeting held 24 March 1939
19 Priestley, J. B.: *English Journey* ([Victor Gollancz], 1934)
20 Edwards, T.: *The Face of Wales* (Batsford, 1950), p18
21 *Great Western Railway Magazine* November 1938, pp457-458
22 'The Railways Ask for a Square Deal' — National Archives: ZLIB15/47
23 *The Times* 12 December 1938
24 Great Western Railway: Minutes of Traffic Committee Meeting held 16 December 1937
25 Great Western Railway: Minutes of Board Meeting held 20 January 1939
26 *Great Western Railway Magazine* October 1939, p423

APPENDICES

Appendix I:
Constituents and subsidiaries

Constituent companies of the Western group as of 1921
Great Western Railway
Alexandra (Newport & South Wales) Docks & Railway
Barry Railway
Cambrian Railways
Cardiff Railway
Rhymney Railway
Taff Vale Railway

Subsidiary companies of the Western group as of 1923
Brecon & Merthyr Tydfil Junction Railway
Burry Port & Gwendraeth Valley Railway
Cleobury Mortimer & Ditton Priors Light Railway
Didcot, Newbury & Southampton Railway
Exeter Railway
Forest of Dean Central Railway
Gwendraeth Valleys Railway
Lampeter, Aberayron & New Quay Light Railway

Liskeard & Looe Railway
Llanelly & Mynydd Mawr Railway
Mawddwy Railway
Midland & South Western Junction Railway
Neath & Brecon Railway
Penarth Extension Railway
Penarth Harbour, Dock & Railway
Port Talbot Railway
Princetown Railway
Rhondda & Swansea Bay Railway
Ross & Monmouth Railway
South Wales Mineral Railway
Swansea Harbour Trust
Teign Valley Railway
Vale of Glamorgan Railway
Welshpool & Llanfair Light Railway
West Somerset Railway
Wrexham & Ellesmere Railway

Appendix II:
Statistical highlights

Traffic and dock receipts

Year	Passenger	Goods	Total	Docks	Total
1913	7,989,000	9,690,000	17,679,000	1,799,000	19,478,000
1923	13,665,000	18,012,000	31,677,000	3,647,000	35,324,000
1925	13,940,000	16,998,000	30,938,000	2,813,000	33,751,000
1926	12,502,000	13,760,000	26,262,000	1,917,000	28,179,000
1927	13,258,000	18,299,000	31,557,000	3,251,000	34,808,000
1929	12,686,000	17,893,000	30,579,000	3,072,000	33,651,000
1930	12,323,000	16,968,000	29,291,000	2,763,000	32,054,000
1931	11,346,000	15,253,000	26,599,000	2,269,000	28,868,000
1932	10.469,000	13,741,000	24,210,000	2,109,000	26,319,000
1933	10,444,000	13,834,000	24,278,000	1,976,000	26,254,000
1934	10,526,000	14,500,000	25,026,000	1,963,000	26,989,000
1935	10,673,000	14,683,000	25,356,000	1,945,000	27,301,000
1936	10,986,000	15,235,000	26,221,000	1,862,000	28,083,000
1937	11,417,000	16,287,000	27,704,000	2,223,000	29,927,000

The Tregenna Castle Hotel in Cornwall, refurbished and updated by the GWR in the 1930s.

Salaries/wages and staff totals

Year	Total wage bill (£)	Staff total
1913	8,221,444	76,480
1923	20,771,199	109,876
1924	21,700,448	117,113
1925	21,602,460	117,850
1926	18,561,526	114,649
1927	20,601,568	110,849
1928	20,175,108	110,591
1929	19,347,632	106,429
1930	19,665,263	110,729
1931	18,489,463	107,970
1932	17,215,540	103,839
1933	16,414,444	96,436
1934	16,570,966	96,642
1935	16,853,752	95,729
1936	17,385,947	98,290
1937	18,329,449	100,614

Dividend paid to GWR shareholders

Year	%
1913	6½
1919	5
1920	6
1921	7½
1922	8
1923	8
1924	7½
1925	7½
1926	3
1927	7
1928	5
1929	7
1930	5½
1931	3
1932	3
1933	3
1934	3
1935	3
1936	3
1937	4
1938	3

Stock of road vehicles

Year	Number
1913	67
1924	441
1927	719
1929	1,148
1930	1,324
1933	1,704
1935	2,010
1937	2,324

Stock of horses

Year	Number
1913	3,386
1924	2,811
1927	2,782
1930	2,449
1933	1,973
1937	1,687

Locomotives available and in use

Year	Average stock during year	Average in use	% of available stock	Max in use in any one day
1913	3,069	2,916	95.01	2,371
1923	3,936	2,852	72.46	3,062
1926	4,023	2,384	59.26	3,019
1927	4,035*	2,909	72.09	3,057
1929	3,908	2,902	74.26	3,124
1931	3,865	2,775	71.80	2,992
1935	3,609	2,688	74.48	2,941
1937	3,604	2,783	77.22	3,007
*highest number in period				

(All statistics taken from GWR General Statistics, General Manager's Office, Paddington, May 1938)

SOURCES & BIBLIOGRAPHY

Information for this book has been drawn from a variety of sources, including Board and Traffic Committee minutes held at the STEAM Museum in Swindon and the minutes of the GWR Chief Officers' Conference meetings, consulted at the Great Western Trust archive at Didcot. The RAIL files at the National Archives at Kew also provided vital information, particularly in relation to docks, GWR air services and the company's centenary. Material collected many years ago for an exhibition on the General Strike at the old GWR Museum was also used in Chapter 6. The Centenary chapter is a much-

enlarged and revised version of an article written for *Steam Railway* magazine in 2010.

The company's own *Great Western Railway Magazine* was an invaluable resource, chronicling much of what the railway did during the interwar period, and copies were consulted both at STEAM and in the Local Studies section of Swindon Central Library, as were books, leaflets and timetables published by the GWR itself and now variously in the Didcot, STEAM and Swindon Library collections.

Listed below are secondary sources consulted; other references are recorded in the notes for each chapter.

General works

Anon: Silver Jubilee —The Story of 25 Eventful Years in Pictures (Odhams Press, 1935)

Gardiner, J.: The Thirties — An Intimate History (Harper Press, 2011)

Graves, R., & Hodge, A.: The Long Week-End — A Social History of Great Britain, 1918–1939 (Hutchinson, 1940)

Harris, M.: Decades of Steam, 1920–1969 (Ian Allan, 1999)

Hattersley, R.: *Borrowed Time — The Story of Britain between the Wars* (Abacus Books, 2007)

Jones. B., & Thomas, B.: *Coal's Domain — Historical glimpses of life in the Welsh Coalfields* (National Museum of Wales, 1993)

Lewis, E. & P.: *The Land of Wales* (Batsford, 1937)

McElwee, W.: *Britain's Locust Years: 1918–1940* (Faber & Faber, 1962)

Mowat, C. L.: *Britain Between the Wars, 1918–1940* (Methuen, 1955)

Pimlott, J. A. R.: *The Englishman's Holiday — A Social History* (Faber & Faber, 1947)

Pugh, M.: *We Danced All Night — A Social History of Britain between the Wars* (Vintage Books, 2009)

Shepherd, J., & Shepherd, J.: *1920s Britain* (Shire Publications, 2010)

Great Western Railway

Adams, W. (Ed): Encyclopaedia of the Great Western Railway (PSL Books, 1993)

Bennett, A.: Great Western Lines and Landscapes (Runpast Publishing, 2002)

Bryan, T.: The Great Western at War, 1939–1945 (PSL Books, 1993)

Jones, G. B., & Jenkins, D.: The Great Western Railway in Wales (National Museums of Wales, 1995)

Kelley, P.: Great Western Road Vehicles (Oxford Publishing Co, 2002)

Nock, O. S.: A History of the Great Western Railway Volume 3 (Ian Allan, 1967)

Roden, A.: Great Western Railway — A History (Aurum Press, 2012)

Semmens, P.: History of the Great Western Railway: 1. Consolidation, 1923–1929 (Allen & Unwin, 1985)

Semmens, P.: History of the Great Western Railway: 2. The Thirties, 1930–1939 (Allen & Unwin, 1985)

Timms, P.: Working at Swindon Works, 1930–1960 (History Press, 2008)

Vaughan, A.: The Great Western at Work, 1923–1939 (PSL Books, 1991)

Wragg, D.: GWR Handbook: The Great Western, 1923–1947 (Haynes Publishing, 2006)

INDEX

A Holiday Season Tickets leaflet issued by Paddington in 1938.
Great Western Trust Collection

A view of a busy Platform 1 at Paddington in the 1930s.

One of a series of folders produced by the GWR to advertise attractions and beauty spots within its territory. This striking design for Wookey Hole, in Somerset, dates from March 1934. *Great Western Trust Collection*